EXPORTING SECURITY

EXPORTING SECURITY

International Engagement,
Security Cooperation,
and the Changing Face
of the U.S. Military

DEREK S. REVERON

Georgetown University Press
Washington, D.C.

Georgetown University Press, Washington, D.C.
www.press.georgetown.edu

Library of Congress Cataloging-in-Publication Data

Reveron, Derek S.
 Exporting security : international engagement, security cooperation, and the changing face of the U.S. military / Derek S. Reveron.
     p. cm.
 Includes bibliographical references and index.
 ISBN 978-1-58901-708-5 (pbk. : acid-free paper)
 1. United States--Military policy. 2. United States--Armed Forces. 3. Engagement (Philosophy)--Political aspects--United States. 4. National security--United States. 5. Security, International. 6. International cooperation. I. Title.
 UA23.R463 2010
 355'.0310973--dc22
                        2010003363

16 15 14 13 12 11 10   9 8 7 6 5 4 3 2
First printing

Printed in the United States of America

There is little that will sober an enemy more surely than the knowledge that somewhere, just over the horizon, lies a force of well-trained, well-equipped Marines in competently manned ships capable of delivering a stunning amphibious blow at a point and time of their choosing. . . . The future of the Corps lies within itself, because, however large or small its problems are, nobody else is going to find solutions to them.

—Lt. Gen. Victor Krulak,
USMC (Ret.), 1984

As capable as our joint forces are today, this will not be enough to meet future challenges. . . . We will need to develop new capabilities and change the capacities of existing ones. We will need to create new joint and Service doctrine, tactics, techniques and procedures. We will need to establish new methods for integrating our actions, both internally and with partners. We will need to select, educate, train, equip and manage our people differently. We will need to envision and create new organizations. We will need to develop new technologies and adapt existing ones to new missions.

—Adm. Michael G. Mullen,
Chairman of the Joint Chiefs of Staff, 2009

The joint force commander will need to function as soldier-statesman in the grand American tradition. He will have to be savvy in all the instruments of national power and should have cross-agency and multinational experience.

—Joint Forces Command,
"Military Contribution to Cooperative Security,"
ver. 1.0, 2008

Contents

Illustrations

Tables

Figures

Preface

BECAUSE I ATTENDED graduate school in the 1990s, it was not unusual that I studied democratization in Eastern Europe and Latin America like many scholars of my generation. After all, the democratic transformation movements of the 1990s were the most significant events in comparative and international politics. Although good governance and transformation politics is an important field, changes in foreign policy in the 2000s highlighted the effects of weak states on international security. So while I took a "governance first" approach in my early work, my recent work has been focused on security first. This book is a comprehensive effort to understand why security has become a more important export from the United States than democracy is. Simply put, without security, democratization and development are not possible.

With a strong background and a deep belief in the importance of good governance, universal human rights, and democracy, I am also keenly aware of the dangers of arming repressive regimes, training militaries that are not grounded in civilian control, or upsetting regional balances of power that could lead to war. Like my critics, I too worry that the military's role in national policy has been changing. Yet, as insurgents, pirates, terrorists, gangs, and organized crime networks in once faraway lands challenge United States' partners and threaten regional stability, promoting partners' militaries has become essential for U.S. national security. Different from direct action or counterinsurgency, security assistance programs attempt to strengthen the partner to provide for its own security, thus enabling political and economic development. To export security, the United States military is gradually shifting from a combat force designed for major war against external threats to a mentor force engaged in cooperation.

As a professor of national security affairs at the U.S. Naval War College, I have learned of how the U.S. military is changing from my military officer students and my own efforts to work with similar colleges around the world. In many ways, the U.S. military's strategy is catching up with U.S. allies such as Canada, the United Kingdom, and other North Atlantic Treaty Organization (NATO) countries. Further, given my position, I have also been able to participate in security cooperation programs. I have witnessed firsthand that U.S. military personnel have a deep understanding of the risks associated with security assistance.

Officers are learning the limits of what they can do and are attempting to impart their skills to partners all around the world. At times security assistance can be limitless, dissatisfying, and futile. At times partners misinterpret the assistance and do not appreciate the transitory nature of the assistance. To convince partners that a cold war logic no longer governs security assistance, U.S. military officers promote human rights, encourage military professionalization, and serve as mentors to military officers in developing countries throughout the world. I have yet to witness programs that do not support U.S. interests on promoting security, stability, and good governance, whether in Argentina, Botswana, Chile, Colombia, Djibouti, Ethiopia, Iraq, Jamaica, Kenya, Madagascar, South Africa, Uganda, or Uruguay. And I have yet to encounter an officer from these countries who was not grateful for the U.S. attention to their security problems. Furthermore, I have yet to witness military programs that did not have the full endorsement and support of the U.S. ambassadors who see fragile security as a serious roadblock to reform and development efforts.

The new model of security assistance is far from what the military practiced in most of the twentieth century. Then, military assistance meant installing U.S.-friendly governments through the power of the bayonet. Although there are some cold war legacy programs that persist, the new security assistance programs do not resemble those of an earlier era that focused on promoting insurgency to overthrow unfriendly governments, or training and arming friendly regimes to repress dissent. With congressional oversight and the importance of soft power, the hard lessons have been learned, and these new programs represent a maturity developed over the last several decades.

The U.S. military officers that I have taught and have worked with are learning the lessons of U.S. history in Latin America, Africa, and Asia. Working with them and understanding the goals of security assistance, I have little concern that the United States is either creating an empire or laying the groundwork for future coups. There is no public support for such actions or strategic rationale to direct them. Adding to the echo of Vietnam is U.S. experience in Iraq and Afghanistan. Those conflicts remind military officers of their limits and of the costs associated with regime change.

Given the current structure of the international system and technological advances, the United States does not need partners in the same way that it did in the past, when partners provided direct benefits through coaling stations, maintenance facilities, or large bases. Rather, the United States aspires to create true partners who can confront their own threats to internal stability, which organized crime and violent actors exploit. The United States also seeks to foster independence by training and equipping militaries to support the global demand for peacekeepers. The United States certainly gets increased access to countries around the world through these programs, but given the overwhelming military dominance of the United States, it does not abuse these relationships or ignore seemingly insignificant states. Instead, it seeks to create partners where sovereignty is respected and all parties derive benefits. Given the challenges in Iraq and Afghanistan, there is a potential for these lessons to be ignored. I hope this book can show those inside and outside the military how the world has changed, how militaries are changing from forces of confrontation to forces of cooperation, and why security assistance is an essential pillar of military strategy.

Acknowledgments

THIS BOOK HAS BEEN A WORK in progress for many years, and I am grateful to Joan Johnson-Freese for encouraging me to complete it and for creating an environment where I can be a practitioner-scholar.

A number of Naval War College colleagues were generous with their time. In particular, Nick Gvosdev and Mac Owens provided great comments on chapter 2, which was revised for *Orbis* (Summer 2009). My officemate, Jim Cook, was an invaluable sounding board throughout the process. Jim and Mike Todd kept me focused on the implications of global security cooperation for how the military trains and equips. Paul Smith and Dana Struckman graciously reviewed several early chapters. Gunfighter Mike Mahony was my sparring partner on the proper use of the military. Sean Sullivan patiently discussed the intricacies of defense acquisition processes. Larry Dinger, Gene Christy, Debbie Bolton, and John Cloud shared their insights on the embassy country team. And Larry McCabe provided me many opportunities to participate in mil-to-mil engagement by helping U.S. partners develop strategies and strengthen professional military education, and by immersing me in security cooperation activities.

My students, as always, kept my argument sharp and my evidence convincing. In particular, I am grateful to Forrest, Mark, Brian, John, Tamara, and Tim.

The security assistance officers that I worked with continue to be the unsung heroes of U.S. military strategy, and I thank them all for sharing their experiences and insights with me.

The anonymous reviewers and the editorial staff at Georgetown University Press were helpful. In particular, I am grateful for Don Jacobs's support through the writing process.

Finally, but not least, I thank Kirie, who continues to create a rich environment for me to think, research, and write. Without a strong family, I would not have had the time for the necessary travel to conduct this research or finish this book.

Acronyms and Abbreviations

CJTF-HOA	Combined Joint Task Force Horn of Africa
CSO	civil society organization
DCMA	deputy to the commander for civil–military activities
DOD	Department of Defense
EASWIO	East African Southwest Indian Ocean
EEZ	exclusive economic zone
FARC	Revolutionary Armed Forces of Colombia
FMF	foreign military financing
GDP	gross domestic product
IMET	international military education and training
IUU	illegal, unreported, and underreported
ISPS	International Ship and Port Security
MNNA	major non-NATO ally
NATO	North Atlantic Treaty Organization
NIC	National Intelligence Council
NGO	nongovernmental organization
SAO	security assistance officer
SFOR	Stabilization Force
SOFA	Status of Forces Agreement
3D	defense, development, and diplomacy
UCP	Unified Command Plan
UN	United Nations
USAID	U.S. Agency for International Development

Introduction

WHEN PRESIDENT BUSH ANNOUNCED in early 2007 that the United States would become more strategically engaged in Africa, it was through the creation of a new military command—U.S. Africa Command—and not through increasing the activities of the U.S. Agency for International Development (USAID) or the State Department's Bureau of African Affairs. Yet this new "combatant" command is not focused on combat at all; it is optimized for promoting international military partnerships through security assistance.[1] In fact, since the announcement was made, the word "combatant" has fallen away with an emphasis on the noncombat functions that this new unified command will fill.

Through the creation of Africa Command, President Bush moved far from his 2000 observation that the military should not do nation building and he continued the post–Cold War practice of using the military in non-warfighting ways. He concluded his eight years not obviating the military's role in noncombat missions but leaving enhanced capabilities and a new paradigm for President Barack Obama to continue the practice of using the military for state-building missions and foreign policy objectives beyond traditional warfare. This was formally acknowledged in the 2010 strategic defense review.

The new paradigm for the U.S. military is epitomized by Africa Command, which is designed to strengthen security cooperation efforts with African partner countries. Africa Command, like the other five geographic combatant commands, has embraced the notion that the military does much more than fight wars. The military trains, equips, and deploys peacekeepers; provides humanitarian assistance and disaster relief; and supports other militaries to reduce the security deficits throughout Africa. With national security focused on weak and failing states, the U.S. military has been changing over the last twenty years from a force of confrontation to one of cooperation. The military has learned that partnership is better than clientism and is adapting its command structure once optimized for waging major combat to one that is focused on conflict prevention.

These changes are reflected in the continued evolution of language to describe how to guarantee national security. President Roosevelt's War Department gave rise to President Truman's Department of Defense. While no formal name change is expected, it is better to think of today's Defense Department as the Cooperative Security Department to emphasize how much effort is now expended supporting other countries' militaries from Afghanistan to Yemen. Security assistance is now a key pillar of U.S. military strategy, which places American officers and noncommissioned officers in more than 150 countries to train, mentor, and professionalize other militaries. The impetus for the change is based on the beliefs that capacity building sets the conditions for conflict prevention and that there is a global need for capable military partners to serve in peacekeeping operations, control their own territory, and preserve regional stability. The military does so under direction of the U.S. ambassador where these programs occur.

New Missions for a New Era

Security assistance programs have broadened the mission set for the military. Some new missions for a new era include

- Providing training and equipment for partners to monitor and control air, land, and sea borders
- Training and equipping partners for peacekeeping operations
- Enabling partners to resolve local conflicts and addressing underlying conditions that spur violent extremism
- Developing bilateral and multilateral military relationships
- Promoting bilateral and multilateral information sharing and interoperability
- Providing training and educational opportunities for partners' officers and noncommissioned officers
- Planning and executing bilateral and multilateral exercises
- Enabling partner countries to provide good governance
- Enabling the success of integrated foreign assistance
- Alleviating human suffering after a natural disaster to counter anti–United States sentiment in regions such as the Middle East and Latin America
- Providing humanitarian assistance such as food, medical care, and veterinarian services
- Building civil infrastructure[2]

For example, soldiers from the 101st Airborne Division assessed hundreds of fish farms in Mahmudiya Qada, Iraq; Combined Joint Task Force Horn of Africa partnered with a Kenyan college to create a Maritime Center of Excellence; and Naval War College professors designed and ran a conference on building maritime safety and security in East Africa and the Southwest Indian Ocean. These examples illustrate that on any given day, U.S. military personnel are engaged in a wide variety of missions not associated with combat. Formerly the domain of Special Forces, general-purpose forces and civilian personnel regularly promote security. For some, these new missions are an anathema for a superpower, which prefers to be feared. However, the U.S. military wants to be feared and loved.[3]

With the most modern military in the world and the capability to deliver sustained attack against any target in the world, the United States is undoubtedly feared. The activist foreign policy of the Bush administration led many traditional allies to disassociate their countries with U.S. actions as evidenced in the run-up to the 2003 Iraq War. The relative decline of favorable views of the United States during the 2000s is well documented and has prompted the United States government to be more proactive in shaping its image.[4] Using the military to respond to humanitarian crises, such as the 2005 tsunami in South Asia or the 2010 earthquake in Haiti, has improved public perceptions of the United States.[5] While short-lived, these lessons are institutionalized in national documents such as the U.S. Navy's 2007 maritime strategy, which upgraded humanitarian assistance and disaster relief as a core capability on par with power projection and sea control.[6] Consequently, many field commanders no longer request aircraft carriers as the hallmark of naval presence but prefer noncombatants such as hospital ships, auxiliary repair ships, and other unarmed support ships to train partners and provide humanitarian assistance. Through nonkinetic military activities such as building schools, providing medical assistance, and digging wells, the United States attempts to improve its international image while facilitating development in nearly three-quarters of the world's countries. At the same time, these same military personnel train partners to combat transnational threats, plan disaster relief operations, and impart basic soldiering skills to support peacekeeping operations.

Changing the face of the U.S. military has not been easy. Mixed results in Somalia, the Balkans, East Africa, and Central Asia led some to question the efficacy of these types of missions. In spite of lacking evidence of success, the United States has embarked on a program to illustrate that its superpower capabilities can be used for good. The same capability that can accurately drop a bomb on an adversary's barracks has been used to deliver food aid in the mountains of Afghanistan. The same capability used to disembark Marines from Navy ships to a foreign shore has been used to host nongovernmental organizations (NGOs) that provide fisheries conservation in West Africa. And the same capability to track an enemy's submarines can detect changes in the migration of fish stocks in response to climate change. To be sure, swords have not been beaten into plowshares, but military capabilities once used for confrontation are now used for cooperation. And this is having an effect on military officers and the international assistance community.

Given the global nature of U.S. foreign policy and the emphasis on promoting security, senior military commanders are as much policy entrepreneurs as they are war fighters providing expertise on security issues within the national security bureaucracy.[7] Officers routinely meet with heads of state and senior cabinet ministers, and are often the public face of the United States during security and humanitarian assistance programs. Officers frequently testify before Congress and work with U.S. ambassadors to develop programs to address security deficits evidenced by piracy, terrorism, illegally armed groups, illicit maritime trafficking, and failing states.

The military's emergence in once civilian-only domains is based on four interrelated ideas. First, weak states have largely supplanted peer competitors as the focus of strategic thinkers. The United States is more concerned that Pakistan will fail than it is that Russia will attack Western Europe. Second, routine diplomatic and development activity mainly occupies USAID and the Department of State, which delegates security assistance programs to the Defense Department. In spite of obvious security deficits around the world, no new bureaucracy was created to deal with health, maritime, and developmental insecurity. Third, the Defense Department has a distinct advantage over the foreign assistance agencies in both size and resources. This is most evident in staff size. For example, Africa Command headquarters is composed of about 1,200 military personnel whereas the State Department's Africa Bureau has about 80. Or, in East Africa, the U.S. military has more than 2,000 personnel, who are primarily noncombat personnel focused on engineering and construction projects, medical and veterinary care, and various forms of military training. In contrast, U.S. Foreign Service and development officers in the region only number in the hundreds. Finally, changes in the U.S. foreign assistance bureaucracy has turned development specialists into contract managers who rely on NGOs to deliver services. In addition to relying on NGOs, the U.S. government uses military personnel to provide international assistance.

While the Defense Department's capacity certainly explains why international assistance missions increasingly have a military face, it is also essential to understand that the new security landscape cannot be navigated by a single bureaucratic entity. The last twenty years illustrate that the changed nature of national security does not easily divide activities between war and peace. Instead, security issues encompass defense, development, and diplomacy. A problem such as Somali piracy is simultaneously military, economic, social, and political. Solutions require unity of effort among the U.S. government, industry, NGOs, and international partners.

The military has been out front in adapting to the new security landscape. Its size and resources—National Guard and Reserve personnel, in particular—enable it to cut across the civil–military divide. Through its organic medical, construction, and logistics capabilities, military personnel perform development missions, which often occur alongside NGOs, USAID, and international partners. Given its size, the military often overwhelms the civilian agencies of government, but it has realized that it must coordinate its activities with USAID and it must support Department of State policy. Furthermore, the Defense Department has recognized that there are limits to what it can do; it understands that a superpower is not a superhero. It needs partners from across the government, allies, and private organizations. Military personnel can build a school, but it needs the Department of State to identify where the school should be built, USAID to train teachers, and NGOs to provide school supplies. The military also knows that it is better at achieving quick victories than it is at resolving underlying conditions that produce instability. Consequently, it builds relationships with partner governments to address sustainability.

Unfortunately, these lessons learned in the military have not moved into the broader policy community. For critics, U.S. military activities in permissive environments bring old memories of invasion or coup. For them, U.S. foreign policy is on a dangerous militarization path. While that part of U.S. military history is real and still resonates in many parts of the world, it is wrong to overlook the changes that have occurred over the last two decades. The United States does not operate an Imperial Office or a Foreign Legion as past dominant powers did. Instead, it offers mentors to create security forces that obviate U.S. presence. In fact, the short-term focus might be the fatal flaw in U.S. security assistance programs because it takes generations for countries to develop. Biannual military personnel rotations and annual budgets inhibit the long-term investments required to build sustainable programs. The military is trying to adapt to the new security landscape not dominated by threatening states.

Civil–Military Space

America's military commands, with their forward presence, large planning staffs, and various engagement tools, are equipping for the new civil–military space that is characterized by the absence of major war. Today, they routinely pursue regional-level engagement by playing host to international-security conferences, promoting military-to-military contacts, and providing American military presence, training, and equipment to nearly every country in the world. In practice, this means that pilots from Singapore train in Nevada, sailors from Ghana ride on U.S. Navy ships off the coast of Nigeria, and officers from more than sixty countries study at America's defense colleges. While the breadth of these activities is new, the military's role in this civil–military space is not.

When he conducted engagement operations in the 1980s, Adm. William J. Crowe, then commander in chief of Pacific Command, said that national leaders frequently told him that without American military presence, their achievements in democracy and development would not have been possible.[8] Security assistance can help democracies consolidate, fragile states avoid failure, and authoritarian states liberalize.[9] This is evidenced in the liberalization of countries such as South Korea or the Philippines. Contemporary lessons in Iraq and Afghanistan illustrate that security is essential for economic and social development. Violence and instability chase out intergovernmental organizations, NGOs, and private individuals and companies. Without security, educated professionals emigrate, foreign direct investment disappears, and economic development stalls. Outside of these anecdotes, there is empirical evidence to support this claim. Carol Atkinson found that U.S. military engagement activities are "positively and systematically associated with liberalizing trends, and provide evidence that these programs play an important role in U.S. national security."[10] Her findings reinforce the civil–military space where what constitutes civilian or military is blurred.

While some argued in the 1990s that military activism is a logical product of a more stable international order and a way to avoid distributing the "peace dividend" by finding a new rationale for militaries, this overlooks both a military's natural predisposition to eschew non-warfighting activities, the current high operational counterinsurgency tempo, and the military's role as a tool of national power that is increasingly used in noncoercive ways. Given the very real combat demands of U.S. forces in Iraq and Afghanistan, one would expect to see a decline in security assistance activities, yet the creation of Africa Command and the transformation of Southern Command illustrate the opposite. If warfighting were the sole function of the military, then the thousands of military personnel in east Africa should be in Afghanistan confronting today's challenges instead of implementing programs designed to prevent future challenges.

British general Sir Rupert Smith captured the change that the Defense Department is responding to, "war as cognitively known to most noncombatants, war as a battle in a field between men and machinery, war as a massive deciding event in a dispute in international affairs; such war no longer exists."[11] Given the importance of this change, there is increasing demand to understand how militaries are adapting their strategies and capabilities to fulfill noncombat roles. This book seeks to analyze the strategic rationale for these activities and explore how these activities take place to analyze the shift from coercive diplomacy to military engagement.

Overview of the Book

In chapters 1 and 2, I explore the tendency to use the military in other than warfare missions and discuss the rationale for these security assistance activities. What many thought was a peculiarity to the Clinton administration turned out to be the hallmark of the Bush administration. President Obama inherited a military focused on security assistance, and he will continue to use it to further his aims of promoting multilateralism and aiding countries in need. No matter a politicians' political stripes, the military will continue to be used in noncombat ways; allies demand it and emerging partners expect it. In a world characterized by increased levels of connectivity, the United States cannot heed the calls by some to disengage.[12] Transnational actors and weak states are increasingly bringing the world's powers together in an unprecedented nonwartime fashion. In 2009, for example, the United States, Europe, Russia, China, India, Japan, and South Korea coordinated actions to deter piracy in the Gulf of Aden. Similar counterterrorism coalitions exist.

Because the changing face of the military is controversial, chapter 3 explores various forms of resistance to security assistance and explains why the military now embraces this as a core function. To be sure, there is a deep skepticism of these new roles and missions coming from Congress, the Department of State, development NGOs, and from some in the military itself. They fear that traditional aid and diplomacy agencies will be marginalized by the military and that government money will be directed away from the NGO development community. And critics within the military fear it will lose its capacity and ethos for major combat operations and it will be ill suited for an uncertain future characterized by the rise of China. Conflict prevention is a shared goal, but critics of the military's security assistance roles claim that the costs are too great, the operations never end, and partners are too slow to develop.

Chapters 4 and 5 examine how the U.S. military has changed through the process of demilitarizing combatant commands and supporting other countries' militaries. The analysis suggests that security assistance is conducted in a tailored way that takes into account differing U.S. interests and local conditions. For example, the United States provides weapons in the Middle East, medical assistance in Africa, and training and education in Latin America. Chapter 6 offers the specific case of how the U.S. Navy is promoting maritime security around the world. These chapters reveal that the military is filling a void in the U.S. foreign assistance community by adapting its command structure to include nonmilitary personnel and private organizations to promote security and stability. Foreign Service officers, development specialists, and other U.S. government civilians now work at military commands attempting to formulate comprehensive policy solutions. In the field, military officers embedded at U.S. embassies have expanded their portfolios to include development and diplomacy working with various ministries to plan medical assistance and civil engineering projects. Given the expanded roles of military officers, language training and cultural studies are obvious deficits to be filled.

With U.S. presidents increasingly relying on the military as a ready foreign policy tool, chapter 7 explores the implications for the military's force structure. While it is relatively easy to determine what capabilities the U.S. military needs to defeat an adversary's submarine, determining what capabilities are necessary to professionalize a partner's military or improve stability is not. This chapter offers a sketch of the force planning implications when designing a military that emphasizes cooperation. Finally, in chapter 8, I highlight the risks of ceding civilian responsibilities to military agencies and the risks of weakening the secretary of state's primacy in setting the agenda for U.S. relations with foreign countries. The implications of these findings are also important for civil–military relations theory.

Conclusion

The changed nature of security no longer allows for an easy divide between war and peace. As General Petraeus told his troops in 2008, "you have contributed significantly to the communities in which you have operated. Indeed, you have been builders and diplomats, as well as guardians and warriors."[13] While his statement was made in a counterinsurgency context, his point is equally applicable to security assistance operations where conflict prevention is the goal.

This has profound implications for how militaries train and equip for future operations. Advanced aircraft, ships, and tanks will not be the main systems to secure political objectives. Rather, the human skills that General Petraeus promoted and tested in Iraq will be the key. Success is not contingent on being warriors alone; instead, military personnel must also be builders, diplomats, and guardians. It is my hope that this book makes a contribution to seeing the military as an instrument for cooperation and informs how militaries should train and equip for the future.

Notes

1. "Africa Command will enhance our efforts to help bring peace and security to the people of Africa and promote our common goals of development, health, education, democracy, and economic growth in Africa." George W. Bush, "President Bush Creates a Department of Defense Unified Combatant Command for Africa,"

The White House website, http://georgewbush-whitehouse.archives.gov/news/releases/2007/02/20070206-3.html.

2. Derek S. Reveron and Kathleen Mahoney-Norris, ""Military-Political" Relations: The Need for Officer Education," *Joint Force Quarterly* 52, no. 1 (2009): 61–66.

3. In chapter 17 of *The Prince*, Machiavelli wrote, "Upon this a question arises: whether it is better to be loved than feared or feared than loved. It many be answered that one should wish to be both, but, because it is difficult to unite them in one person, it is much safer to be feared than loved, when, of the two, either must be dispensed with."

4. See Pew Global Attitudes Project at http://pewglobal.org.

5. Dennis Lynn, "Strategic Communication and the Diplomacy of Deeds," in *Shaping the Security Environment*, ed. Derek S. Reveron (Newport, RI: Naval War College Press, 2007).

6. Department of the Navy, "A Cooperative Strategy for 21st Century Seapower," October 2007, www.navy.mil/maritime/MaritimeStrategy.pdf. See page 15: "Human suffering moves us to act, and the expeditionary character of maritime forces uniquely positions them [naval assets] to provide assistance."

7. See Derek S. Reveron and Judith Hicks Stiehm, eds., *Inside Defense: Understanding the 21st Century Military* (New York: Palgrave Macmillan, 2008).

8. William J. Crowe Jr. "U.S. Pacific Command: A Warrior-Diplomat Speaks," in Derek S. Reveron, ed., *America's Viceroys: The Military and U.S. Foreign Policy* (New York: Palgrave Macmillan, 2004), 74.

9. "Security assistance refers to a group of programs by which the United States provides defense articles, military training, and other defense-related services to foreign nations by grant, loan, credit, or cash sales in furtherance of national policies and objectives." Programs include: Foreign Military Sales, Foreign Military Financing, International Military Education and Training, and the Economic Support Fund. See U.S. Department of Defense, "Joint Operations," Joint Publication 3-0 (Washington, DC: Department of Defense, September 17, 2006), VII-7.

10. Carol Atkinson, "Constructivist Implications of Material Power: Military Engagement and the Socialization of States, 1972–2000," *International Studies Quarterly*, 50 (2006): 509–37.

11. Rupert Smith, *The Utility of Force: the Art of War in the Modern World* (New York: Vintage, 2007), 3.

12. Eugene Gholz, Daryl G. Press, and Harvey M. Sapolsky, "Come Home America: The Strategy of Restraint in the Face of Temptation," *International Security* 21, no. 4 (Spring 1997): 5–48.

13. David Petraeus, "Farewell Letter," Multi-National Force Iraq, September 15, 2008. Available at *New York Times* website, http://graphics8.nytimes.com/images/2008/09/15/world/20080915petraeus-letter.pdf.

1

Beyond Warfare

GIVEN THE LARGE NUMBER OF U.S. military forces deployed around the world and the casualties sustained in Iraq and Afghanistan, it is easy to miss that the military does much more than engage in combat. On any given day, military engineers dig wells in East Africa, medical personnel provide vaccinations in Latin America, and Special Forces mentor militaries in southeast Asia. By doing so, the United States seeks to improve its international image, strengthen the state sovereignty system by training and equipping security forces, preempt localized violence from escalating into regional crises, and protect U.S. national security by addressing underlying conditions that inspire and sustain violent extremism.

Far from preparation for major war, these activities rely on a unique blend of charitable American political culture, latent civil–military capacity, and ambitious military officers who see the strategic landscape characterized by challenges to human security, weak states, and nonstate actors. Furthermore, changes are informed by U.S. partners that conceive of their militaries as forces for good and not simply for combat. The United States has been slow to catch up to European governments that see the decline of coercive power and the importance of soft power today. This chapter analyzes the debate about U.S. power, explores the shift from traditional to human security challenges, and explains why weak states matter for U.S. national security. Fundamentally, this chapter offers theoretical support for the movement beyond preparation for warfare and embeds security assistance in contemporary U.S. military strategy.

End of U.S. Primacy?

U.S. foreign policy activism over the last twenty years has revived interest in power and the nature of security. For decades some scholars have been forecasting the end of U.S. primacy and waiting for the unipolar moment to end.[1] Taken to the extreme, these behaviors can give way to a tripolar world composed of the

United States, China, and India.[2] The U.S. National Intelligence Council (NIC) echoed a multipolar future in 2004 when it noted that the rise of China and India would be reminiscent of Germany's ascent in the twentieth century, which will have profound implications on the geopolitical landscape.[3] The NIC reiterated the end of unipolarity in 2008 when it reported that "the whole international system—as constructed following WWII—will be revolutionized. Not only will new players—Brazil, Russia, India and China—have a seat at the international high table, they will bring new stakes and rules of the game."[4] And China optimistically agreed in its defense white paper: "a profound readjustment is brewing in the international system."[5]

These statements are largely consistent with realist theory that tends to see a great power such as the United States provoking balancing behavior by potential victim states.[6] As early evidence of balancing against the United States, realists point to China's military modernization program, Russia's coercive energy policy, and general reactions to NATO enlargement as signs that great power competition is reappearing. Christopher Layne sees that his earlier predictions of multipolarity were premature but now predicts balancing coming from Asia.[7] Xenia Dormandy suggests that China's and India's growing economies, developing naval capabilities, and expanding spheres of influence in the Indian Ocean are early signs that American unipolarity is waning.[8]

Additionally, some scholars have also noted soft balancing, which Robert Pape defines as measures that "do not directly challenge U.S. military preponderance but that use nonmilitary tools to delay, frustrate, and undermine aggressive unilateral U.S. military policies."[9] T. V. Paul sees that "soft balancing involves tacit balancing short of formal alliances."[10] For Stephen Walt, soft balancing is the "conscious coordination of diplomatic action in order to obtain outcomes contrary to U.S. preferences, outcomes that could not be gained if the balancers did not give each other some degree of mutual support."[11] For this group of scholars, the United States provoked a backlash (evidenced in the 2003 opposition to the Iraq War), and the international system will eventually return to equilibrium, bringing the era of U.S. primacy to an end. The 2009 global recession was expected to hasten the decline.

The Absence of Balancing

The United States cannot dominate the geopolitical landscape as colonial empires once did, but to date, potential rivals such as China, India, Russia, or the European Union are not balancing U.S. power. They either lack the resources to catch up to U.S. military supremacy or the strategic rationale to balance the United States. Robert Kagan wrote, "The world's failure to balance against the superpower is more striking because the United States, notwith-standing its difficult interventions in Iraq and Afghanistan, continues to expand its power and military reach and shows no sign of slowing this expansion."[12] Far from being a unipolar moment, this era of U.S. military dominance is entering its third decade.

While Russia, India, and China pursue national interests apart from the United States, their behavior does not suggest military balancing.[13] Rather, integration is occurring. The United States and these potential great powers have been increasing diplomatic and trade ties, giving way to another era of globalization. Keir Lieber and Gerard Alexander see soft balancing as "much ado about nothing" and consistent with normal diplomatic friction.[14] There is no cold war–like rivalry that centers around ideological differences on how to organize society or economy. These great powers do not fight proxy wars in the developing world. Instead, it appears that there are financial disincentives for states to risk war.[15] China's rise is contingent on U.S. consumer demand. Likewise, a resurgent Russia depends on European energy consumption. China's defense white paper noted this: "factors conducive to maintaining peace and containing war are on the rise, and the common interests of countries in the security field have increased."[16] Likewise, there have been no conflicts among the great powers over natural resources.[17] Instead there is energy interdependence for both consumer countries such as the United States and China and producer countries such as Russia and Iran. Inasmuch as resource scarcity can produce competition, it can also induce cooperation. Supposed flashpoints in the Caspian Sea, Spratly Islands, or East China Sea have not produced armed conflict. Thus, it is not certain that competing claims in the Arctic will give rise to war either. Four of the competing states are NATO allies and the fifth, Russia, is dependent on European energy imports.

The Changing Nature of Power

In the absence of great power war and interstate military competition, an industrial-age understanding of power is not as relevant today in a globally connected information age.[18] Large economies and populations or advanced militaries will not be enough to dominate a changed international system. Far from challenging the existing international order, the development of Brazil, Russia, India, and China is dependent on the Western economic system. In spite of political opposition during the Bush years, the United States still finds itself in a dominant military and economic position for the foreseeable future. Its military operations in Iraq and Afghanistan did not bankrupt the United States or destroy its dominant military position. Instead, the wars gave way to massive military modernization, vastly increased the war experience base of the U.S. military, and altered how the military thinks about future operations.

The 2008 global economic crisis did not see new structures or alternative economic centers of power emerge. China, Russia, India, and European countries continue to work with the United States to create a common approach. Yet the United States does find it increasingly difficult to advance and defend its national interests. In reaction to U.S. activism, Andrew Bacevich sees that "American power has limits and is inadequate to the ambitions to which hubris and sanctimony have given rise."[19] However, this is not simply a reaction to the rise of new powers or anti-Americanism generated by the Bush administration but is a part of the changing conceptions of power that began twenty years ago.

Writing soon after the Berlin Wall fell, former assistant secretary of defense Joseph Nye commented that "although the United States still has leverage over particular countries, it has far less leverage over the system as a whole."[20] Nye observed that not only was the international system changing from bipolar to unipolar but power itself, which is the ability to shape the outcomes you want and change the behavior of others, was also changing. Joseph Nye and Walter Mead accurately predicted that lethal military power would not be enough to affect outcomes.[21] Instead, outcomes are more likely to be affected through non-coercive measures or soft power, which Nye defines as "the ability to get what we want through attraction rather than coercion or payments."[22] To achieve national objectives, the United States must use all its tools of national power—military, diplomacy, economy, and culture.

While soft power is often inaccurately equated with the "softer side" of the military or diplomacy, it is better thought of as attractiveness or magnetism. Soft power is a byproduct of diplomatic, informational, military, and economic actions. The Center for Strategic and International Studies dubbed this "smart power."[23] The goal of those actions is to inspire countries to bandwagon with the United States because the balancing alternative is too expensive or simply unattractive.

Influence, not Dominate

Predictions about the changing nature of power bore out in the late 1990s when coercive diplomacy did not produce the desired effects, and in the early 2000s with negative reactions to a post-9/11 U.S. foreign policy. It appears that hard power worked better in a coherent state system and not well with new and traditional partners, in under-governed spaces, or with weak states. Terrorists in the trans-Saharan arc, pirates in Somalia, and drug traffickers in Latin America simply do not care that the United States is a military superpower. Ballistic missile defense, space dominance, and fifth generation fighters are irrelevant in conflicts characterized by nonstate actors, insurgent cells, and improvised explosive devices.

There are few direct kinetic military solutions to crises in the Middle East, South Asia, or East Africa. Consequently, the U.S. government has placed renewed emphasis on generating soft power to serve as a reservoir from which to draw nonlethal solutions to U.S. foreign policy problems. One way to do this is through global military engagement, which can build trust among societies and strengthen weak states that threaten international security. As Robert Art notes, "short of waging war or playing chicken in a crisis, then, military power shapes outcomes more by its peacetime presence than by its forceful use."[24] Beyond deterrence, military forces engage in security assistance to strengthen sovereignty by reducing security deficits.

These insights on power have profound implications for international relations theory in general, and for power in particular. It moves thinking about power beyond coercion and explains the expansive use of the military in non-warfighting roles. The policy implications of these changes are explored in chapter 2, but Secretary of Defense Robert Gates captured it succinctly: "Success will be less a matter of imposing one's will and more a function of shaping behavior of friends, adversaries, and most importantly, the people in between."[25] Consequently, the United States has greatly increased the number of countries it cooperates with on security issues. While it is obvious why Mongolia or Georgia would seek alliance with the United States, it is less obvious why the United States would develop relationships with these countries for fear of provoking Russia or China. Yet the United States does.

To explain the nonexclusive nature of U.S. security relations, some scholars have equated these activities with empire. The argument seems bolstered by American military dominance and the global nature of American military activities but is inconsistent with American values. Dimitri Simes brushes off those Americans that are offended by the term empire: "Whether or not the United States now views itself as an empire, for many foreigners it increasingly looks, walks, and talks like one, and they respond to Washington accordingly."[26] Yet Simes misses the point that U.S. partners regularly exercise independence from Washington (e.g., Turkey's refusal of U.S. requests to use its territory to invade Iraq in 2003, Israel's reluctance to accept a two-state solution, and NATO countries' reluctance to increase troop levels in Afghanistan). Scholars interpret events such as these as evidence that the United States is in decline. Yale Ferguson wrote, "United States capabilities appear to be gravely waning today and its exercise of both hard and soft power has recently been so inept as to limit its current influence and possibly future role in global politics."[27] Charles Kupchan has concluded that "American primacy is already past its peak."[28] Many of these arguments are based on Paul Kennedy's argument in *The Rise and Fall of Great*

Powers, an argument that accepts the inevitability of American decline.[29] Instead of imperial incompetence, however, pessimistic interpretations of U.S. power may be wrong.

Thus, the United States is not an incompetent empire; rather, the term empire does not adequately describe the United States. While the current international system speaks with an American accent, the United States and Americans are also vulnerable to the same international system that causes concern around the world. This leads to Max Boot's conclusion: "[The United States] is a country with interests to protect and enemies to fight all over the world."[30] The United States cannot govern the world and has no strategic ambition for empire. While American power is checked in the economic, diplomatic, and cultural spheres, its ideology still dominates the international system. Far from rejecting it, many leading states of the world crave and demand continued U.S. leadership. For example, the 2008 global financial crisis did not precipitate a foreign sell-off of American holdings but resulted in a flight to the U.S. dollar. In spite of its economic problems, the United States is still seen as a safe investment, and foreign banks and governments continue to finance U.S. debt. Foreign corporations continue to invest in the United States, making it one of the top destinations for foreign direct investment. Furthermore, the 2008 election of Barack Obama was hailed around the world as a global success and new leadership in the United States to confront global challenges was welcomed.[31] Overall confidence in President Obama increased by 37 percentage points during Obama's first six months in office.[32] His receipt of the 2009 Nobel Peace Prize suggested that the United States still has soft power and still inspires others around the world.

Likewise, the United States' emphasis on promoting and supporting democracy has not produced reversals of the third wave or a backlash against democratization. Even illiberal governments still retain democratic processes. Writing in reaction to the cottage industry of seeing the United States in decline, Alan Dowd noted that "America has a magnetic pull on peoples of every race, religion and region."[33] This is evident in emigration patterns, international students in American colleges, and the desirability of American companies as joint venture partners. In short, the United States still has soft power.

U.S. military presence has increased in dozens of new countries. Old allies such as Germany and South Korea protest efforts to reduce the U.S. military presence there. As Robert Kagan wrote, "Overall, there is no shortage of other countries willing to host U.S. forces, a good indication that much of the world continues to tolerate and even lend support to American geopolitical primacy if only as a protection against more worrying foes."[34] It is true that these allies can constrain the United States, but this is far from balancing. Constraints occur through institutions that the United States helped create or through binding agreements that the United States negotiated and accepted. U.S. diplomats certainly dislike Sudan's presence on the UN Human Rights Council, but U.S. diplomats did see it more important to be included in discussions and eventually sought a seat.

Consistent with Zeev Maoz's thinking, trade interdependence has a dampening effect on systemic conflict.[35] Objections to U.S. foreign policy are caused by the ways the United States acts, not necessarily by the desired outcomes or the United States itself.[36] For John Ikenberry, American hegemony is liberal, which "makes it acceptable to other countries that might otherwise be expected to balance against hegemonic power, and it is also what makes it so stable."[37] Outright balancing is negated by general international agreement that human security concerns are supplanting traditional military threats. Keir Lieber and Gerard Alexander argue that "the great powers, as well as most other states, either share the U.S. interest in eliminating the threats from terrorism or WMD or do not feel that they have a significant direct stake in the matter."[38] John Mueller believes that "war . . . is merely an idea, an institution, like dueling or slavery, that has been grafted onto human existence. It is not a trick of fate, a thunderbolt from hell, a natural calamity, or a desperate plot contrivance dreamed up by some sadistic puppeteer on high. And it seems to me that the institution is in pronounced decline, abandoned as attitudes toward it have changed, roughly following the pattern by which the ancient and formidable institution of slavery became discredited and then mostly obsolete."[39] Among great powers, war as a way of settling grievances or advancing national interests seems to be disappearing.[40] Yet conflict continues. In 2009 the Uppsala Conflict Data Program tracked twenty-nine intrastate conflicts (e.g., Sudan), zero interstate conflicts, and five internationalized internal conflicts (e.g., Congo) that are occurring in just twenty-five countries.[41] Separating crisis from conflict, there were eight wars in 2008, and only Russia's invasion of Georgia was new.[42] Conflict, it appears, tends to be internal, tends to occur in poor countries, and requires external actors to provide for or supplement security.[43]

From Traditional Security to Human Security

The decline in great power competition, prevalence of internal conflict, and increases in external actors providing global security are important characteristics of the modern security landscape. These changes are also important to the world's militaries that see human security concerns largely supplanting traditional security. In the age of globalization, Jonathan Kirshner sees the United States attracting "more violent resistance and political opposition to its international ambitions."[44] "To a large extent the most obvious consequence of globalization is the diminishing power and influence of the sovereign state."[45] Even a superpower such as the United States is "not immune to the powerful forces of globalization."[46] Yet developed states are more immune than developing states to the negative aspects of globalization. Developing states are less equipped to prevent their territories from becoming safe havens for violent political actors, and they lack ready access to international capital markets necessary to finance government social and military spending. Thus, the process of globalization contributes to political violence, which makes vulnerable states weaker.[47]

The National Intelligence Council has forecasted that within the next decade "weak governments, lagging economies, religious extremism, and youth bulges will align to create a perfect storm for internal conflict in certain regions."[48] Weak states are those wracked by civil war or insurgency and have a comparative advantage in international crime and terrorism.[49] Aidan Hehir noted that weak states suffer from both coercive incapacity and administrative incapacity.[50] Robert Rotberg explained that weak states cannot provide political goods that are expected of modern governments, such as personal security, economic stability, and a functioning bureaucracy to provide for education, trash removal, and transportation services.[51]

Because weak states cannot provide law and order, transnational security issues have emerged as key challenges for all states in the twenty-first century. Paul Smith defined these challenges as "non-military threats that cross borders and either threaten the political and social integrity of a nation or the health of that nation's inhabitants."[52] These threats are very different from traditional threats. In many cases, nonstate actors such as terrorist groups or criminal enterprises cause these threats; they find either sanctuary or support within weak states. For example, most law enforcement agencies regard West African criminal networks as dangerous adversaries with global reach.[53] The transnational gang Mara Salvatrucha (MS-13) and drug trafficking organizations challenge governments from Colombia to Mexico. And the meteoric rise of Somali piracy in 2008 threatened a key maritime trade route. These transnational security challenges often represent the "dark side" of globalization, which "seems to foster conflicts and resentments."[54]

In almost every country in the world, transnational actors wage "wars of globalization," which Moisés Naim defines as the illegal trafficking of drugs, small arms, and humans, violations of intellectual property, and money laundering.[55] Svante Cornell and Niklas Swanström argue that among transnational criminal activities, illegal drug production and trafficking pose a full spectrum of threats to state sovereignty and human security. For example, narcotics trafficking affects societies through addiction, crime, and disease.[56] Drug production also undermines or weakens effective governance by fostering corruption and providing financial support to terrorism and insurgency. For example, the resurgence of the Taliban in Afghanistan was enabled by profits from the heroin trade, and the Revolutionary

Armed Forces of Colombia (FARC) in Colombia sustains itself through cocaine trafficking. And democratic societies tend to be more vulnerable to drug traffickers because they can bribe, corrupt, and influence politics in regular ways.[57]

Many of Africa's fifty-three countries have been plagued with famine, disease, internal conflict, and population displacement that cross national borders, which have generated further security destabilization.[58] Most of the costs of state failure accrue to neighboring states; "state failure is a regional public bad."[59] Gen. Bantz Craddock testified before Congress that "the large ungoverned areas in Africa, HIV/AIDS epidemic, corruption, weak governance, and poverty that exist throughout the continent are challenges that are key factors in the security stability issues that affect every country in Africa."[60] Even the once isolated trans-Saharan arc is increasingly seen as a breeding ground for violent conflict, terrorism, and instability that "poses a serious challenge to African and global peace and security."[61]

In general, transnational groups or networks are the sources of these threats. These nonstate actors have an inherent advantage over governments. Small private groups can more readily harness off-the-shelf technology such as satellite phones, encryption, and transportation technology. For example, semisubmersible vehicles carrying cocaine are increasingly common in the Caribbean. And in Nigeria, organized crime illegally trades one hundred thousand barrels of stolen oil every day, which costs the government billions of dollars every year. Whether state-supported, local, transnational, narcoterrorist, Islamist, or neocommunist, these groups have access to a variety of underground economies, religious charities, and illicit government sponsorship.

Given the sophistication of the threats, Naim argues that "in one form or another, governments have been fighting these five wars for centuries [against transnational actors]. And losing them."[62] With these illegal groups operating at a subnational level, police forces are underequipped to effectively confront these groups and are too frequently co-opted through corruption. To fill the security void, advanced militaries are beginning to think beyond warfare and are developing core competencies to meet the challenges of transnational threats to better address human security concerns. Paul Smith argued in 2000, "Because military troops are the ultimate instrument of the state in maintaining its security, it is logical that military forces would be involved in combating such [transnational] threats."[63] These formerly distant internal security concerns have been elevated to that of international security concerns, and they threaten national unity, stability, and internal peace—but also with implications for regional and global security.[64] The Pentagon largely accepts this view and sees the United States as more threatened by and vulnerable to nontraditional threats.[65]

Over the last twenty years, human security concerns gained currency in U.S. defense circles and became the basis for thinking about security. A 2008 Defense

Science Board study on the industrial base (not the typical venue for such discussions) saw a holistic view of security as the number one driving force underneath defense transformation, which is characterized by "world-wide terrorism, pandemics; weapons proliferation; rogue nuclear states; energy dependence; insurgencies; environment; mass migration; regional conflicts; transnational threats; resource access (i.e., water, oil, critical materials)."[66]

Even climate change cannot escape national security discussions. The military advisory board of National Security and the Threat of Climate Change, which is composed of distinguished retired senior military officers, said: "Climate change can act as a threat multiplier for instability in some of the most volatile regions of the world, and it presents significant national security challenges for the United States."[67] The group's findings see the United States intervening to minimize the impact of disasters, conduct stability operations, or deny sanctuary to extremists who may exploit weakened states. At an operational level, this is already occurring, according to commander of the 13th Air Force, Lt. Gen. Loyd S. "Chip" Utterback: "More often than not out there in the Pacific we deal with disasters. If there is not an earthquake, there is certainly a volcano erupting. There are landslides in the Philippines, floods in Vietnam and Burma. India and Bangladesh deal with flooding, cyclones, and typhoons."[68] In a region challenged by North Korea's nuclear program, on edge because of the China-Taiwan situation, or concerned about the frozen conflict between India and Pakistan, it is astonishing that so much attention is paid to human security challenges.

Thinking about the future, "The U.S. government should use its many instruments of national influence, including its *regional* [military] *commanders*, to assist nations at risk build the capacity and resiliency to better cope with the effects of climate change."[69] The connection between climate change and military intervention is based on the assumption that extremists can gain sanctuary where governments are weak. And climate change will further weaken vulnerable states. Former U.S. commander of naval forces in Europe Adm. T. Joseph Lopez captures this connection: "More poverty, more forced migrations, higher unemployment. Those conditions are ripe for extremists and terrorists."[70] Consequently, the logic goes, the military should strengthen regimes around the world to prevent the emergence of sanctuaries where nonstate actors can thrive.

Prioritizing Weak States

At least since the early 1990s state failure was identified as a risk to international peace and security. This view continued throughout the 2000s when policymakers saw a direct connection between weak states and international terrorism.[71] For Secretary of Defense Gates, "the recent past vividly demonstrated the consequences of failing to address adequately the dangers posed by insurgencies and failing states. Terrorist networks can find sanctuary within the borders of a weak state and strength within the chaos of social breakdown. The most likely catastrophic threats to the U.S. homeland, for example, that of a U.S. city being poisoned or reduced to rubble by a terrorist attack, are more likely to emanate from failing states than from aggressor states."[72] This moved formerly subnational or regional crises to the international level where it was assumed that failed states or states at risk pose an acute risk to national security.[73] This produced external intervention into weak states in the name of human security (e.g., the United States and the Philippines; the United Kingdom and Sierra Leone, France, and the Ivory Coast; or Australia and East Timor). And it expanded the number of recipients of security assistance.

Prioritizing weak or failing states represents a profound shift in strategic thinking. Historically, countering the Soviet Union or economic interests drove U.S. foreign policy decisions and military deployments.[74] Yet since the 1990s, weak states and the struggle to bring stability to countries such as the Democratic Republic of Congo, Haiti, and Somalia has captured the world's attention. At a time when populations are less vulnerable to nuclear annihilation or traditional war, transnational forces have instilled a "pervasive sense of insecurity, which may be as much based on psychological perceptions as physical threats."[75] "The difficulty today is that material threats are more difficult to perceive. Terrorism is an 'immanent' rather than an 'imminent' threat. It is present potentially everywhere in sleeper cells and illegal arms networks, but it is not visible actually in any specific location until it happens."[76] These concerns are captured in terms beyond warfare—human security, maritime security, food security, environmental security, and energy security. Consequently, it is important for the United States to understand what threatens friends, adversaries, and those countries in between. With few exceptions, the United States willingly forms security assistance agreements with almost every country in the world.

Given the significance of this, a robust debate has been occurring inside academia and government. Important critiques came from Ken Menkhaus and Karin von Hippel who warned of reading too much into Afghanistan serving as a safe haven for al-Qaeda. They argued that failed or weak states are undesirable locations because terrorists need a functioning infrastructure to train, equip, and deploy terrorists internationally. Chaotic environments are destabilizing even for those that seek to create chaos. Instead, Menkhaus argued that "quasi-states" are better suited for international terrorist operations because terrorists can use the functioning government to support its ends through bribery.[77] In contrast, von Hippel saw authoritarian states as the breeding grounds for transnational actors because the alienated and disgruntled are ideal recruits for terrorist movements.[78] While these are important theoretical insights, differentiation of terrorist groups is required to fully understand the relationship between state failure and terrorism. We should not treat all terrorist groups the same; the Irish Republican Army (IRA) is very different from the Tamil Tigers.

Complicating understanding of the relationship between terrorism and weak states is the high-profile nature of attacks in developed countries (e.g., 9/11 in the United States, 3/11 in Spain, or 7/7 in the United Kingdom). It is easy to see the "West" as the target of terrorists and the terrorists coming from the "East," but terrorism is more widespread in weak states such as Iraq, Afghanistan, Pakistan, India, Thailand, and Somalia.[79] U.S. cooperation with these governments will benefit those countries more than it will benefit the United States, which remains too distant a target for many groups to attack. Furthermore, "homegrown terrorists" in the United Kingdom have proven to be more deadly than those who emanate from weak states.

James Piazza empirically tested the relationship between terrorism and weak states and concluded that states plagued by failure are statistically more likely to host terrorist groups that commit transnational attacks or have their citizens commit transnational attacks, and they are more likely to be targeted by transnational terrorist groups.[80] Prior to Piazza's study, theoretical arguments pointed in this direction. Ray Takeyh and Nikolas Gvosdev argued that weak states provide safe haven for terrorists not only because of their inability to act but also through "outward signs of sovereignty" that prevented external actors from attacking.[81] In addition to weak states shielding groups from external attack, weak governments provide legal documentation such as passports or end-user certificates for weapons. The international community has generally been reluctant to withdraw sovereignty protections from weak states, but this may be changing with the emerging doctrine of the "responsibility to protect."[82]

The Changing Face of the U.S. Military

The foundation of America's post–Cold War foreign policy is based on the fusion of interests and ideals.[83] While there was considerable opposition to U.S. foreign policy during the Bush years, there was also unprecedented cooperation to address transnational concerns such as nuclear proliferation, terrorism, and weak states.[84] It appears that insecurity unites. It makes sense for small states to bandwagon with the United States, but it is not clear why the United States continues to expand its security relationships when it is already the dominant power.[85] Since there are significant costs associated with expanding security ties (especially with poor militaries), instrumental explanations are inadequate.[86] Instead, new ideas about U.S. motives and American national interests are needed. The United States does not invade countries to take territory or install puppet regimes but instead sets in place, no matter how flawed, democratic processes to allow self-determination. And it aids new (e.g., Kosovo), struggling (e.g., Mexico), or transforming states (e.g., Georgia) with security and development assistance programs. The United States provides some form of security assistance to about 150 countries.[87] And with the rest of the world, the United States cooperates with its NATO allies, Japan, and other advanced militaries that would not qualify for U.S. assistance.

At least since World War II, it has been the interest of the United States to guarantee American security by reducing threats from abroad and encouraging a system of global trade to promote American prosperity and create global interdependence. This has continued over the last twenty years and is giving way to the prominence of internal security issues in developing countries. Former secretary of state Condoleezza Rice said, "it is clear that managing the problems of state failure and ungoverned spaces will be a feature of U.S. foreign policy for the foreseeable future—whether we like it or not."[88] Consequently, preparations for war are giving way to military operations that focus on humanitarian assistance, stability operations, and security assistance. These operations attempt to preempt impacts on the United States, but they also follow American idealist thinking to make the world safer.

With weak governments unable to control their territory or channel social frustration in nonviolent ways, academics and policymakers recognized a need to address states at risk, but there were no good answers. "Neither the United States nor the UN has developed an adequate system for preventing or even containing such calamites [such as Darfur] in the future. Article 8 of the Genocide Convention, an injunction to prevent genocide, is the most important responsibility in the convention, much more so than acting after genocide has happened."[89] This will be discussed in detail in chapter 2, but the formal acknowledgment came in the 2002 National Security Strategy that noted "America is now threatened less by conquering states than we are by failing ones."[90]

The implications of this view of security are profound. It immediately brings once-local conflicts into international view and thrusts the military to the front of U.S. foreign policy to provide security assistance. Because security is the essential precondition for stability and development, the military literally became the tip of the spear on U.S. efforts to reduce the global consequences of weak states. With few exceptions, indigenous security forces are too small, poorly equipped, and ill trained to effectively monitor and secure their long and remote borders.[91] Consequently, the United States has stepped up its security assistance efforts and finds its military forces in more countries than ever. The forces seldom engage in direct combat operations but are training, equipping, and mentoring partner countries' militaries. These programs are a part of the U.S. grand strategy that emphasizes military-to-military relations to confront transnational actors while strengthening weak states.

Notes

1. Christopher Layne, "The Unipolar Illusion: Why New Great Powers Will Rise," *International Security* 17, no. 4 (Spring 1993): 5–51; John J. Mearsheimer, "Back to the Future: Instability in Europe after the Cold War," *International Security* 15, no. 1 (Summer 1990): 5–56; and Kenneth Waltz, "The Emerging Structure of International Politics," *International Security* 18, no. 2 (Fall 1994): 44–79.

2. Arvind Virmani, "A Tripolar Century: USA, China, and India," March 2005. Indian Council for Research on International Economic Relations, www.icrier.org/pdf/wp160.pdf.

3. "Mapping the Global Future: Report of the National Intelligence Council's 2020 Project," December 2004. National Intelligence Council, www.dni.gov/nic/NIC_globaltrend2020.html.

4. "Global Trends 2025: The National Intelligence Council's 2025 Project," November 2008. National Intelligence Council, www.dni.gov/nic/NIC_2025_project.html.

5. "China's National Defense in 2008" (Beijing: Information Office of the People's Republic of China, 2009), 3.

6. Kenneth Waltz, *Theory of International Politics* (New York: McGraw-Hill, 1979).

7. Christopher Layne, "The Unipolar Illusion Revisited," *International Security* 31, no. 2 (Fall 2006): 7–41.

8. Xenia Dormandy, "Is India, or Will It Be, a Responsible International Stakeholder?" *The Washington Quarterly* 30, no. 3 (Summer 2007): 117–30; see also Aaron L. Friedberg, "Ripe for Rivalry: Prospects for Peace in a Mulitpolar Asia," *International Security* 18, no. 3 (Winter 1993/94): 5–53.

9. Robert A. Pape, "Soft Balancing against the United States," *International Security* 30, no. 1 (Summer 2005): 7–45. See also Stephen M. Walt, "Keeping the World 'Off Balance,'" in *America Unrivaled*, ed. G. John Ikenberry (Ithaca, NY: Cornell University Press, 2002); T. V. Paul, "The Enduring Axioms of Balance of Power Theory," in *Balance of Power Revisited: Theory and Practice in the Twenty-first Century*, ed. T. V. Paul, James J. Wirtz, and Michel Fortmann (Stanford, CA: Stanford University Press, 2004); Josef Joffe, "Defying History and Theory: The United States as the 'Last Superpower,'" in *America Unrivaled*, ed. G. John Ikenberry (Ithaca, NY: Cornell University Press, 2002); Yuen Foong Khong, "Coping with Strategic Uncertainty: The Role of Institutions and Soft Balancing in Southeast Asia's Post–Cold War Strategy," in *Rethinking Security in East Asia: Identity, Power, and Efficiency*, ed. Allen Carlson, Peter J. Katzenstein, and J. J. Suh (Stanford, CA: Stanford University Press, 2004); and Erik Voeten, "Resisting the Lonely Superpower: Responses of States in the United Nations to U.S. Dominance," *Journal of Politics* 66, no. 3 (May 2004): 729–54.

10. Paul, "Enduring Axioms of Balance of Power Theory," 3.

11. Stephen Walt, "Can the United States Be Balanced? If So, How?" Paper presented at the annual meeting of the American Political Science Association, Chicago, IL, www.allacademic.com//meta/p_mla_apa_research_citation/0/5/9/9/6/pages59968/p59968-1.php, 14.

12. Robert Kagan, "End of Dreams, Return of History," *Policy Review*, no. 144 (August and September 2007), www.hoover.org/publications/policyreview/8552512.html.

13. The most noteworthy and prescient prediction on the decline of great power struggles came from John Mueller, *Retreat from Doomsday* (New York: Basic Books, 1989).

14. Keir A. Lieber and Gerard Alexander, "Waiting for Balancing: Why the World Is Not Pushing Back," *International Security* 30, no. 1 (Summer 2005): 109.

15. Jonathan Kirshner, *Appeasing Bankers: Financial Caution on the Road to War* (Princeton, NJ: Princeton University Press, 2007).

16. "China's National Defense in 2008," 3.

17. David G. Victor, "What Resource Wars?" *The National Interest Online*, November 12, 2007, www.nationalinterest.org/Article.aspx?id=16020.

18. Daniel M. Gerstein, *Securing America's Future: National Strategy in the Information Age* (Westport: CT: Praeger Security International, 2005).

19. Andrew Bacevich, *The Limits of Power* (New York: Metropolitan Books, 2008), 11.

20. Joseph Nye, "Soft Power," *Foreign Policy* (Autumn 1990): 156. "Soft power" is something that a country has that can be generated from cultural, political, and economic behavior, but it is better thought of as a byproduct rather than a raw material. Soft power is noncoercive, not simply nonmilitary. On this point, see Joseph Nye, "Think Again: Soft Power," *Foreign Policy Web Exclusive*, February 23, 2006. Available at http://yaleglobal.yale.edu/content/think-again-soft-power.

21. Walter Russell Mead, *Power, Terror, Peace, and War: America's Grand Strategy in a World at Risk* (New York: Knopf, 2004).

22. Joseph S. Nye, *Soft Power: The Means to Success in World Politics* (New York: Public Affairs, 2004), x.

23. CSIS Commission on Smart Power. See www.csis.org/smartpower.

24. Robert Art only views the military as a coercive force. He does not consider the noncoercive dimensions of the military that I address in this book. Robert J. Art, "The Fungibility of Force," in *The Use of Force: Military Power and International Politics, sixth edition*, ed. Robert J. Art and Kenneth N. Waltz (New York: Rowman and Littlefield, 2004), 4.

25. Robert Gates, "Remarks as Delivered by Secretary of Defense Robert M. Gates," Landon Lecture (Kansas State University), November 26, 2007. Reprinted in *Military Review* (January–February 2008) and available at www.defense.gov/speeches/speech.aspx?speechid=1199.

26. Dimitri K. Simes, "America's Imperial Dilemma," *Foreign Affairs* 82 (November–December 2003): 93, www.foreignaffairs.com/articles/59370/dimitri-k-simes/americas-imperial-dilemma.

27. Yale H. Ferguson, "Approaches to Defining "Empire" and Characterizing United States Influence in the Contemporary World," *International Studies Perspectives* 9, no. 3, (2008): 272.

28. Quoted in Alan W. Dowd, "Declinism," *Policy Review*, no. 144 (August/September 2007), www.hoover.org/publications/policyreview/8816802.html.

29. Paul Kennedy, *The Rise and Fall of Great Powers* (New York: Random House, 1987).

30. Max Boot, "The Struggle to Transform the Military," *Foreign Affairs* 84, no. 2 (March–April 2005): 103–18.

31. R. Nicholas Burns, "The Ascension," *National Interest Online*, January 21, 2009, www.nationalinterest.org/Article.aspx?id=20488.

32. "Obama Rockets to Top of Poll on Global Leaders," June 29, 2009, WorldPublicOpinion.Org, www.worldpublicopinion.org/pipa/pdf/jun09/WPO_Leaders_Jun09_longart_emb.pdf.

33. Dowd, "Declinism."

34. Kagan, "End of Dreams."

35. Zeev Maoz, "Network Polarization, Network Independence, and International Conflict, 1946–1986," *Journal of Peace Research* 43, no. 4 (2006): 391–411.

36. Christopher Layne argues the opposite is true and doubts that other states view U.S. primacy as nonthreatening. See Layne, "The Unipolar Illusion Revisited," *International Security* 31, no. 2 (Fall 2006): 7–41.

37. G. John Ikenberry, "Introduction," in *America Unrivaled: The Future of the Balance of Power*, ed. G. John Ikenberry (Ithaca, NY: Cornell University Press, 2002), 10.

38. Keir A. Lieber and Gerard Alexander, "Waiting for Balancing: Why the World Is Not Pushing Back," *International Security* 30, no. 1 (Summer 2005): 134.

39. John Mueller, *Remnants of War* (Ithaca, NY: Cornell University Press, 2007), 2.

40. Since the early 1990s, there has been a steady decline of conflict from a high of more than fifty armed conflicts. Ted Robert Gurr and Monty Marshall, *Peace and Conflict* (College Park, MD: Center for International Development, 2005).

41. Uppsala codes "internationalized internal armed conflict as conflict "between the government of a state and one or more internal opposition group(s) without intervention from other states." Uppsala Conflict Data Program, Centre for the Study of Civil Wars, International Peace Research Institute, *UCDP/PRIO Armed Conflict Dataset Codebook* (Oslo, 2008).

42. Heidelberg Institute for International Conflict, *Conflict Barometer 2008* (Heidelberg: HIIK, 2008).

43. In 2009 about ninety-two thousand UN peacekeepers were serving in twenty operations, NATO was providing forces in the Balkans and Central Asia, and military coalitions around the world were conducting land, air, and sea activities. See www.un.org/Depts/dpko/dpko/bnote.htm.

44. Jonathan Kirshner, "Globalization, American Power, and International Security," *Political Science Quarterly* 123, no. 3 (Fall 2008): 363.

45. Ibid., 367.

46. Jean-Marie Guehenno, "The Impact of Globalization on Strategy," *Survival* 40 (Winter 1988–89): 16.

47. Mary Kaldor, *New and Old Wars: Organized Violence in a Globalized Era* (Stanford, CA: Stanford University Press, 2001).

48. "Mapping the Global Future," 14.

49. Paul Collier, *The Bottom Billion: Why the Poorest Countries Are Failing and What Can Be Done about It* (New York: Oxford University Press, 2007), 31.

50. Aidan Hehir, "The Myth of the Failed State and the War on Terror: A Challenge to the Conventional Wisdom," *Journal of Intervention and State Building* 1, no. 3 (2007): 307–32.

51. Robert I. Rotberg, "The New Nature of Nation-State Failure," *The Washington Quarterly* 25, no. 3 (2002): 85–96; and Robert I. Rotberg, ed. *State Failure and State Weakness in a Time of Terror* (Washington, DC: Brookings Institution Press, 2003).

52. Paul J. Smith, "Transnational Security Threats and State Survival: A Role for the Military," *Parameters* (Autumn 2000): 78.

53. Gail Wannenburg, "Organised Crime in West Africa," *African Security Review* 14, no. 4 (2005), Institute for Security Studies, www.issafrica.org/pgcontent .php?UID=15553.

54. Stanley Hoffmann, "Clash of Globalizations," *Foreign Affairs* 81 (July–August 2002), 111.

55. Moisés Naim, "The Five Wars of Globalization," *Foreign Policy* 134 (January–February 2003): 29–37.

56. Svante E. Cornell and Niklas L. P. Swanström, "The Eurasian Drug Trade: A Challenge to Regional Security," *Problems of Post-Communism* (July–August 2006): 10–28.

57. Horace A. Bartilow and Kihong Eom, "Busting Drugs While Paying with Crime," *Foreign Policy Analysis* 5, no. 2 (April 2009): 93–116.

58. James E. Shircliffe Jr., "Tip of the African Spear: Forging an Expeditionary Capability for a Troubled Continent" *RUSI Journal* 152, no. 4 (Aug 2007): 58–62.

59. Collier, *Bottom Billion*, 130.

60. "Testimony of General Craddock to the Senate Armed Services Committee," September 19, 2006. http://armed-services.senate.gov/e_witnesslist.cfm?id=2064.

61. Stephen A. Emerson, "The Trans-Saharan Arc," in *Flashpoints in the War on Terrorism*, ed. Derek S. Reveron and Jeffrey Stevenson Murer (New York: Routledge, 2006), 250.

62. Naim, "Five Wars of Globalization."

63. Smith, "Transnational Security Threats," 88.

64. Gates, Landon Lecture. Reprinted in *Military Review* (January–February 2008).

65. Defense Department, "Quadrennial Defense Review" (Washington, DC: Pentagon, 2006), www.defense.gov/qdr/report/Report20060203.pdf.

66. Defense Science Board, *Creating an Effective National Security Industrial Base for the 21st Century: An Action Plan to Address the Coming Crisis* (Washington, DC: Office of the Under Secretary of Defense for Acquisition, Technology, Logistics, 2008), 4.

67. See "National Security and the Threat of Climate Change," http:// securityandclimate.cna.org/report/SecurityandClimate_Final.pdf. The group is composed of Gen. Gordon Sullivan, Adm. Frank "Skip" Bowman, Lt. Gen. Lawrence P. Farrell Jr., Vice Adm. Paul G. Gaffney II, Gen. Paul J. Kern, Adm. T. Joseph Lopez, Adm. Donald

L. Pilling, Adm. Joseph W. Prueher, Vice Adm. Richard H. Truly, Gen. Charles F. Wald, and Gen. Anthony C. Zinni.

68. Quoted in Bryan Bender, "Pentagon Flexes Its Altruism Muscle: Aims to Win Trust with Soft Power," *Boston Globe*, July 28, 2008.

69. See "National Security and the Threat of Climate Change," 7.

70. T. Joseph Lopez, "On Climate Change and the Conditions for Terrorism," in "National Security and the Threat of Climate Change," 17.

71. Chuck Hagel, "A Republican Foreign Policy," *Foreign Affairs* 83, no. 4 (2004): 64–76.

72. Robert M. Gates, "A Balanced Strategy: Reprogramming the Pentagon for a New Age," *Foreign Affairs* (January–February 2009): 31.

73. Stephen D. Krasner and Carlos Pascual, "Addressing State Failure," *Foreign Affairs* 84, no. 4 (July–August 2005): 153–63.

74. This was especially true in Africa. See Letitia Lawson, "U.S. Africa Policy since the Cold War," *Strategic Insights* 6, no. 1 (January 2007), www.nps.edu/Academics/centers/ccc/publications/OnlineJournal/2007/Jan/lawsonJan07.html.

75. "Mapping the Global Future," 93.

76. Henry Nau, "Conservative Internationalism: Jefferson to Polk to Truman to Reagan," *Policy Review*, no. 150 (August–September 2008), www.hoover.org/publications/policyreview/26105009.html.

77. Ken Menkhaus, "Quasi-States, Nation-Building and Terrorist Safe Havens," *Journal of Conflict Studies* 23, no. 2 (2003): 7–23.

78. Karin von Hippel, "The Roots of Terrorism: Probing the Myths," *Political Quarterly* 73, no. 25 (2002): 1–39.

79. In 2007 the top target countries for terrorism (by fatalities) were Iraq, Afghanistan, Pakistan, India, Thailand, Somalia, Sudan, Chad, Colombia, Sri Lanka, Philippines, Algeria, Congo, and Russia. See National Counterterrorism Center, "2007 Report on Terrorism," April 30, 2008, http://wits.nctc.gov/reports/crot2007nctcannexfinal.pdf.

80. James A. Piazza, "Incubators of Terror: Do Failed and Failing States Promote Transnational Terrorism?" *International Studies Quarterly* 53, no. 3 (2008): 469–88.

81. Ray Takeyh and Nikolas Gvosdev, "Do Terrorist Networks Need a Home?" *The Washington Quarterly* 25, no. 3 (2002): 97–108.

82. Gareth Evans, *The Responsibility to Protect: Ending Mass Atrocity Crimes Once and for All* (Washington, DC: Brookings Institution Press, 2008). An early version of the argument was made by UN Secretary General Bhoutros-Bhoutros Ghali in 1992 with his *Agenda for Peace: Preventive Diplomacy, Peacemaking and Peace-keeping*, Report of the Secretary-General pursuant to the statement adopted by the Summit Meeting of the Security Council on January 31, 1992, (June 17, 1992).

83. USAID highlights this relationship on its web page. "The idea of democracy is inextricably linked to the national identity of the United States. Even during the most isolationist periods in our early history, our relatively young country was seen as a shining beacon to individuals and families seeking personal freedoms." See www.usaid.gov.

84. Derek S. Reveron, "Old Allies, New Friends: Intelligence-Sharing in the War on Terror," *Orbis* 50, no. 3 (Summer 2006): 453–68.

85. Waltz, *Theory of International Politics*; and Stephen M. Walt, *The Origins of Alliances* (Ithaca, NY: Cornell University Press, 1987).

86. J. T. Richelson, "The Calculus of Intelligence Cooperation," *International Journal of Intelligence and Counterintelligence* 4, no. 3 (1990): 307–23.

87. Department of State, Bureau of Political-Military Affairs, www.state.gov/t/pm.

88. Condoleezza Rice, "Remarks at the Civilian Response Corps Rollout," U.S. Department of State, July 16, 2008.

89. Anthony Lake and Christine Todd Whitman, "More than Humanitarianism: A Strategic U.S. Approach toward Africa," Independent Task Report No. 56 (New York: Council on Foreign Relations Press, 2006), 24.

90. National Security Strategy of the United States, (Washington, DC: The White House, 2002), http://georgewbush-whitehouse.archives.gov/nsc/nss/2002/index.html.

91. Emerson, "The Trans-Saharan Arc."

2

Military Engagement, Strategy, and Policy

MANY STATES INCREASINGLY rely on the United States for either the actual provision of security or the training and equipment necessary to perform security functions. While militaries historically have cooperated against a common adversary, the decline of interstate war and the rise of transnational threats have made the prospect of exporting security more compelling.[1] Paul Collier argues that the role for advanced militaries of the world is "to supply the global public good of peace in territories that otherwise have the potential for nightmare."[2] Militaries conducting security assistance activities are rooted in the lessons of the Cold War, which taught that by providing for other countries' security, the United States could advance its trade agenda and prevent the emergence of military competitors. Likewise, countries protected by American security guarantees could focus on their own political and economic development while allowing the United States to solve their countries' security dilemmas. While world political systems did not quite "reach the end of history" in 1989, no peer competitors have emerged to challenge Western-oriented democratic–capitalist systems.[3] However, weak countries are still threatened by internal instability and transnational forces, so the United States and its allies provide these countries the tools to improve regime security. Today, the United States provides security assistance to about 150 countries (see table 2.1).

Although the focus on providing for allies' security has been common since World War II, after the Cold War ended, the military's prominence in international affairs has greatly increased. Far from giving way to a peace dividend, transnational forces have produced less security. Weak states provide sanctuary for terrorists, pirates, drug traffickers, and criminal gangs who challenge state authority in many countries. Consequently, U.S. strategy has shifted from containment to engagement and has generated greater demand for the U.S. military to train other militaries to either supplement its force or serve as peacekeeping surrogates. As former secretary of state Madeleine K. Albright put it, what was "the point of having this superb military you're always talking about if we can't

Table 2.1 Expanding Security Programs

	2000	2009
Status of Force Agreements	40	90
NATO members	15	28
Security partners	125	150
Foreign military financing budget	$3.6 billion (FY01 est.)	$5.2 billion (FY10 request)
International military education and training budget	$58 million (FY01 est.)	$110 million (FY10 request)

Source: 2000 budget data from: "All Fund Sources 'Spigot' Report," http://www.state.gov/documents/organization/4018.pdf.

2009 budget data from: Department of State, "Congressional Budget Justification for Foreign Operations Fiscal Year 2010," http://www.state.gov/f/releases/iab/fy2010cbj/pdf/index.htm

use it?"[4] Albright's view prevailed in the 1990s, which resulted in stepped up military activities in countries such as Haiti, Yugoslavia, East Timor, and Colombia. During the Clinton years, the U.S. military was engaged in dozens of military deployments with missions that varied from providing logistic support to UN peacekeeping missions to conducting stability operations in the Balkans. Very few of these activities resembled traditional combat, but when President Clinton deployed the military, he was accused of tomahawk diplomacy or "wag the dog" military actions to distract the public from domestic issues. Setting aside underlying political motivation for military actions, critics simply missed that the military became an essential non-warfighting tool of national power. And this is largely consistent with United Nations thinking marked by the 1992 *Agenda for Peace* that charged its members "to stand ready to assist in peace-building in its differing contexts: rebuilding the institutions and infrastructures of nations torn by civil war and strife; and building bonds of peaceful mutual benefit among nations formerly at war."[5]

While Gov. George Bush stated during the 2000 presidential election that he abhorred this "misuse" of the military, President Bush did not alter course. In fact, use of the military in non-warfighting ways actually escalated at the same time traditional uses of the military occurred in Iraq and Afghanistan. Combined Joint Task Force Horn of Africa, located in Djibouti, shifted its mission from counterterrorism operations to civil affairs. U.S. Southern Command reorganized away from a warfighting command to better reflect the security cooperation missions it conducts. And U.S. Africa Command was created with a deliberate security assistance mission.

To formalize these activities, President Bush issued National Security Presidential Directive 44 in 2005, which directed the United States to "work with other countries and organizations to anticipate state failure, avoid it whenever possible, and respond quickly and effectively when necessary to promote peace, security, development, democratic practices, market economies, and the rule of law."[6] Consequently, the Bush administration stepped up Clinton-era programs in Africa, Asia, and Latin America. The Defense Department suddenly found itself building militaries in Liberia, Georgia, Rwanda, Yemen, the Trans-Sahara, East Africa, and the Philippines; providing disaster relief in Indonesia, Pakistan, and the U.S. Gulf Coast (post Hurricane Katrina); and leading reconstruction efforts in Iraq and Afghanistan. Up until 2005, the institutional military saw these operations as distractions to its core function of fighting and winning the nation's wars. However, with the inadequacies of international institutions, long-time partners, and other U.S. government agencies (Department of State and U.S. Agency for International Development in particular), the military embraced the mission to bridge the gap between national ends, ways, and means. At least through the midterm, the Defense Department has accepted its role in noncombat missions and is building capacity to perform the roles and missions it expects civilians to perform but do not.

Military officers have gradually learned that they cannot rely on international organizations, nongovernmental organizations, or other U.S. government departments to provide the capabilities for the military to reject noncombat operations. Instead they learned that the military needs to incorporate capabilities expected in civilian organizations. All too often the president deploys military forces until U.S. national objectives to create stable, democratic regimes with functioning economies are realized. Consequently, Secretary of Defense Robert Gates observed, "One of the most important lessons of the wars in Iraq and Afghanistan is that military success is not sufficient to win: economic development, institution-building and the rule of law, promoting internal reconciliation, good governance, provided basic services . . . along with security, are essential ingredients for success."[7] With few institutional alternatives to ensuring national success, the military increasingly finds itself in the non-warfighting roles of promoting development, assisting institutional reform, and facilitating restoration of social harmony after conflict. This chapter traces the roots of military engagement, analyzes the strategic case of this role for the military, and outlines the strategic rationale for preventive military deployments.

The More Things Change

Even though the threat of nuclear war has been greatly reduced since 1986, U.S. security commitments to other countries have increased.[8] Today, the United States formally pledges to protect the sovereignty of twenty-seven NATO countries and five Asian countries. Under mutual defense treaties, the United States has assumed an obligation to assist its treaty partner in the event of an armed attack. Driven by U.S. security concerns of an expansionist Soviet Union, the treaties deterred Soviet attack by promising to retaliate on an ally's behalf. In spite of the disintegration of the Soviet Union in 1991, NATO did not disappear. The same was true with the ANZUS Treaty of 1952, which includes Australia, New Zealand, and the United States, and the Rio Treaty of 1947.[9] After the Cold War, there seemed to be little relevance to these treaties, let alone a rationale for invoking them or expanding them. Yet the opposite occurred.

NATO increased its membership three times, from sixteen to nineteen in 1999, to twenty-six in 2006, and again to twenty-eight in 2009. There are plans to further expand NATO in the next decade, in spite of Russia's provocations. At the same time that the number of NATO members increased, NATO changed from its traditional mission of territorial defense to one of global security engagement. Having never used military force during the Cold War, NATO engaged in combat operations for the first time in 1995 by attacking targets in Bosnia-Herzegovina followed by a ground deployment of thirty-two thousand peacekeepers. In 1999 NATO waged a more aggressive seventy-eight-day air campaign against Yugoslavia followed by a stability force of fifty thousand ground troops. In 2001 NATO invoked Article 5 of its charter by declaring that the 9/11 attacks were an attack on all, and NATO aircraft were deployed to the United States to monitor airspace while American aircraft went to Central Asia. NATO crossed into new territory by even deploying military forces outside of Europe into Afghanistan and assuming responsibility for stability and reconstruction operations there. To be clear, NATO is breaking new ground and does not resemble the mutual defense organization of the Cold War. With every change NATO has undertaken, stresses have occurred, but so far, the organization and European leaders have been committed to this new organizational focus. Depending on how NATO fares in Afghanistan will determine whether European leaders have an appetite for the new security focus of the alliance.

Changes in defense commitments in Asia were not as dramatic as in Europe, but there were clearly changes not anticipated by international relations theory. Although there were tensions with New Zealand, the United States–Australia military alliance was never in doubt and greatly increased in relevance. Remarking on the ANZUS Treaty's relevance fifty years after it was signed, Australian prime minister John Howard said in 2001, "ANZUS lies at the heart of a wide ranging and deep co-operation between our two nations which extends across all fields of common security. It is not simply to be taken literally. It is the foundation stone to what has become a vital, comprehensive and evolving security relationship."[10] About four months after the speech, Australia invoked Article IV of ANZUS, recognizing the 9/11 attack on the United States as an attack on Australia. Australia also responded to U.S. requests for military forces for Afghanistan and Iraq, where it contributed the third-largest component of the initial force in 2003.[11] Australia also assumed a much more military activist role in its region with deployments and was characterized as America's deputy, attempting to bring law and order to untamed regions of the Pacific.

In addition to formal treaties of alliance, an additional dozen countries are offered protection under the U.S. security umbrella either by law, such as the Taiwan Relations Act, or by policy, such as United States support for Israel.[12] Another dozen countries are offered special security provisions through major non-NATO ally (MNNA) status. MNNA does not confer a mutual defense relationship, but the largely symbolic act implies a close working relationship with another country's defense forces.[13] It is more akin to a preferred buyer's program that allows countries such as Argentina, Kuwait, and Pakistan access to advanced weapons systems.

The treaties and security guarantees undoubtedly hold deterrent value, but the security guarantees have also ensured U.S. military primacy over former rivals such as Japan and Germany. Since many European and Asian governments can rely on the United States to protect or at least to promote stability in the region, they invest very little in their own capabilities. U.S. military spending is the highest in the world, at about 4.5 percent of gross domestic product (GDP); most European countries spend just under 2 percent. As table 2.2 highlights, only six countries even meet the NATO target of 2 percent of GDP to support defense. NATO's supreme allied commander warned that if the trend continues, NATO countries "jeopardize their ability to make long-term strategic military commitments to meet the Alliance's 21st century missions."[14] Previous NATO commanders have made similar statements for many years, but there is little political rationale for European governments to increase defense spending.

Differences in defense spending are evident in European military capabilities and capacity. This is obvious during multinational military operations such as the war for Kosovo. During the 1999 Operation Allied Force, thirteen allies flew just 39 percent of the missions and were limited by predictable Balkan weather. The United States flew the preponderance of missions and dropped 70 percent of the munitions. Only the United States could conduct attacks on cloudy, rainy nights.[15] Not much improved two years later when the United States attacked the Taliban in Afghanistan. Instead of including European allies in air combat operations, they were largely excluded since the political costs of their inclusion outweighed the benefits of their capabilities. This of course changed when stresses on the U.S. military fighting two wars in Iraq and Afghanistan led to the deployment of a NATO force to Afghanistan in 2003. However, the NATO force focused on reconstruction and stability operations while American forces undertook combat missions against the Taliban and al-Qaeda. Furthermore, national caveats placed on European forces inhibited their full use and operational integration. Some countries forbid their militaries from engaging in combat.

Table 2.2 NATO Countries' Defense Expenditures as Percentage of GDP

Country	Average 1985–89 (%)	2008 (%)
Belgium	2.8	1.1
Bulgaria	---	2.6
Canada	2.1	1.4
Czech Republic	---	1.4
Denmark	2.0	1.3
Estonia	---	1.9
France	3.7	2.3
Germany	3.0	1.3
Greece	4.5	2.8
Hungary	---	1.2
Italy	2.2	1.3
Latvia	---	1.7
Lithuania	---	1.1
Luxembourg	0.8	0.4
Netherlands	2.8	1.4
Norway	2.9	1.3
Poland	---	1.9
Portugal	2.5	1.5
Romania	---	1.5
Slovak Republic	---	1.5
Slovenia	---	1.5
Spain	2.1	1.2
Turkey	3.3	1.8
United Kingdom	4.5	2.2
United States	6.0	4.0

Note: Countries without data were not NATO members during the period 1985–89.

Source: "NATO-Russia Compendium of Financial and Economic Data Relating to Defence," Table 3, "Defence Expenditures as % of GDP," February 19, 2009, p. 7, www.nato.int/docu/pr/2009/p09-009e.html.

The high rate of U.S. military spending has not only given U.S. presidents a ready foreign policy tool but it can also defuse potential flashpoints between historic rivals such as Japan, China, and North Korea. The United States fills the gap in Japan's security capabilities by basing tens of thousands of marines, an aircraft carrier with accompanying escorts, and sophisticated aircraft in Japan. In the absence of this relationship, Japanese rearmament could give rise to an arms race in northeast Asia. But instead of developing its own nuclear weapons to deter China or North Korea, Japan can rely on the United States to provide this deterrent capability through the mutual defense treaty, U.S. forces based in Japan, and a cooperative defense relationship. More recently, the United States is encouraging Japan to increase defense spending, but it is far from encouraging an independent Japanese Defense Force. By providing security for its friends and allies such as Japan, the United States continues to use military engagement as an essential component of its national strategy.

Military Engagement and Strategy

President Bill Clinton's 1996 National Security Strategy of Engagement and Enlargement directed the military to engage with international partners and to provide a credible overseas presence. "Such overseas presence demonstrates our commitment to allies and friends, underwrites regional stability, ensures familiarity with overseas operating environments, promotes combined training among the forces of friendly countries, and provides timely initial response capabilities."[16] Engagement includes supporting democracy, providing economic assistance, and increasing interactions between U.S. and other militaries around the world. In short, the United States wants to be viewed as a partner of choice. This approach has its roots in American military policy of building and maintaining an international coalition of democracies "not as a political nicety . . . but a matter of national survival."[17]

President George W. Bush was initially opposed to the Clinton-era practice of using the military for engagement purposes. In his 2000 campaign he said, "I'm not so sure the role of the United States is to go around the world and say this is the way it's got to be. We can help. I just don't think it's the role of the United States to walk into a country and say, we do it this way, so should you."[18] Once elected, the Bush administration attempted to rein in engagement activities through largely symbolic acts. Engagement activities were recast as "security cooperation" to emphasize the security dimension of these activities. There would be no engagement for the sake of engagement. Secretary of Defense Donald Rumsfeld reduced the stature of the primary leaders responsible for engagement by preserving the title commander in chief, or CINC, for the president alone. While largely symbolic, these leaders reverted to their Title 10 designations, combatant commanders, with an emphasis on the combat role they are supposed to fill. And the office of secretary of defense asserted greater control of combatant command's activities by clearly articulating security cooperation goals. In short, President Bush tried to bind U.S. foreign policy along strict lines of national interest reminiscent of the Weinberger Doctrine.[19] However, Bush's efforts were largely ineffective at curtailing security assistance programs; when he left office, state building missions were enshrined in doctrine, and his secretary of defense stayed on to continue this for President Obama. With three presidential administrations accepting the importance of preventing national security threats by helping partners, engagement is here to stay as a bipartisan program.

Andrew Bacevich argued that there was little difference between the Clinton and Bush administrations, which were both grounded in the idea of American exceptionalism.[20] President Bush's objections proved to be very much short-lived and his language became reminiscent of President Clinton's secretary of state, Madeline Albright, who called the United States the indispensable nation. Echoing President Clinton's ideas about engagement, President Bush declared in his 2002 National Security Strategy: "The presence of American forces overseas is one of the most profound symbols of the U.S. commitment to allies and friends.... To contend with uncertainty and to meet the many security challenges we face, the United States will require bases and stations within and beyond Western Europe and Northeast Asia, as well as temporary access arrangements for the long-distance deployment of U.S. forces."[21]

The call was repeated in the 2006 National Security Strategy and energized military engagement: "We choose to deal with challenges now rather than leaving them for future generations. We fight our enemies abroad instead of waiting for them to arrive in our country. We seek to shape the world, not merely be shaped by it; to influence events for the better instead of being at their mercy."[22] There are many examples of what this meant for the Bush administration in practice. One from 2007 was the deployment of a hospital ship to Latin America because "these are people that might not otherwise get the basic health care they need to realize a better tomorrow."[23] Another from 2008 was the deployment of an amphibious ship to West Africa to improve the region's maritime capabilities to interdict smuggling and combat piracy. During this deployment the Navy hosted other government agencies to chart the waters for commerce and NGOs to facilitate fisheries conservation.

Taking its cue from national strategy, the Defense Department sought to codify engagement as a key element in the national military strategic outlook. Positing a new foundation of "shape-respond-prepare," the 1997 strategic defense review not only emphasized the capability to fight and win wars but also placed "greater emphasis on the continuing need to maintain continuous overseas presence in order to shape the international environment."[24] A major goal of engagement, then, is to reduce the drivers of conflicts. At the extreme end, U.S.-led forces respond to state failures to prevent the creation of regional crises. At the middle, U.S. forces provide the necessary skills and equipment to facilitate states resolving their own crises before they lead to state collapse and regional turmoil.

For 1990s conflicts born from state failure in Central Europe, Africa, and Southeast Asia, military forces were directed to conduct stabilization, security, transition, and reconstruction operations in weak or failed states. Former State Department policy planning staff director Stephen Krasner made this point:

"weak and failed states pose an acute risk to U.S. and global security."[25] This represents a key shift in U.S. national strategic thinking. In the past, the United States could filter out internal crises in countries that posed no ready threat to core national interests. The logic changed, however; now all states matter, and those states with an inability to police themselves matter more. With weak states now viewed as threats to the international system, the military stepped up its efforts. Former deputy commander of European Command Gen. Charles Wald explained the U.S. military's role in this. "I think that we cannot allow environments like that to exist anymore."[26] His statement was well grounded in defense strategy as articulated nearly a decade earlier in the 1997 defense review: "In addition to other instruments of national power, such as diplomacy and economic trade and investment, the Defense Department has an essential role to play in shaping the international security environment in ways that promote and protect U.S. national interests. Our defense efforts help to promote regional stability, prevent or reduce conflicts and threats, and deter aggression and coercion on a day-to-day basis in many key regions of the world."[27]

These ideas matured during the 2000s and were widely tested not only in the combat zones of Iraq and Afghanistan but also in regional flashpoints such as the Horn of Africa and Southeast Asia. Defense Secretary Robert Gates underscored the importance of engagement and made promoting partners' security one of his five strategic objectives.[28] "Just about every threat to our security in the years ahead will require working with or through other nations. Success in the war on terror will depend less on the fighting we do ourselves and more on how well we support our allies and partners."[29] For Stephen Emerson, this means breaking the bonds that link conflict, weak states, and terrorism into a "deadly cocktail of political instability and violence."[30] Consequently, the slogan "by, with, and through partners" became the new mantra.

In addition to formal strategic direction from presidential administrations, the military's experiences in Somalia, Haiti, and Bosnia-Herzegovina forced recognition that it is far more effective to prevent state failure than to respond to its aftermath. Thus, the military stepped up its engagement efforts, but military officers learned that training and equipping for major combat is different from the mission of building partnership capacity. The 2008 national defense strategy echoed this finding, "To succeed, we must harness and integrate all aspects of national power and work closely with a wide range of allies, friends, and partners. We cannot prevail alone."[31]

With this in mind, the military developed a doctrine for security cooperation that is driven by combating terrorism, transforming alliances and building coalitions, influencing the direction of key powers, cooperating with parties to resolve regional disputes, deterring and isolating problem states, combating weapons of mass destruction, and realigning forward presence. While some of these objectives are based on the political agenda of the White House, there is remarkable continuity in U.S. national security strategies since Ronald Reagan. Before he was nominated as the Democratic Party's vice presidential candidate, Senator Joseph Biden said, "The events of September 11 made it clear that our armed forces could not focus solely on traditional challenges—threats from traditional states with traditional military capabilities. This new world we have found ourselves in has compelled us to think in a very different way."[32] This has meant changing the U.S. military's focus from traditional warfare to preventive engagement.

Preventive engagement necessitates that the military relocate from its traditional main operating bases in developed countries such as Germany, Korea, and Japan to many smaller locations in less developed countries around the world. Over the last decade, the number of Status of Forces Agreements (SOFAs) has increased from forty to about ninety.[33] With access to military sites around the world, the military has found it essential to advance American interests by building partners' capabilities to generate security, influencing potential adversaries, mitigating the underlying causes of conflict, and enabling rapid action when military intervention is required. For example, a U.S. military base in Okinawa, Japan, simultaneously provides a forward base to deter North Korea, prevents Japan from increasing defense spending and becoming a potential military rival to the United States, and provides U.S. Marines an important training area.

The current focus on transnational threats has been the impetus for engagement in order to build new partnerships. The goal of capacity building is for partners to contain their own security challenges and perform missions of common interest with the United States. With an objective of enabling African countries to solve African crises, the United States has not directly intervened in Sudan. Instead, the United States largely trained and supported African Union forces that deployed to Darfur. The American personnel benefit by training in new environments and building relationships with their foreign counterparts who often rise to their countries' senior levels of influence. The international participants obviously benefit from American training and financial assistance. In this example, the international community has the capability to respond to genocide in Darfur when Sudan's government will not prevent it or stop it. These activities are consistent with U.S. national interests and are advanced not from the Pentagon but by military officers that lead large, joint combatant commands.

Military Engagement and Foreign Policy

The bulk of the literature on the formulation of U.S. foreign policy does not recognize the growing influence of the military and its commanders, which has grown significantly over the course of the last two decades.[34] Scholars typically view the military as adjunct to the executive branch and ignore the important role it plays in the policy process. Although the State Department is America's lead foreign policy organization, U.S. military commanders are as much policy entrepreneurs as they are war fighters, and they increasingly fulfill important diplomatic roles.[35] Epitomized by the activities of geographic combatant commanders, military diplomacy brings all instruments of power to bear to develop relationships and form partnerships.[36] "The current norm of 'been there, done that' visits should be transformed into *persistent, personal, and purposeful* contacts that yield results."[37] For example, Adm. Dennis Blair was credited with opening up greater military-to-military channels between the United States and Taiwan, thereby greatly expanding communications between the two countries' armed forces.[38] The current commander at Pacific Command is attempting to do the same with Beijing. Likewise, in Central Command, the commander saw part of his job as trying to influence states and organizations to contribute to regional stability and ensure the free flow of commerce and positive economic growth.[39]

Military commanders have the resources and reputation necessary to be effective in foreign capitals. This is especially true in regions where security issues dominate such as in the Near East, and in countries that have a tradition of the military dominating society such as Indonesia. Since militaries play important roles in many societies, senior American military officers sometimes command more respect than civilian ambassadors might when dealing with Jakarta, Kampala, or Ankara. With combat experiences that cut across national lines, military leaders share a common language that is used by the Defense Department to create and maintain a global network of military partners.

The prominent role of military commanders has also been a shock to civilians in the Pentagon. An assistant secretary of defense called *Washington Post* reporter Dana Priest to complain about the actual influence of the commanders that he encountered. "I went to graduate school and earned a doctorate in international relations," he said. "I worked in government for 10 years, and no one mentioned these guys to me. I get over here and they are the elephant in the living room!"[40] When it comes to foreign policymaking, the military plays a key role. For example, Gen. Charles Wilhelm testified before Congress seventeen times in support of increasing support to Colombia, and Gen. Wesley Clark testified fourteen times during the Kosovo crisis.[41] No other senior U.S. official, civilian or military, testified as much as these two generals did, and they can champion policy without political affiliation. This gives an officer in uniform tremendous credibility with politicians. More recently, Adm. Jim Stavridis testified that the Senate should ratify free trade agreements with Panama and Colombia, address drug demand in the United States, and continue to support security assistance for Colombia. These policies have little to do with a traditional military portfolio, but given the expansive nature of security today, military commanders do advo-cate for policies like these.

Military leaders typically command more attention than civilian leaders do, and they see themselves as policy actors. For example, in 2006–8, when there was consensus that there was no purely military solution to U.S. policy in Iraq, Gen. David Petraeus dominated policy debates with his frequent public appearances. Much less attention was paid to the top U.S. leader in Iraq, Ambassador Ryan Crocker, who is the president's representative in country and is charged with facilitating the development of Iraq's government and economy.[42] Ironically, the military became the focus of solving nonmilitary problems. A *Wall Street Journal* headline captured this, "Petraeus Shifts Focus to Economy, Politics."[43] This is the central premise of this book, that security and stability are essential for socioeconomic development. To do this, the military employs its latent civilian capabilities to achieve national objectives.

In addition to influence, military leaders also command more capabilities than leaders from other government departments and are consistently viewed by presidential administrations as capable of "getting the job done." But this is not without peril to the military; civilian control is the law. When military leaders do get out of step with the administration, however, they are let go as Adm. William "Fox" Fallon was in spring 2008 because of perceived differences with President Bush on Iran. And in 2009 Gen. David McKiernan was replaced to bring fresh ideas to Afghanistan. His successor, Gen. Stanley McCrystal, precariously navi-gated the civil–military divide during key policy debates on Afghanistan.

The increased role of the military in foreign policy was aided by official actions like the 1986 Goldwater–Nichols Act, by budgetary increases as friends in the neoconservative movement sought to increase the Pentagon's power, and by advances in technology that allow commanders to meet with heads of state easily. When Republicans became the majority in Congress in 1995, "the military came to outrank its civilian chain of command in influence, authority, and resources in many parts of the world."[44] The trend continued under a Republican White House and even further when the Democrats retook control of the Congress in 2005. Despite this growing power, there is very little scholarly analysis of the extent to which military commanders actually influence policy formation.[45] Congress, when it has been controlled by a single party, has been predisposed to fund the military vastly better than any other foreign assistance agency. About one-third of the budget is devoted to personnel costs, which gives the Defense Department a sizable force for conducting diverse activities. The military continues to respond to this funding preference by retooling its force to conduct noncombat opera-tions and to formulate and implement national security policy.

In spite of the size disparity between the departments of State and Defense, the two organizations are mainly mutually supporting. American ambassadors are the president's representatives to particular countries, and U.S. military commanders assist in formulating and implementing the president's foreign policy. Both departments advance and defend national interests. Gen. Anthony Zinni captured the military's perspective on this: "I was asked to carry out presidential and other diplomatic missions that would normally have fallen to diplomats. I'm sure such things frustrated the State Department, but I don't think they disapproved. In fact, they were very supportive. It was more a case of, 'Well, if we can't do it, at least somebody is taking care of it. If it's the CINCs [heads of U.S. military commands], then God bless them.'"[46] Former deputy secretary of state John Negroponte testified to this point; in hard circumstances "the State Department and U.S. Agency for International Development (USAID) have benefited greatly from the Defense Department's cooperation and resources."[47] Military commanders are not autonomous proconsuls or viceroys but conduct missions in support of broader foreign policy objectives and act in accordance with the president's strategy.

General Zinni's comments likely strike a nerve among some foreign service officers, but they have learned to deal with the military's diplomatic and development activities, and U.S. ambassadors ensure that the military programs support larger national security objectives within a particular country. The State Department is well aware of its congressionally limited capacity, but embassies are still the focal point for all U.S. government activities within a particular country. The military does not ignore this and is aware of its supporting role.

Military Diplomacy

Military involvement in foreign policy does not obviate the role of the foreign service officer.[48] However, implementing foreign policy is complex. General Zinni describes his experience: "I never found a way to effectively join forces with the State Department to link their plans with mine. I had no way to get answers to questions like, What's the diplomatic component of our strategy? What's the economic component? How is aid going to be distributed?"[49] Ideally, military activities are driven by national strategy objectives and run parallel with other U.S. government activities, which are also guided by national strategy. Yet generating unified action through the interagency process remains a contemporary national security challenge with repeated calls for organizational realignment for the interagency.[50] To overcome this, the Joint Staff established interagency coordination as a high priority in 2005, and two combatant commands (U.S. Africa Command and U.S. Southern Command) have a decidedly interagency orientation (see chapter 4). Additionally, the Department of State is placing more of its foreign service officers in military commands.

Driven by national security strategy objectives, military diplomacy with a primary mission of developing relationships and partnerships with other militaries or their governments is increasingly common. Reflecting on his command, General Zinni remarked, "As my experiences throughout the region in general and with [Pakistan's former President] Musharraf in particular illustrate, I did not intend to sit back and say, 'Hey, my job is purely military. When you're ready to send me in, coach, that's when I go in.' When I assumed command of CENTCOM [Central Command] and had the ability to choose between fighting fires or preventing them, I chose prevention."[51]

Military commanders have learned that they need to be more than an emergency force responding to crises. In an age of interconnectedness, prevention matters. And when a crisis occurs, military commanders need international partners to be successful. If a common foundation does not exist between the United States and its partners prior to a crisis, then motivations are questioned and action can be more difficult. Many leaders have found that it is much better to consult with allies and partners between crises, not just after one begins. One commander told me that his role was to "build trust and reliability."[52] To gain entry into partners' military establishments, U.S. commanders host regional conferences, build allies' capabilities, and enhance the education of military leaders in partner countries.

Military leaders also have common experiences and common frames of reference that facilitate dialogue and relationships that are less hindered by political realities. Foreign military leaders have often attended U.S. military schools and developed their own networks of U.S. officers as their careers progressed. However, networking is fundamentally different from warfighting. Engagement is about managing relationships, not command and control; it is about cooperation, not fighting; and it is about partnership, not dominance. Success often relies on fully comprehending the influence of warrior-diplomats and these leaders' penchant for intercultural communication.

Warrior-Diplomats

In her September 2000 *Washington Post* series, Dana Priest highlighted the prominent role combatant commanders play in foreign policy. Noting the importance in Central Command of now retired Marine Corps general Tony Zinni, Priest reported that General Zinni routinely engaged in foreign policy activities such as hosting a conference for Persian Gulf states to regionalize defense issues, providing counterterrorism training for Kyrgyzstan, and establishing an engagement strategy with Uzbekistan. Throughout his travels in his twenty-five-country region, General Zinni behaved like an ambassador. He promoted U.S. interests while falcon hunting with Saudi royals, discussed U.S. policy while dining with tribal leaders in Africa, and provided American equipment while drinking vodka and eating horse meat with the Uzbek defense minister.

Because the Central Commander is responsible for an entire region, he takes a macro view of U.S. interests to coordinate policy with twenty-five countries in mind. Noting the importance of the Central Commander to U.S. foreign policy, Zinni remarked that U.S. government agencies "don't have a way to say, 'Okay, Central Asia is a problem, let's all get together, each agency, and build a program.' The geography of the agencies [doesn't] even match up. If I go over to the State Department, I have four bureaus to visit."[53] Things are not much better at the Pentagon, where he had to visit two bureaus: the Office of African Affairs and the Office of Near East and South Asian Affairs.

In other commands, subregional approaches are pursued too. For example, Africa Command aligns its organization around African Union subregional organizations: North Africa, West Africa, Central Africa, East Africa, and Southern Africa. In Southern Command, the organization differentiates its approach in the Caribbean, Central America, the Southern Cone, the Andean Ridge, and the Amazon basin.

Having one commander responsible for an entire region allows combatant commanders to implement national strategy with all of their countries of responsibility in mind. For example, engagement programs developed by Central Command were critical to ensuring access to Afghanistan in 2001. Since it is a part of Zinni's area of focus, Central Command paid attention to Central Asia before it mattered to prosecute the war against the Taliban and al-Qaeda. When it was time for the United States to request basing rights in Central Asia, the United States already had a solid foundation on which to secure bases in Uzbekistan and Kyrgyzstan.

A comparable diplomatic dimension of a combatant commander's duties can be found in the Pacific Command. Before he retired in 2001, Adm. Dennis Blair led America's Pacific forces and proved that he was a valuable American diplomat. When the United States and China confronted each other over the collision between an American reconnaissance aircraft and a Chinese fighter aircraft, Admiral Blair was the point man for the U.S. government who worked directly with the Chinese government to secure the aircrew's release. In 2008 Adm. Tim Keating also found himself as a key foreign policy actor who worked to improve military relations between the United States and China. For him, engagement with his Chinese counterparts is "the best means to reduce the chance of miscalculation, increase our mutual understanding, and encourage cooperation on areas of common concern."[54] Pacific Command continues to work in a trilateral way to bridge historic grievances between South Korea and Japan. This is not simply a case of a rogue commander or renegade viceroy but an American warrior-diplomat pursuing a strategic dialogue to build understanding, improve communication, and reduce the risk of miscalculation.[55] The breadth of Keating's portfolio is demonstrated by his travel schedule, which brought him to twenty-one Pacific countries in 2008.[56]

These brief examples highlight the increased importance of combatant commanders in U.S. foreign policy–making. As a single voice, a regional commander
provides clear, unambiguous policy to an entire region. No other office in the
U.S. government is as sweeping or as well funded. Largely funded through the
Department of State's international assistance budget, military-to-military contacts, military equipment transfers, and combined training activities build partnerships with cooperative governments and increase U.S. access to other countries' bases, intelligence, and resources. Military commanders see these programs
as an ideal way to minimize interoperability problems. The departments of State
and Defense, with the U.S. Embassy Country Team initiating proposals, run the
programs cooperatively. Security assistance is predicated on an interconnected
world assumption where U.S. partners "are better positioned to handle a given
problem because they understand the local geography, social structures, and culture better than we [the United States military] do or ever could."[57] The ultimate
goal is to reduce security deficits that can enable socioeconomic development.

These non-warfighting activities do fulfill important training, basing, and operational requirements for American forces. To advance American interests, combatant commands build partners' capabilities and capacity to generate security,
influence nonpartners and potential adversaries, mitigate the underlying causes
of conflict and extremism, and enable rapid action when military intervention is
required. Because combined operations are the norm today, U.S. forces also need
regular interactions with their international partners who increasingly fill roles in
U.S.-led missions. These activities fulfill current military strategic requirements
of assuring friends and allies, dissuading potential competitors, and deterring
conflicts in nonlethal ways. Military engagement has become one tool—and an
increasingly important one—in the arsenal of American "soft power."

Preventative Engagement

In addition to increasing U.S. influence through military engagement, both policymakers and senior military officers have learned that it is far more effective to
prevent state failure than to respond to its aftermath. Consequently, the military
stepped up its engagement efforts in the early years of the George W. Bush administration. Secretary of State Condoleezza Rice described the new thinking: "In a
world as increasingly interconnected as ours, the international state system is only
as strong as its weakest links. We cannot afford another situation like the one that
emerged in 2001 in Afghanistan."[58] This perception of interdependence was codi-
fied in official military strategy. The 2008 national defense strategy notes, "The
security of the United States is tightly bound up with the security of the broader
international system. As a result, our strategy seeks to build the capacity of fragile or

vulnerable partners to withstand internal threats and external aggression."[59] And the 2010 Quadrennial Defense Review declared, "Preventing conflict, stabilizing crises, and building security sector capacity are essential elements of Amercia's national security approach."[60] Adds Admiral Stavridis, "Throughout U.S. history, our nation has depended upon external partners to help maintain our own security."[61]

The 2007 maritime strategy declares that "preventing war is as important as winning wars." And the 2008 U.S. Marine Corps Strategy and Vision notes that "our future Corps will be increasingly reliant on naval deployment, *preventive in approach*," to achieve national objectives.[62] In practice, preventive military engagements take the form of security cooperation, which is the ability of militaries to interact together to build defense relationships that promote specific security interests, develop allied and friendly military capabilities for self-defense and coalition operations, and provide foreign forces peacetime and contingency access. These activities are in part funded by the State Department to "promote the principles of democracy, respect for human rights, and the rule of law."[63] Chapters 4 and 5 trace the evolution of the military's concepts and doctrine to support these operations, but it is worth exploring how engagement became a central feature of U.S. defense strategy and policy.

During the Bush years, all engagement had to be under the guise of preventing terrorism by getting at root causes. However, as the loaded "global war on terrorism" language fades from the policy lexicon, activities are being recentered around improving social conditions and sovereignty. It is unlikely that program focus will change; it will remain focused on building the security capacity of other countries. While it is politically expedient to characterize a maritime security operation as counterterrorism or counterpiracy, the same activities can reduce illegal smuggling and illegal, unregulated, and unreported fishing, which are primary concerns for many maritime countries. The latter resonates more closely with U.S. partners who do not feel the same level of terrorist threat that the Bush administration did. It remains to be seen how the Obama administration will package security assistance programs, but retaining President Bush's secretary of defense hints at continuity.

In Africa Command, security cooperation has been framed as "active security," which is defined "as a persistent and a sustained level of effort on security assistance programs that prevent conflict and foster continued dialogue and development."[64] This approach attempts to strengthen the sovereignty of governments by increasing their militaries' capacities to protect territory and prevent subnational actors from challenging the government. Furthermore, because militaries can be sometimes the source of social instability through inciting corruption, challenging the government, being a repressive arm of the government, or even spreading HIV/AIDS, military professionalism programs are embedded throughout Africa Command. The programs are designed to bring security to ineffective or vulnerable governments.

The notion of "security first" is based on the idea that societies can only flourish in safe, stable environments.[65] There are obvious limits to this approach, as evidenced by U.S. military assistance to Persian Gulf states such as Saudi Arabia, where regime survival is based on commodity prices and not social development. In much of the world, however, stability has given way to economic development. Given this, defense, development, and diplomacy have been linked as essential elements to bring coherence to U.S. foreign policy. For example, if the Coast Guard assists a country in improving port security, it should also look left and right for diplomatic and development opportunities with other governmental and nongovernmental partners. This can include linking country X with neighboring country Y in a diplomatic agreement to improve information sharing, or linking formal development programs to military construction projects such as airfields or roads to enable private commercial activity.

From a practical standpoint, there are many opportunities for dual-use infrastructure and activities. For a military command to be effective, it needs to have the ability to travel throughout a region and work with its partner countries. In regions of the world with developed infrastructure, training teams can fly via commercial air to their destination. However, some theaters such as Africa are not developed. The lack of infrastructure creates real operational challenges. For example, African airlines account for 4 percent of world travel, but 25 percent of air disasters.[66] Consequently, to improve its effectiveness, Africa Command is likely to assist countries in improving airline safety through training and financial assistance to develop a transportation infrastructure. This may include developing an air traffic control system to improve civilian aviation and cutting down on illegal smuggling. The command likely will also assist countries in improving the quality of their airports, which has obvious consequences for economic development.

Conclusion

Presidents of all political persuasions continue to use the military as a preferred tool of national power in noncoercive ways. Given the strategic rationale and the paradigm shift from traditional to human security, the military has reluctantly embraced this new role, but it has not been easy. There is a natural tendency for the military to eschew non-warfighting activities. Given the very real combat demands of U.S. forces in Iraq and Afghanistan, one would expect to see a decline in nontraditional military activities, yet the creation of U.S. Africa Command and the transformation of U.S. Southern Command, which operates in the Western Hemisphere, illustrate the opposite. National strategies underscore the interdependence of security and prioritize building the capacities of partners as the basis for long-term security. These activities are prevalent in hot war zones such as Iraq, Afghanistan, and the southern Philippines. Candidate Obama echoed these concerns by emphasizing threats that "come from weapons that can kill on a mass scale and from global terrorists who respond to alienation . . . from rogue states . . . from weak states that cannot control their territory or provide for their people."[67] President Obama reinforced this view:

> We have learned from recent experience that when a financial system weakens in one country, prosperity is hurt everywhere. When a new flu infects one human being, all are at risk. When one nation pursues a nuclear weapon, the risk of nuclear attack rises for all nations. When violent extremists operate in one stretch of mountains, people are endangered across an ocean. And when innocents in Bosnia and Darfur are slaughtered, that is a stain on our collective conscience. That is what it means to share this world in the 21st century. That is the responsibility we have to one another as human beings.[68]

Current views of the security environment require that the United States "address security from a holistic perspective and integrate our efforts horizontally across the U.S. government."[69] But the military has painfully learned that it cannot rely on international organizations, allies, or other government departments to fill the void among national ends, ways, and means. It is accepted in doctrine that civilians should perform civilian tasks, but civilians (NGOs included) have limited ability to deploy in sufficient numbers in violent or poorly developed areas of the world.[70] The president, the national security advisor, and prominent cabinet secretaries have failed to create government solutions to national security problems. Consequently, the U.S. military has changed to deliver comprehensive solutions through a new model of defense—security cooperation. To do this, the activities are evolving beyond old models of military assistance that transferred weapons or occasional military interventions. Instead, commands are demilitarizing to be better equipped to address non-warfighting challenges and are incorporating civilians into their command structures. Before discussing the implications of this, it is essential to review the arguments against civilizing the military that inform future strategy, doctrine, organization, and capabilities.

Notes

1. A version of this chapter appeared as Derek S. Reveron, "Military Engagement, Strategy, and Policy," *Orbis* 53, no. 3 (2009): 489–505.

2. Paul Collier, *The Bottom Billion: Why the Poorest Countries Are Failing and What Can Be Done about It* (New York: Oxford University Press, 2007), 125.

3. Francis Fukuyama, *The End of History and the Last Man* (New York: Free Press, 1992).

4. Colin Powell with Joseph E. Persico, *My American Journey* (New York: Random House, 1995), 576.

5. "An Agenda for Peace: Preventive Diplomacy, Peacemaking and Peace-keeping," Report of the Secretary-General pursuant to the statement adopted by the Summit Meeting of the Security Council on 31 January 1992 (June 17, 1992). United Nations Rule of Law, http://es.unrol.org/doc.aspx?n=A_47_277.pdf.

6. "National Policy on Management of Interagency Efforts Concerning Reconstruction and Stabilization." National Security Presidential Directive 44, December 7, 2005. www.fas.org/irp/offdocs/nspd/nspd-44.pdf.

7. Robert Gates, "Remarks as Delivered by Secretary of Defense Robert M. Gates," Landon Lecture (Kansas State University), November 26, 2007. Reprinted in *Military Review* (January–February 2008) and available at www.defense.gov/speeches/speech .aspx?speechid=1199.

8. While the year is arguable, I think the 1986 U.S.-Soviet summit in Reykjavik between Ronald Reagan and Mikhail Gorbachev signaled a clear change in relations. Although political tensions increased in the early Reagan years, Reagan's chairman of the Joint Chiefs of Staff argued publicly that things were different since 1983. Adm. William Crowe testified to Congress that he was not going to be the Paul Revere of the Pacific, saying the "Russians are coming." Politically, that was a difficult position to take for Crowe until after the Reykjavik Summit. In 1987 Admiral Crowe reached agreement with his Soviet counterpart, Marshal Sergei Akhromeyev, to establish a military-to-military relations program. As Crowe tells the story, Akhromeyev initiated the idea in 1987 as a way to reduce tensions between the two superpowers. See chapter 16 in William J. Crowe Jr., *The Line of Fire* (New York: Simon and Schuster, 1993).

9. In 1985 the nature of the ANZUS alliance changed after the government of New Zealand refused access to its ports by nuclear-armed and nuclear-powered warships of the U.S. Navy. After extensive efforts to resolve the issue, the United States suspended its ANZUS security obligations to New Zealand in August 1986. The U.S.-Australia alliance under the ANZUS Treaty remains in full force, as does the Australia–New Zealand alliance. In acknowledgment of New Zealand's contributions to U.S. security goals, the United States in 1996 designated the government of New Zealand a "major non-NATO ally," which allowed increased access to the U.S. defense establishment.

10. John Howard, "50 Years of ANZUS," May 30, 2001. AustralianPolitics.com, www.australianpolitics.com/foreign/anzus/01-05-30howard.shtml.

11. Australia deployed Special Air Service troops for combat operations in Afghanistan and contributed air-to-air refueling aircraft and F/A-18 fighter aircraft (deployed to Diego Garcia to backfill U.S. aircraft deployed elsewhere). Australia also maintained a naval task group of two frigates in the Persian Gulf.

12. Congress enacted the Taiwan Relations Act "to resist any resort to force or other forms of coercion that would jeopardize the security, or the social or economic system, of the people on Taiwan." *Taiwan Relations Act*, Public Law 96-8, 96th Congr., 93 Stat. 14; H.R. 2479 (April 10, 1979).

13. Title 10 U.S. Code Sec. 2350a authorizes the secretary of defense, with the concurrence of the secretary of state, to designate MNNAs for purposes of participating with the Department of Defense (DOD) in cooperative research and development programs. MNNA status does not entail the same mutual defense and security guarantees afforded to NATO members. MNNA status makes a nation eligible to receive priority delivery of excess defense articles; to buy depleted uranium ammunition; to have U.S.-owned war reserve stockpiles on its territory; to enter into agreements with the USG for the cooperative furnishing of training on a bilateral or multilateral basis under reciprocal financial arrangements; to use U.S.-provided foreign military financing for commercial leasing of certain defense articles; to receive loans of materials, supplies, and equipment for cooperative research and development projects, testing, and evaluation; and to receive expedited processing of export licenses of commercial satellites as well as their technologies, components, and systems.

14. Bantz J. Craddock, "United States European Command before the House Armed Services Committee," March 13, 2008, www.dod.mil/dodgc/olc/docs/testCraddock080313.pdf.

15. Derek S. Reveron, "Coalition Warfare: The Commander's Role," *Defense and Security Analysis* 18, no. 2 (June 2002): 107–22.

16. Executive Office of the President, "A National Security Strategy of Engagement and Enlargement," February 1996, 17. Available at www.fas.org/spp/military/docops/national/1996stra.htm#II.

17. Attributed to Dwight D. Eisenhower in Robert Gates, "Reflections on Leadership," *Parameters* (Summer 2008): 6.

18. "Excerpt of Presidential Debate October 12, 2000," www.pbs.org/newshour/bb/politics/july-dec00/for-policy_10-12.html.

19. Ronald Reagan's defense secretary, Casper Weinberger, posited conditions to limit the military's use and to avoid repeating Vietnam and Lebanon. There are six tenets based on a speech Weinberger gave at the National Press Club in 1984: (1) The United States should not commit forces to combat unless the vital national interests of the United States or its allies are involved; (2) U.S. troops should only be committed wholeheartedly and with the clear intention of winning. Otherwise, troops should not be committed; (3) U.S. combat troops should be committed only with clearly defined political and military objectives and with the capacity to accomplish those objectives; (4) the relationship between the objectives and the size and composition of the forces committed should be continually reassessed and adjusted if necessary; (5) U.S. troops should not be committed to battle without a "reasonable assurance" of the support of U.S. public opinion and Congress; and (6) the commitment of U.S. troops should be considered only as a last resort.

20. Andrew J. Bacevich, *American Empire: The Realities and Consequences of U.S. Diplomacy* (Cambridge, MA: Harvard University Press, 2002).

21. Executive Office of the President, "The National Security Strategy of the United States of America," September 2002, 29, http://georgewbush-whitehouse.archives.gov/nsc/nss/2002.

22. Executive Office of the President, "The National Security Strategy of the United States of America," March 16, 2006, i, http://georgewbush-whitehouse.archives.gov/nsc/nss/2006.

23. "President Bush Discusses Western Hemisphere Policy," March 5, 2007, http://georgewbush-whitehouse.archives.gov/news/releases/2007/03/20070305-6.html.

24. William S. Cohen, "Secretary's Message," in "1997 Quadrennial Defense Review," www.fas.org/man/docs/qdr/msg.html.

25. Stephen D. Krasner and Carlos Pascual, "Addressing State Failure," *Foreign Affairs* 84, no. 4 (July–August 2005): 153.

26. Quoted in "U.S.-Trained Force Scour Sahara for Terror Links," *Boston Globe*, December 12, 2004.

27. Department of Defense, "Quadrennial Defense Review," May 1997, www.defense.gov/qdr.archive/index.html.

28. The five objectives of the 2008 national defense strategy are defend the homeland, win the long war, promote security, deter conflict, and win the nation's wars.

29. Gates, "Reflections on Leadership," 7.

30. Stephen A. Emerson, "The Trans-Saharan Arc," in *Flashpoints in the War on Terrorism*, eds. Derek S. Reveron and Jeffrey Stevenson Murer (New York: Routledge, 2006), 257.

31. Department of Defense, "National Defense Strategy of the United States," June 2008, www.defense.gov/news/2008%20National%20Defense%20Strategy.pdf, 1.

32. Joseph Biden, "Military's Expanding Role in U.S. Foreign Policy," Hearing before the Committee on Foreign Relations, United States Senate, 110th Congress, Second Session, July 31, 2008, http://foreign.senate.gov/testimony/2008/BidenStatement0807731.pdf.

33. SOFAs are not basing agreements but are essential when there is long-term U.S. military presence within a country to define the legal rights of military personnel and establish jurisdiction for criminal and civil matters involving military personnel. In cases where SOFAs do not exist, U.S. military personnel can be granted diplomatic immunity under normal bilateral relations.

34. Christopher J. Fettweis, "Militarizing Diplomacy: Warrior-Diplomats and the Foreign Policy Process," in *America's Viceroys: The Military and U.S. Foreign Policy*, ed. Derek S. Reveron (New York: Palgrave Macmillan, 2004).

35. See Derek S. Reveron and Judith Hicks Stiehm, eds., *Inside Defense: Understanding the 21st Century Military* (New York: Palgrave Macmillan, 2008).

36. Military diplomacy is defined as "the ability to support those activities and measures U.S. military leaders take to engage military, defense and government officials of

another country to communicate policies and messages and build defense and coalition relationships." See "Joint Capability Areas Tier 1 U.S. government and Supporting Tier 2 Lexicon, Post 24 August 2006 JROC," available at www.dtic.mil/futurejointwarfare/.

37. Joint Forces Command and European Command, "Draft Military Support to Shaping Operations, Joint Operating Concept," June 5, 2007, 13, www.dtic.mil/futurejointwarfare/joc.htm.

38. Charles Snyder, "U.S. Plan for Defending Taiwan Disclosed," *Taipei Times*, June 5, 2006, 3.

39. "Statement of Admiral William J. Fallon, U.S. Navy, Commander, U.S. Central Command before the Senate Armed Services Committee," March 4, 2008, 14, http://armed-services.senate.gov/e_witnesslist.cfm?id=3158.

40. From Dana Priest's remarks in "Open Forum: The Changing Roles of the Regional Commanders in Chief," March 23, 2001, available at www.state.gov/documents/organization/4398.doc.

41. Fettweis, "Militarizing Diplomacy," 53.

42. A Lexis-Nexis search of the *New York Times* from January 1, 2007, to July 28, 2008, illustrated this. David Petraeus's name appeared 115 times and Ryan Crocker's name appeared only 41 times.

43. Gina Chon, "Petraeus Shifts Focus to Economy, Politics," *Wall Street Journal*, August 21, 2008, A6.

44. From Priest's remarks. See note 41.

45. See Derek S. Reveron, ed., *America's Viceroys: The Military and U.S. Foreign Policy*, (New York, Palgrave Macmillan, 2004).

46. Tom Clancy with Tony Zinni and Tony Koltz, *Battle Ready* (New York: Putnam, 2004), 319.

47. "Testimony for Deputy Secretary John D. Negroponte," Senate Foreign Relations Committee, July 31, 2008, 5. http://foreign.senate.gov/testimony/2008/NegroponteTestimony080731p.pdf.

48. This was noted in the 1997 QDR, Section III. "DoD's role in shaping the international environment is closely integrated with our diplomatic efforts." DOD, "Quadrennial Defense Review," May 1997, www.defense.gov/qdr.archive/index.html.

49. Tony Zinni, *The Battle for Peace: A Frontline Vision of America's Power and Purpose* (New York: Palgrave Macmillan, 2006), 135.

50. Michele Flournoy, "Navigating Treacherous Shoals: Establishing a Robust Interagency Process for National Security Strategy, Planning, and Budgeting," in *Defense Strategy and Forces: Setting Future Directions*, ed. Richmond M. Lloyd (Newport, RI: Naval War College Press, 2007).

51. Tony Zinni, "Military Diplomacy," in *Shaping the Security Environment*, ed. Derek S. Reveron (Newport, RI: Naval War College Press, 2007), 14.

52. Author interview with a combatant commander.

53. Quoted in Dana Priest, "An Engagement in 10 Time Zones; Zinni Crosses Central Asia, Holding Hands, Building Trust," *Washington Post*, September 29, 2000.

54. House Armed Services Committee, "Statement of Admiral Timothy J. Keating, U.S. Navy," March 12, 2008, 5, http://armedservices.house.gov/pdfs/FC031208/Keating_Testimony031208.pdf.

55. DOD, "National Defense Strategy," 10.

56. "Statement of Admiral Keating."

57. DOD, "National Defense Strategy," 8.

58. "Remarks at the Civilian Response Corps Rollout," U.S. Department of State, July 16, 2008.

59. DOD, "National Defense Strategy," 6.

60. DOD, "Quadrennial Defense Review" (Washington, DC, February 2010), 75, http://www.defense.gov/QDR/QDR%20as%20of%2029JAN10%201600.pdf.

61. "The Posture Statement of Admiral James G. Stavridis, United States Navy, Commander, United States Southern Command Before the 110th Congress," 2008, http://armed-services.senate.gov/e_witnesslist.cfm?id=3134.

62. "Marine Corps Vision and Strategy 2025" (Washington, DC: Office of Naval Research, 2008), emphasis added; www.onr.navy.mil/en/~/media/Files/About%20ONR/usmc_vision_strategy_2025_0809.ashx, 6.

63. "Foreign Military Training in Fiscal Years 2005 and 2006," vol. I. U.S. Department of Defense and U.S. Department of State Joint Report to Congress, released September 2006, www.state.gov/t/pm/rls/rpt/fmtrpt/2006.

64. William E. Ward, Commander, United States Africa Command, "Statement before the House Armed Services Committee," March 13, 2008, 7, www.armedservices.house.gov/pdfs/FC031308/Ward_Testimony031308.pdf.

65. Amitai Etzioni argues that U.S. foreign policy should focus on removing security dilemmas for regimes that would allow for social and economic development. His argument is squarely aimed at criticizing the Bush administration's regime change policy, but he fails to miss all of the other defense programs outside of Iraq and Afghanistan. Amitai Etzioni, *Security First: For a Muscular, Moral Foreign Policy* (New Haven, CT: Yale University Press, 2007).

66. Ward, "Statement before Senate," 20.

67. Barack Obama, "Renewing American Leadership," *Foreign Affairs*, July–August 2007, 3.

68. "Remarks of President Barack Obama in Egypt," June 4, 2009, www.whitehouse.gov/the-press-office/remarks-president-cairo-university-6-04-09.

69. William E. Ward and Thomas P. Galvin, "U.S. Africa Command and the Principle of Active Security," *Joint Force Quarterly*, no. 51 (4th quarter, 2008): 62.

70. U.S. Army and U.S. Marine Corps, *Counterinsurgency Field Manual* (Chicago: University of Chicago Press, 2007), 67.

3

Resistance to Military Engagement

OVER THE LAST TWENTY YEARS, as militaries have shifted from a core responsibility of preparing for and prevailing in major war to more direct foreign policy engagements and training partners' militaries, a natural opposition arose. Security scholars and practitioners have been debating the proper use of the armed forces for decades. While some policymakers call for a conservative approach for the use of military power based upon a careful calculation of national interests reminiscent of the Weinberger Doctrine of the 1980s, others seek to apply the military instrument of power to an increasing range of non-warfighting missions such as civil engineering, humanitarian assistance, and disaster relief.

The debate begins with national strategy, which largely determines how presidents use the military. Because of the timing and character of the Clinton administration (see chapter 2), Clinton's 1990s "shape-respond-prepare" strategy gave rise to the "superpowers don't do windows" counterargument. Some identified diplomatic engagement by generals Wesley Clark, Tony Zinni, or Charles Wilhelm in the 1990s or state-building missions in Haiti, Bosnia, and Kosovo as apostasy for an organization that is supposed to prepare for and win the nation's wars. The first year of the Bush administration emphasized this— militaries fight wars and do not conduct foreign policies or do peacekeeping. By the last years of the Bush administration, however, things were very different. His two defense secretaries added security assistance as a strategic pillar by institutionalizing stability operations in 2005 and then irregular warfare in 2008. And security assistance had expanded from 49 to 149 countries over eight years. Finally, the military found itself doing state building in several countries, including Iraq and Afghanistan. In spite of the demand for the U.S. military in these areas, resistance to these missions continued throughout the 2000s.

Civilian Opposition

Former secretary of state Condoleezza Rice said, "Stabilization and reconstruction is a mission that civilians must lead. But for too long, our civilians have not had the capacity to lead, and investments were not made to prepare them to lead. As a result, over the past 20 years, over the course of 17 significant stabilization and reconstruction missions . . . too much of the effort has been borne by our men and women in uniform."[1] In the case of Africa Command, the State Department and the U.S. Agency for International Development (USAID) have exhibited an institutional reluctance to support the new command because Africa Command is seen by many within these organizations to be infringing on their traditional responsibilities.[2] Even after the command stood up in 2008, it still had difficulty filling its billets with nonmilitary personnel or contractors. Other federal departments did not prioritize these positions and minimized their personnel at this military command.

Vice President Joe Biden voiced similar concerns that "there has been a [undesirable] migration of functions and authorities from U.S civilian agencies to the Department of Defense. This has led to concern . . . about what's seen as a creeping militarization . . . of America's foreign policy."[3] Former Clinton-era assistant secretary of defense for public affairs Kenneth Bacon said, "Our [foreign] policy is out of whack. It is too dominated by the military and we have too little civilian capacity. The military should not take on what [USAID] does or the State Department."[4] Representative John Tierney (D-Mass), Chairman of the House Oversight and Government Reform subcommittee on national security and foreign affairs said, "I'm not comfortable that the military is the right entity to be leading all the civilian aspects of this [security cooperation in Africa] and I'm not sure it's fair to put that on the military."[5] Government leaders were nothing short of ambivalent about the changing roles and missions of the U.S. military. But they also did not take any action to replace military personnel with civilian personnel.

Policy analysts also reacted negatively to what was sometimes cast as postmodern imperialism, a failure in civilian control of the military, or a major problem with the interagency process. A report by the Center for Strategic and International Studies, headed by former deputy secretary of state Richard Armitage and former assistant secretary of defense Joseph Nye, lends insight into this dilemma when it warned that "the Pentagon is the best trained and resourced arm in the federal government and as a result it often fills every void . . . expanding the role of the military [in foreign assistance] makes the weaknesses of the civilian tools a self-fulfilling prophecy."[6] Retired U.S. ambassador David Passage goes further and challenges the premise of non-warfighting commands such as Africa Command and Southern Command. He wrote, "We do not permit our military to train our own police and law enforcement personnel and do economic development work in the U.S.," so it should not be done by the military in Africa or Latin America.[7] Retired ambassador Charles Ray wrote, "Military units, particularly those deployed abroad for short-term missions, cannot be expected to be sensitive to or even aware of the foreign policy situation."[8] His concerns extended to differences in organizational culture: "Military organizations are mission oriented and tend toward linear thinking. To the military professional there is a problem, and some action must be taken to solve it. While external factors might be given some consideration, the mission always comes first. It is understandably difficult for a military commander to worry about future bilateral diplomatic relations in the face of an immediate problem requiring a solution."[9]

Reacting to the preventive intent of security assistance, Justin Logan and Christopher Preble found that the United States "has been overly prone to military intervention, without a proper appreciation of the costs ahead of time."[10] John Hillen raised this concern about fears of overextension: "Most Americans would agree that the United States must be active in the world, but not so active that the effort wastes American resources and energies in interventions that yield little or no payoff and undermine military preparedness."[11] Andrew Bacevich linked the tendency for the military to do it all with a disturbing trend within American politics that linked "a militaristic cast of mind with utopian ends," which leads to an increased propensity to use force.[12] Some see the military undermining the authority of the secretary of state by setting the U.S. foreign policy agenda.[13] One sitting combatant commander made the explicit point that he does not make foreign policy but implements policy made by the State Department.[14] In actuality, combatant commanders work for the secretary of defense, but they have become extremely sensitive to the misperceived disconnects between the Department of State and the Department of Defense.

In addition to policy opposition, international public opinion on the increasing uses of the U.S. military is mixed. Majorities in thirteen out of fifteen different countries polled say the United States is "playing the role of world policeman more than it should be." This is the sentiment of nearly three-quarters of those polled in France (89 percent), Australia (80 percent), China (77 percent), Russia (76 percent), Peru (76 percent), the Palestinian territories (74 percent), and South Korea (73 percent).[15] While negative feedback to U.S. activities is substantial, negative reactions appear to be based on the mode of U.S. involvement rather than on U.S. involvement itself.[16] Publics around the world do not want the United States to disengage from international affairs but rather to participate in a more cooperative and multilateral fashion.[17] Majorities in thirteen out of fifteen publics polled support U.S. involvement in a more cooperative and multilateral fashion through international institutions instead of what they perceived as irresponsible unilateralism.[18] This is highly correlated with the unpopular

Bush administration, and it remains to be seen how the Obama administration will be viewed over time.

Concerns about security assistance activities of the military, which dwarfs other federal departments, inevitably fuel calls for interagency reform. Critics contend that if only the State Department were on equal footing with the Defense Department, the United States would have a more balanced, less belligerent foreign policy. The effects of this imbalance were recognized by a Senate Foreign Relations Committee report: "As a result of inadequate funding for civilian programs, U.S. defense agencies are increasingly being granted authority and funding to fill perceived gaps."[19] Consequently, the military runs human rights initiatives, HIV/AIDS programs, and hosts conferences on natural resource management. A National Defense University conference on Africa Command elicited concerns about these activities; its attendees were concerned "that Africa Command risked becoming simply another competitor in the interagency race for scarce resources, and part of an improper trend in the militarization of U.S. foreign aid."[20] Development specialists point out that the military personnel in the field are about ten times more expensive than aid workers are.[21]

Analysis of the international assistance budget does not support this perception. Most U.S. assistance goes to nonsecurity programs. In contrast to public perceptions, the United States does not dole out suitcases filled with cash to allies. Instead, foreign assistance typically takes the form of U.S. goods and services. Because of support to Israel and Egypt, the largest line item is foreign military financing (see chapter 5). The effect of this is profound. For example, every American president since Jimmy Carter has supported Israel with billions of dollars of weapons annually while seeking a permanent two-state solution. Providing weapons to Israel, promoting regional stability, or developing a Palestinian state are decidedly unlinked in U.S. national strategy and are a constant rallying cry for those that see U.S. foreign policy filled with hypocrisy. The United States accepts Israel's view of the Middle East and will not even try to use the assistance as leverage in peace negotiations. Critics of U.S. policy in the Middle East do make these connections.

Before she left government, Secretary of State Rice bemoaned the inability of civilian institutions to be more engaged in security programs, but her solution was much too limited and could not relieve the military of its non-warfighting roles. "Though significant changes in the U.S. government's bureaucratic organization and performance have taken place since 11 September 2001, we have yet to see a serious reform of our non-kinetic departments and agencies in order to put them on a war footing."[22] Since Rice was President Bush's national security advisor as well as his security of state, her statement is as much a criticism of her own efforts as it is of the U.S. government. One attempt to fix this is the Office of the Coordinator for Stabilization and Reconstruction (S/CRS). Since 2004 strategy, planning, and budgeting that would enable the United States to assess long-term threats and opportunities, set clear priorities, allocate and manage risk, develop long-term 'whole of government' approaches, identify critical capability areas in which to invest, and make course corrections along the way."[28]

For many it is obvious that "the United States is hugely over-investing in military tools and under-investing in diplomatic tools. The result is a lopsided foreign policy that antagonizes the rest of the world and is ineffective in tackling many modern problems."[29] Stephen Emerson lamented, "Over-reliance on military and security tools is likely to prove counterproductive and destabilizing in the long run."[30] In the case of Africa, many countries welcome the increased attention and resources that will go with the new Africa Command. However, there are concerns that African military establishments do not deserve increased support given that about one-third of the current regimes came to power through military means.[31] Somehow the United States has to ensure that it does not support the next Idi Amin, Mobutu Sese-Seko, or Olusegun Obasanjo. Almost all African countries have made it clear that they want nothing to do with hosting Africa Command, while others have even warned that it should not be stationed in any country neighboring them.[32] South African defense minister Mosiuoa Lekota described African animosity to the U.S. military's changing role. "The Africa Command initiative has raised a lot of attention because at some point there is a certain sense that Africa has to avoid the presence of foreign forces on its soil."[33] Countries with a colonial heritage have difficulty seeing foreign military forces in nonimperial ways. Furthermore, countries with their own regional ambitions do not welcome the competition.

Military Opposition

There is also substantial debate on proper roles and missions within the military.[34] Sam Sarkesian's analysis of the Army officer corps in Vietnam provides a useful structure to understand broader military culture. He saw three types of officers: traditionalists, transitionalists, and modernists.[35] The traditionalists were largely World War II veterans who were frustrated that the United States was not applying conventional warfare practices to achieving victory in Southeast Asia. For example, Gen. William Westmoreland, who ran military operations in Vietnam, thought that "the United States failed in Vietnam because it did not use its military power to maximum advantage."[36] The transitionalists cut their teeth in the 1950s and envisioned technology enhancing conventional warfare. Along these lines, the era of strategic aviation rose to combat larger Soviet conventional forces. And the modernists, largely affected by their Vietnam experience, believed that conventional militaries were somewhat irrelevant to insur-

S/CRS within the Department of State has been working toward pɪ civilian reconstruction staff under the Active Reserve Corps, Standby ł Corps, and Civilian Response Corps. These groups are designed to "buil« effective partnerships among our government's many civilian departmen agencies, among our civilian and military institutions, together with our friends and allies abroad, and perhaps most importantly, with foreign leː and citizens whose countries are in crisis, or approaching crisis, and who ᵥ and need our support."[23]

With an ambitious goal of having civilian experts deploy to crisis zones ᵢ coordinate whole of government responses, the corps' proposal suffered frᵢ limited resources. With a requested 2009 budget of $249 million to fund jᵤ 250 personnel, this Corps is more suitable for a relatively permissive, smɑ environment such as Haiti and not postconflict zones such as the Balkans, th Middle East, or Central Asia. Staffing for stabilization and reconstruction in the Active Reserve Corps has been a tough sell for mid-career foreign service offi-cers. A Government Accountability Office report in October 2007 described the difficulty that S/CRS had in recruiting only eleven of the fifteen then-authorized positions.[24] At the end of 2009 the corps included 78 active and 554 reserve per-sonnel.[25] In the field, S/CRS has yet to actually form a provincial reconstruction team or provide staff for extended duty in either Iraq or Afghanistan. Even with the proposed two thousand reserve personnel, the Corps could still not replace a modest size military-led civil affairs effort such as the one based in Djibouti. Even before this initiative, it was obvious that the creation of a civilian nation-building organization would not let the military off the hook; "the bulk of the manpower for any nation building assignment would still have to come from the Pentagon."[26] In late 2009 the Department of State was looking to the military reserves to fill these billets.

Mitchell Thompson argues that to remedy this political and budgetary imbal-ance necessarily entails "breaking the proconsulate." Thompson writes, "Our current geographic Combatant Commands should be redesigned to break their heavy military orientation, and be transformed into truly interagency organiza-tions, under civilian leadership, and be prepared to conduct the full spectrum of operations using all elements of national power within their assigned regions."[27] This call is echoed by current strategy to combat international terrorism that sees the military playing only a supporting role to other federal departments, which can counter terrorists' ideology, interdict terrorist financing, and promote devel-opment among vulnerable populations—tasks that are not core military func-tions. As discussed in chapter 4, Thompson's view underlies how U.S. Southern Command is changing and U.S. Africa Command is being constructed, but these roles are still filled by military personnel conducting non-warfighting missions. Michelle Flournoy argued for establishing "a robust interagency process for gencies. For them, economy of violence, small unit tactics, and civil–military cooperation were essential to securing the population from insurgents.

Sarkesian's typology is historically important, but in today's environment, the debate is focused on two core questions. First, what went wrong after major combat in Iraq and Afghanistan? For some, the Iraq and Afghanistan wars have been a rude awakening for the military's shortcomings.[37] Second, what are the implications of these lessons for how the military trains and equips for the future? Andrew Bacevich saw answers divided into two basic camps and labeled the protagonists as either crusaders or conservatives.[38] The basic division is right, but if the question of military strategy is expanded beyond counterinsurgency to include security assistance and building partners' capacity, there is an important faction of conservatives that I call modernists. Modernists are devout followers of military transformation and effects-based operations. Modernists see a natural trade-off between personnel and technology, which undermines the ability to conduct personnel-intense security assistance programs or irregular campaigns. The remainder of this section examines resistance to the changing face of the U.S. military, and I posit three schools: traditionalist, modernist, and irregular.

The Three Schools

The traditionalist school sees challenges from potential peer competitors that require preparation for high-end warfare reminiscent of D-day and the Battle of Midway. For Army chief of staff Gen. George Casey, traditionalists see that "lethality is our core competency."[39] Traditionalists object to soft uses of the military and worry that these "feel good" operations undermine the military's warfighting ethos. This tends to be the default position in the military. Gen. Tony Zinni remarked, "The Service Chiefs have minimal interests in, and little insight into, engagement programs."[40] Consequently, there was much outrage and foot dragging in response to non-warfighting missions conducted in the 1990s. When pushed, the Pentagon could deploy the National Guard or Reserve forces to conduct soft missions.

The modernist school sees similar challenges in potential peer competitors but sees preparation for major combat leveraging technology to overmatch potential challengers' large standing militaries. Modernists object to the high levels of manpower required for stability and engagement operations because they negatively impact acquisition accounts. The military spends more money on health care than warships. For modernists, mass is not a principle of warfare but a liability.

The irregular school, which is largely discussed in this book, sees the security environment dominated by weak states and nonstate actors, which necessitates a military optimized for small wars. In irregular warfare, it is better to address underlying conditions or confront local crises before they become regional ones.

The rest of this chapter analyzes the debate among the three schools. The remaining chapters will consider the implications of the irregular school on military strategy, doctrine, and force structure.

Traditionalist View

The non-warfighting roles of the U.S. military have attracted substantial criticism from within the military itself as being contradictory to the military's warfighting ethos. For example, John Hillen writes, "To maintain the skills necessary to execute this [warfighting] function requires strategy, doctrine, training, and force structure focused on deterrence and war fighting, not on peacekeeping missions."[41] Air Force general Charles Dunlap wrote "forget the lessons of Iraq" and reject the idea that soldiers should be social workers, engineers, schoolteachers, nurses, and boy scouts.[42] The Army's own 2008 strategy echoed this: "We have focused our training and leader development almost exclusively on counter-insurgency operations (COIN) to the detriment of major combat operations."[43] And Army brigade commanders weighed in from Iraq charging that the Army is "mortgaging [its] ability to fight the next war."[44] Chairman of the Joint Chiefs of Staff Adm. Mike Mullen erected a signpost, "We've converted from a conventional force to focus on counterinsurgency. That said, I think we've got to broaden our training and readiness with respect to full spectrum conflicts, put in balance the counterinsurgency requirement, which is very much in evidence in Iraq and Afghanistan, and preserve the capability to prosecute a conventional war."[45] Fundamentally, traditionalists are concerned about transforming a warfighting organization into a police organization that serves and protects— one that is ill suited for major combat.

The traditionalists cling to the military's historic role as defender of the state with deterring or waging combat as its sole purpose. For them, small wars or military engagement activities are simply costly distractions. Traditionalists see major war against another military power as the greatest potential threat to national security. For example, Colin Gray argues that great power politics, regional nuclear wars, and traditional conflict will return.[46] In general, the Defense Department develops a military in line with Gray's predictions, and it is more interested in preparations for two major theater wars than peacetime engagement or stability operations.[47] After all, "only peer competitor nations have the ability to end the existence of the United States."[48] For the Army perspective of this view, Col. Gian Gentile captures the frustration with the changing face of the U.S. military. For him, there are very real limits to what can be accomplished and great strategic risk: "By placing nation building as its core competency over fighting, our Army is beginning to lose its way, and we court strategic peril as a result."[49]

Gentile reaches back to doctrine from his formative years that saw military operations involving "fundamental decisions about when and where to fight and whether to accept or decline battle."[50] Gentile has become the traditionalists' traditionalist, arguing, "The Army has been steamrolled by a process that proposes its use as an instrument of nation building in the most unstable parts of the world."[51] For Gentile and other traditionalists, shifting capabilities away from traditional warfare tempts "the fate of many past states and their militaries that thought they had become smarter than war and had divined its future, only to find out they were wrong after squandering much blood and treasure."[52]

The Marine Corps is also debating the meaning of current missions for its future, and there is genuine concern that the core competency of amphibious operations has sufficiently eroded. Since 2001 Marines fly into combat zones on chartered airliners instead of coming ashore via landing craft across the beach. As combat operations wound down in Iraq in 2008 and were increasing in Afghanistan, the Marine Corps tried to formally extricate itself from counter-insurgency and nation building in Iraq. Marine Corps commandant Gen. James Conway stated that the Marine Corps is a "fighting machine," and it needs to be in Afghanistan "where there's a fight" and where it can be used better.[53] Speaking as the head of the Marine Corps, he said, "It's our view that if there is a stiffer fight going on someplace else in a much more expeditionary environment where the Marine Air-Ground Task Force really seems to have a true and enduring value, then that's where we need to be."[54]

Opposition to nation building or stability operations is so strong that the deputy secretary of defense issued a directive mandating that the services treat stability operations equal to major combat for purposes of force planning. The Defense Department directed that "U.S. military forces shall be prepared to perform all tasks necessary to establish or maintain order when civilians cannot do so."[55] This 2005 directive, which elevated stabilization and reconstruction missions to equal footing with warfighting, made it clear that such efforts were a national security priority for the military equal with high-intensity combat operations. A similar directive in 2008 mandated that irregular warfare is as "strategically important as traditional warfare."[56] Secretary of Defense Gates said, "The wars we are in clearly have not earned much of a constituency in the Pentagon as compared to the services' conventional modernization programs."[57] Consequently, the secretary of defense believed it was essential to institutionalize those capabilities.

Others have questioned whether military officers have or can reasonably be expected to acquire the linguistic skills and political and cultural knowledge to operate effectively as surrogate diplomats. A senior diplomat told me, "It's a silly military officer who thinks he can operate as he wishes in a foreign environment."[58] The military brings a security mindset and asks the question, "what is the threat," as opposed to a diplomatic or development perspective, which asks "what is the need."[59] Consequently, Secretary of Defense Gates noted, "if we are to meet the myriad challenges around the world in the coming decades, this country must strengthen other important elements of national power, both institutionally and financially, and create the capability to integrate and apply all of the elements of national power to problems and challenges abroad."[60] This idea is repeated in the 2008 National Defense Strategy: "We as a nation must strengthen not only our military capabilities, but also reinvigorate other important elements of national power."[61] For Vice President Joseph Biden, the military's non-warfighting role

> is problematic for several reasons. First, the increasing dominance of the military in our foreign policy may inadvertently limit our options—when the military is the most readily available option, it is more likely to be used, whether or not it is the best choice. Second, how we balance economic and military aid to a country influences perceptions about U.S. priorities and how we choose to project our power. A foreign policy that overemphasizes the military runs the risk of displacing or overshadowing broader policy and development objectives. Third, focusing on the immediate military dimensions of combating extremism instead of pursuing a long-term strategy in vulnerable countries could have the unintended consequence of purchasing short-term gains at the expense of long-term stability and sustained development. Finally, militaries are good at winning wars and training armies. But, in my view, we do not want soldiers training lawyers or setting up court systems. Or instructing health-care workers on HIV/AIDS prevention. Or running a micro-finance program. Out of necessity, our men and women in uniform have gotten very good at this. But it is not their primary mission; war-fighting is."[62]

From an institutional perspective, privileging building partners is seen as diversion from warfighting. The 2008 national defense strategy underscores this point. "In the long run the Department of Defense is neither the best source of resources and capabilities nor the appropriate authority to shoulder these tasks."[63] To coordinate the military and civilian agencies operating in geographic theaters, the president should appoint a civilian theater commander of sufficient experience and authority to understand and integrate all facets of the interagency community, especially the traditionally domestically oriented agencies that have so far been largely sidelined.[64]

Modernist View

The modernist school is a subset of the traditional school. It sees preparing for and prevailing in major war the military's sole purpose, but the key difference for the modernist school is the role of technology. For the traditionalist, mass through personnel numbers matters and is a principle of war. For the modernist, technology replaces mass and focuses on an operation's effects. Through technology, the military assumes that its technological prowess prevents challengers to U.S. dominance.[65] The role of technology was essential during the Cold War to counter numerically superior Soviet forces, but technology really took hold after Desert Storm, enabled by the information technology revolution. During the 1990s the military services became transfixed on technology under a program called "transformation," which was defined as "a process that shapes the changing nature of military competition and cooperation through new combinations of concepts, capabilities, people, and organizations that exploit our nation's advantages and protect against our asymmetric vulnerabilities to sustain our strategic position."[66]

Scholars and practitioners debated transformation and the existence of a revolution in military affairs, that information technology could propel a new type of warfare.[67] Moving beyond the American way of attrition warfare, the new method "eschews the bloody slogging matches of old. It seeks a quick victory. . . . Its hallmarks are speed, maneuver, flexibility, and surprise."[68] Future military operations would emphasize "stand-off firepower over physical movement, software over hardware, and extensive deployment of light infantry as well as special forces over armored or mechanized forces."[69] The key advocate was Vice Adm. Art Cebrowski, who argued that through networked sensors, dominant battlespace awareness, and precision weapons, "you can achieve your initial military ends without the wholesale slaughter" endemic to traditional warfare.[70] Former vice chairman of the Joint Chiefs of Staff, Adm. William Owens, contended that technology could eliminate the fog and friction inherent in warfare, which would reduce overall risk to using the military.[71] The meaning of this was clear for Vice Admiral Cebrowski:

We are entering a new era of military operations and capabilities. The very character of warfare is changing to account for the massive implications of the information age. It embodies the new decision logic with attributes we will become increasingly familiar with and comfortable. We can already see its effects in current operations. The last time we witnessed change of this magnitude was with the advent of the industrial age and the levee en masse (the mobilization of entire societies for war). Both of these events are rapidly receding into the past. A new American way of war has emerged—network centric operations.[72]

During the 1990s, the technologists prevailed in defense debates; personnel numbers declined overall, but investments in technology continued. The rationale was clear; technology could make warfighting more efficient, which was needed because of shrinking defense budgets that saw deep personnel cuts. As opposed to mass as a principle of war, network-centric war espoused "demassed" forces that substituted information and effects obviating the need to concentrate physical forces.[73] Gen. Charles Dunlap argued that in the future, "air strikes to demolish enemy capabilities complemented by short-term, air assisted raids and high-tech Air Force surveillance" would be needed, not "colossal, boots on the ground efforts."[74]

Transformation has had a profound effect on how the United States and other countries think about and wage war. China, for example, wants to "informationize" and modernize its national defense by 2020. The U.S. Navy could claim that its next-generation destroyer has the same capabilities of twelve current *Arleigh Burke*–class destroyers and that it could get by with fewer ships because of technology. The U.S. Air Force has illustrated that through better targeting and precision weapons, one modern aircraft is as effective as a squadron was during the 1990s or as effective as hundreds of aircraft were in World War II.

Overall, modernists argue that U.S. military strength rests on the foundation of technological superiority, not raw numbers or mass, and that the 2001 war in Afghanistan was the test case for the modernist way of war.[75] In that war a very small U.S. force supporting Afghan groups, including the Northern Alliance, and linked through technology to U.S. airpower captured much of the country in less than two months.[76] Likewise, 2003 combat operations in Iraq were also seen as validation of the modernist way of war. After all, Baghdad was captured in just three weeks. Max Boot wrote in 2003 that U.S. victory in Iraq "must rank as one of the signal achievements in military history."[77] Ralph Peters wrote, "The basic lessons that governments and militaries around the world just learned was this: Don't fight the United States. Period. This stunning war did more to foster peace than a hundred treaties could begin to do."[78]

For Boot and others at the time, U.S. general Tommy Franks was in the pantheon of military leaders. Yet in both Iraq and Afghanistan, what happened after major combat is what mattered most. The lack of preparation for postcombat and counterinsurgency exposed the limits of a high-tech military that sacrifices manpower for technology. As Marine lieutenant general Paul Van Riper pointed out, "once you understand how you're going to fight, then you bring the technology to it. If you lead with the technology, I think you're bound to make mistakes."[79] Maj. Gen. Robert Scales argued that "net-centric warriors are best able to make their arguments in big wars against enemies who depend on the electromagnetic spectrum and uncluttered mediums such as air, sea, and space."[80] H. R. McMaster saw a "wide disparity between prewar military thought and the reality of those conflicts that also helps explain why the overextension and strain on U.S. land forces was described as a temporary 'spike,' why senior military and defense officials resisted reinforcing forces that were clearly overtasked, and why leaders repeatedly denied the need to expand the size of the Army and Marine Corps despite the strain on these forces."[81] This includes poor planning assumptions and bad policy decisions. Consequently, the irregular warfare school gained popularity to explain why and how the military should think beyond major combat as a core mission.

Irregular View

Retired Army lieutenant colonel John Nagl epitomizes the irregular warfare school for his expansive view of the security environment and the broad role that the military should play in preventing local conflicts that impact U.S. national security. The logic of this view is embedded in national security thinking today, as discussed in chapter 2. Instability creates alienated populations and ungoverned spaces that can become incubators for international security challenges that range from anti-Americanism to terrorism. In Nagl's influential 2002 book, *Counterinsurgency Lessons from Malaya and Vietnam*, he identified the military implications of this.[82] The U.S. military should not just be able to dominate land, sea, and air domains but should "change entire societies." For Nagl, "the Army today is out of balance, but not just because of a stressful operational tempo and certainly not because of a long-overdue increase in counterinsurgency training and education. Rather, it is because the Army, along with the broader defense establishment it is a part of, remains rooted in an organizational culture that continues to prioritize the requirements for a hypothetical future big war over the irregular conflicts the force is currently fighting."[83] This is consistent with Thomas Hammes's ideas about fourth-generation warfare, which focused on nonstate actors waging political and social warfare against states.[84] Given the insurgencies that arose after major combat concluded in Afghanistan and Iraq, fourth-generation theorists gained currency. Tim Benbow sees the concept of fourth-generation warfare as a useful corrective for the military's tendency to focus on interstate warfare.[85] And this view of warfare is not new.

The Army Field Manual says of stability operations, "Contrary to popular belief, the military history of the United States is one characterized by stability operations, interrupted by distinct episodes of major combat."[86] The last major American sea battle was Leyte Gulf in 1944 and the last serious air-to-air engagement was Linebacker II in 1972.[87] World War III with the Soviet Union only happened in war games and not the real world, yet many military officers are affected by that virtual war.

Before World War II, specialized civil affairs units did not even exist and combat operations and governance operations occurred in tandem.[88] It was not until after Vietnam that training and advising indigenous forces, establishing police and local governance, and developing dual-use civil infrastructure largely migrated to the Special Forces community. Since 2001 the demand for these operations has outpaced Special Forces' ability to conduct these operations alone, and the scope of warfare has changed.

Fred Kagan argued that "the ability to simply sit on some spot and hold it without killing anyone is one of the most important aspects of the Army's contribution to war, and it is critical to peacekeeping."[89] Thus the Army in particular, and the military in general, has the capabilities and capacity for non-warfighting operations. The military simply chooses to forget it. Nagl and others have argued, "rather than rethinking and improving its counterinsurgency doctrine after Vietnam, the Army sought to bury it, largely banishing it from its key field manuals and the curriculum of its schoolhouses."[90] The irregular warfare school is fighting today to ensure that history is not repeated.

Likewise, the modernist school, with its emphasis on technology over manpower, severely limited the military in Iraq. Even after it was clear that the ground forces were too small and severely strained, the Defense Department's strategic review prescribed the same size force as if the operations in Iraq and Afghanistan did not exist. Soon after the results were released, Max Boot wrote: "The U.S. lead in high-tech warfare is even greater than the British Empire's was in the nineteenth century. . . . But when it comes to old-fashioned nation building and counterinsurgency operations, the United States lags behind both the Victorian British army and its modern successor."[91] The failure for the Pentagon to realize this and the missteps in Iraq likely led President Bush to accept Secretary of Defense Donald Rumsfeld's resignation in November 2005.

Thus the irregular warfare school highlights the dangers of ignoring history and the historic change that is reflected in the lessons of Iraq and Afghanistan. Nagl reminds us that "inadequate contingency planning by both civilian leaders and military commanders to secure the peace contributed to the chaotic conditions that enabled insurgent groups to establish themselves. With some notable lower level exceptions, the institutional Army did not adapt to these conditions until it was perilously close to losing these wars."[92] The House of Representatives Committee on Armed Services noted that "the Provincial Reconstruction Team experience in Afghanistan and Iraq demonstrates that, where inadequate civilian capacity to deploy for postconflict stabilization and reconstruction operations exist, military and Department of Defense civilian personnel will be employed to carry out stability operations, regardless of whether they possess the requisite skills, expertise or training."[93]

This is reflected in the Army's counterinsurgency strategy, which states unequivocally that nonmilitary factors are primary and suggests a ratio of 80 percent political to 20 percent military in counterinsurgency activities. In spite of this, the military provides 99 percent. But there is no easy division of labor between a "Marine Corps" and a "Peace Corps."[94] Unlike conventional warfare where "military (lethal) action . . . is generally the principal way to achieve the goal" and "politics as an instrument of war tends to take a back seat," in unconventional warfare, "politics becomes an active instrument of operation" and "every military move has to be weighed with regard to its political effects and vice versa."[95] David Galula argues that, due to the centrality of politics to this type of warfare, counterinsurgent forces must craft a political and non-warfighting strategy that is sensitive to the needs of the population; that seeks to secure their loyalty to the government; that mobilizes the community to identify, expel, or fight the insurgent; and that extends the authority and reach of the central government.[96]

These ideas took center stage when Gen. David Petraeus executed it in Iraq. In his farewell letter to U.S. forces in Iraq, he set the tone of future debate on the U.S. military. He wrote, "You have not just secured the Iraqi people, you have served them, as well. By helping establish local governance, supporting reconstruction efforts, assisting with revitalization of local businesses, fostering local reconciliation, and conducting a host of other non-kinetic activities, you have contributed significantly to the communities in which you have operated. Indeed, you have been builders and diplomats, as well as guardians and warriors."[97] For Michael Vlahos, the military "must now rule as well as fight."[98] As will be discussed later, lessons coming from nonpermissive environments such as Afghanistan are being applied in permissive environments such as East Africa.

Hybrid Wars

In spite of the three schools' attempts to define three unique wars of the future, there is an emerging consensus that future war will have elements of all three or will be hybrid wars. A hybrid war has the "lethality of state conflict with the fanatical and protracted fervor of irregular warfare."[99] While the term did not gain currency until 2008, modern hybrid wars trace their roots to Marine general Charles Krulak's three-block war idea. Influenced by his experience in Somalia in the early 1990s, Krulak wrote, "At one point in time, one block, they've got a child in their hands, they're wrapping that child in swaddling clothes, they're feeding it, and it's called humanitarian assistance. The next moment, they're keeping two factions apart—that's called peacekeeping. And what you're seeing is the third block, every once in a while coming into the second, and the third block in the three-block war is what we call mid-intensity, highly lethal conflict."[100]

The institutional military attempted to run away from a three-block war depiction of the future and left it dependent on other organizations to be relieved. The 1990s are instructive. In Somalia, the military was able to hand off relief operations to the United Nations. In Rwanda, the military was able to avoid conflict and peacekeeping altogether. And in the Balkans, NATO and American National Guard and Reserve units primarily conducted the stabilization operations after the high-intensity air campaign concluded. Active forces largely remained in reserve for potential war with Iraq or North Korea. But for Krulak and others like him, this was a mistake. He said, "We're not going to see the son of Desert Storm anymore. You're going to see the stepchild of Chechnya."[101] But the Pentagon ignored this.

In a hybrid world, "Microsoft coexists with machetes, and stealth is met by suicide bombers."[102] Hybrid war, like almost all wars in history, can be chaotic. It is not only defined by fog and friction, it is fraught with ambiguity of objective. Preparation for hybrid war underlies significant change in the military. Secretary of Defense Gates told an audience at the Air War College, we "need to think about future conflicts in a different way. To recognize that the black and white distinction between irregular war and conventional war is an outdated model."[103] The chairman of the Joint Chiefs of Staff echoed this. "In every operational situation, the joint force commander will have to develop a concept of operations that integrates—and reconciles the frequently competing demands of—combat, security, engagement, and relief and reconstruction as they apply."[104] In short, the military can no longer disaggregate war and assign certain responsibilities to particular forces or agencies. Instead, all personnel need the capability to adapt to a variety of missions.

Conclusion

The traditionalist school and irregular warfare school do agree on at least one thing—prevailing in Iraq and Afghanistan is essential. Defeat, perceived or otherwise, would have catastrophic impact on the United States' image and negative impact on the military's morale. Where the schools differ is on future defense planning. To date, the assumption has been if the military is prepared for high-end, major combat, it can conduct lesser contingencies such as counterinsurgency or security assistance. Traditionalists argue that preparing only for lesser contingencies will undermine the military's future ability for high-end conflict. Marine major general Larry Taylor explains:

> Complex, irregular warfare may be the most likely fight . . . but are you prepared to guarantee that? It may be that nobody can beat us in a conventional fight today, but what we buy today is what we will have to fight with in 2020. Furthermore, advertising that our focus of effort is on the low-to-mid intensity fights of the future reduces the deterrence that powerful

conventional capabilities demonstrate to traditional state actors. Remember, phase 1 of the plan for any big fight is to, hopefully, deter the enemy from even starting the fight. Non-state actors, guerrillas, terrorists, whatever, are not likely to be deterred by our capabilities. Nation-states are. We had better damn well have the capability to fight the guerrilla *and* the nation-state, regardless of which of these is more or less likely.[105]

In contrast, Marine general James Mattis said this: "If we don't set up some kind of magnet to pull the [Defense] Department out of its good old 'mano-a-mano' conventional war focus, then we won't shift the budgeting, we won't shift the focus over where it has to go."[106] His view is embedded in the vision of the Marine Corps, which sees itself as training and equipping two-fisted fighters "capable of offering an open hand to people in need or a precise jab to an adversary in an irregular warfare environment; while at the same time, ready to wield a closed fist in the event of major combat operations."[107] Security assistance gives marines (and soldiers, sailors, and airmen) ready opportunities to practice giving people an open hand.

As this chapter suggests, the concerns about the changing face of the military are very real, and the debate on appropriate roles and missions is ongoing. Much of this is informed by operational challenges evident in counterinsurgency, but this is important in the security assistance missions the military conducts outside of war zones. However, given the size and depth of the U.S. military, this is not a simple zero-sum game. The United States can field next generation aircraft, such as the F-22 or a Joint Strike Fighter, and personnel who are bilingual instructors skilled in border control. The Navy is large enough to conduct antisubmarine warfare and build coast guards and navies around the world to combat piracy. And the Army is adaptable enough to fight potential ground adversaries and provide counterterrorism training to partners in North Africa. With a government that spends more than $700 billion on defense, trade-offs between preparing for major combat and non-warfighting missions have not occurred in a substantial way to make the United States vulnerable to attack from competing states. Cutbacks in large acquisitions have more to do with cost overruns than from competition with non-warfighting programs. But the three schools are engaged in serious debate, which will determine the future size and shape of the U.S. military. Since 2005 the irregular warfare school seems to be winning, but, as discussed in this chapter, this has provoked its own set of objections within the U.S. government, the policy community, and the military.

While the reactions have been real and sometimes dramatic, efforts to reduce the non-warfighting roles of the military have largely failed. In contrast to objections during the 2000 presidential election, the Bush administration could not escape from the reality that there is a global demand for U.S. engagement programs and that the military is the most capable federal department to do the engaging. In fact, Congress in the FY 2007 National Defense Authorization Act recognized this: "Civilian agencies of the United States Government lack the capacity to deploy rapidly, and for sustained periods of time, trained personnel to support . . . operations in the field."[108] While President Obama has pledged to rebalance the tools of power in a "smart" way, he also sees that the United States "must also consider using military force in circumstances beyond self-defense in order to provide for the common security that underpins global stability—to support friends, participate in stability and reconstruction operations, or confront mass atrocities."[109] The next four chapters explore how irregular warfare considerations are reshaping the U.S. military from a force of confrontation to one of cooperation.

Notes

1. Condoleezza Rice, "Remarks at the Civilian Response Corps Rollout," U.S. Department of State, July 16, 2008.

2. National Defense University, "Transforming National Security: Africa Command—An Emerging Command Synopsis and Key Insights," February 19–20, 2008. www.ndu.edu/ctnsp/NCW_course/AFRICOM%20Summary%20Notes.pdf.

3. Senator Joseph Biden (D-Del), Chairman of the Senate Foreign Relations Committee at a hearing on "Defining the Military's Role toward Foreign Policy." www.gpo.gov/fdsys/pkg/CHRG-110shrg764/pdf/CHRG-110shrg764.pdf.

4. Quoted in Bryan Bender, "Pentagon Flexes Its Altruism Muscle: Aims to Win Trust with Soft Power," *Boston Globe,* July 28, 2008.

5. Quoted in Michael Hoffman, "U.S. Lawmakers: Too Few Civilians in Africa Command," *Inside Defense News,* July 21, 2008, 23.

6. Richard L. Armitage and Joseph S. Nye, "Implementing Smart Power: Setting an Agenda for National Security Reform" Testimony to the Senate Committee on Foreign Relations, 110th Congress, April 24, 2008. Report compiled by the *Center for Strategic and International Studies,* http://csis.org/files/media/csis/congress/ts0804024armitage-nye.pdf.

7. David Passage, "Speaking Out: Africa Command & Southern Command: Reliquaria from an Earlier Age," *Foreign Service Journal,* February 2009, 13.

8. Charles Ray, "Defining Lines of Authority," *Armed Forces Journal,* 2009, www.afji.com/2009/02/3875360/.

9. Ibid.

10. Justin Logan and Christopher Preble, "The Case against State's Nation Building Office," *Foreign Service Journal,* November 2006, 55.

11. John Hillen, "Superpowers Don't Do Windows," *Orbis* 41, no. 2 (Spring 1997): 257.

12. Andrew J. Bacevich, *The New American Militarism* (New York: Oxford University, 2005), 3.

13. Biden, "Defining the Military's Role."

14. Author private interview.

15. World Public Opinion, "World Publics Reject U.S. Role as the World Leader," April 17, 2007, available at www.worldpublicopinion.org/pipa/articles/views_on_countriesregions_bt/345.php?nid=&id=&pnt=345&lb=btvoc.

16. Lisa Haugaard argues that a tarnished U.S. image in Latin America is nothing new but that this reflects historical frustration with interventions and U.S. trade policy. Frustrations have been exacerbated by reductions in military assistance, disputes over the International Criminal Court, and the Guantanamo Bay detention center. See Lisa Haugaard, "Tarnished Image: Latin America Perceives the United States," The Latin America Working Group Education Fund, March 2006, www.lawg.org/storage/lawg/documents/tarnished%20image.pdf.

17. Steven Kull, "America's Image in the World," Testimony before House Committee on Foreign Affairs, Subcommittee on International Organizations, Human Rights, and Oversight, March 6, 2007, www.worldpublicopinion.org/pipa/articles/views_on_countriesregions_bt/326.php?nid=&id=&pnt=326&lb=btvoc.

18. Argentines and Palestinians disagreed that the United States should be so active.

19. "Embassies as Command Posts in the Anti-Terror Campaign," A Report to Members of the Committee on Foreign Relations, United States Senate, December 15, 2006, www.fas.org/irp/congress/2006_rpt/embassies.pdf, 2.

20. Armitage and Nye, "Implementing Smart Power."

21. Rupp, "Defining the Military's Role."

22. Dan Green, "Harnessing the Islamist Revolution: A Strategy to Win the War against Religious Extremism," *Strategic Studies Quarterly* (Fall 2008): 139.

23. "Remarks at the Civilian Response Corps Rollout," U.S. Department of State, July 16, 2008.

24. U.S. Government Accountability Office, "Stabilization and Reconstruction—Actions Needed to Improve Government Wide Planning and Capabilities for Future Operations, Report to Congress" (Washington, DC: GAO, October 2007), 19.

25. Office of the Coordinator for Reconstruction and Stabilization, "2009 Year in Review: Smart Power in Action," March 1, 2010, www.state.gov/s/crs/rls/rls/137259.htm.

26. Max Boot, "The Struggle to Transform the Military," *Foreign Affairs* (March–April 2005).

27. Mitchell J. Thompson, "Breaking the Proconsulate: A New Design for National Power," *Parameters, U.S. Army War College Quarterly* (Winter 2005–6): 63.

28. Michelle Flournoy, "Navigating Treacherous Shoals: Establishing a Robust Interagency Process for National Security Strategy, Planning, and Budgeting," in *Defense Strategy and Forces: Setting Future Directions*, ed. Richmond M. Lloyd (Newport, RI: Naval War College Press, 2008), 271.

29. Nicholas D. Kristof, "Make Diplomacy, not War," *New York Times*, August 10, 2008.

30. Stephen A. Emerson, "The Trans-Saharan Arc," in *Flashpoints in the War on Terrorism*, eds. Derek S. Reveron and Jeffrey Stevenson Murer (New York: Routledge, 2006), 261.

31. Robert E. Gribbin, "Implementing Africa Command: Tread Carefully," *Foreign Service Journal*, May 2008: 25–31.

32. Dr. Wafula Okumu, Head, African Security Analysis Program, Institute for Security Studies, South Africa, Testimony given to the House Committee on Foreign Affairs, Subcommittee on Africa and Global Health, August 2, 2007, 7, www.internationalrelations .house.gov/110/oku080207.htm.

33. Quoted in Greg Mills, "The U.S. and Africa: Prisoners of a Paradigm," *Current History*, May 2008: 229.

34. Michael P. Noonan, "Next-war-itis, This-war-itis, and the American Military," Foreign Policy Research Institute E-Notes, January 2009, www.fpri.org/enotes/200901 .noonan.waritisamericanmilitary.html.

35. Sam C. Sarkesian, *Beyond the Battlefield: The New Military Professionalism* (New York: Pergamon Press, 1981).

36. George C. Herring, "American Strategy in Vietnam: The Postwar Debate," *Military Affairs*, April 1982: 88.

37. Andrew J. Bacevich, "The Petraeus Doctrine," *The Atlantic*, October 2008.

38. Ibid.

39. "An Interview with George W. Casey, Jr.," *Joint Force Quarterly*, no. 52 (1st Quarter, 2009): 19.

40. Tony Zinni, *Battle Ready* (New York: Palgrave MacMillan, 2006), 323.

41. Hillen, "Superpowers Don't Do Windows," 242.

42. Charles J. Dunlap Jr., "Forget the Lessons of Iraq," *Armed Forces Journal*, January 2009.

43. U.S. Army, "The Army Strategy," August 22, 2008, 7, http://pksoi.army.mil/ training_education/documents/Army_Strategy_20081.pdf.

44. Sean McFarland, Michael Shields, and Jeffrey Snow, "The King and I: The Impending Crisis in Field Artillery's Ability to Provide Fire Support to Maneuver Commanders," U.S. Army White Paper, n.d., available at www.npr.org/documents/2008/ may/artillerywhitepaper.pdf.

45. Quoted in "Executive Summary," *Joint Force Quarterly*, no. 52 (1st Quarter 2009): 13.

46. Colin Gray, "Future Warfare or the Triumph of History," *RUSI Journal* (October 2005): 16–19.

47. Two major theater wars (2MTWs) was a notional force planning construct used to determine the appropriate size of the U.S. military.

48. Charles J. Dunlap, "Roles, Missions, and Equipment: Military Lessons from Experience in This Decade," Foreign Policy Research Institute E-Notes, June 2008, www .fpri.org/enotes/200806.dunlap.militarylessons.html.

49. Gian Gentile, "Let's Build an Army to Win All Wars," *Joint Force Quarterly*, no. 52 (1st Quarter 2009): 27.

50. Field Manual 100-5, "Operations," 1986, quoted in ibid.

51. Gentile, "Let's Build an Army."

52. Gian P. Gentile, "Think Again: Counterinsurgency," Foreignpolicy.com, January 2009.

53. Quoted in Cami McCormick, "'High Time' to Move Marines to Afghanistan," CBSNews.com, December 31, 2008, www.cbsnews.com/stories/2008/12/31/terror/main4694266.shtml.

54. Quoted in Donna Miles, "Anbar Handover Could Free Marines for Afghanistan Missions, General Says," American Forces Press Service, August 27, 2008. www.centcom.mil/en/news/anbar-handover-could-free-marines-for-afghanistan-missions-general-says.html.

55. DOD, "Stability Operations," Directive 3000.05, November 2005, www.dtic.mil/whs/directives/corres/pdf/300005p.pdf.

56. DOD, "Irregular Warfare (IR)," Directive 3000.07, December 2008, www.dtic.mil/whs/directives/corres/pdf/300007p.pdf.

57. Robert Gates, "Remarks as Delivered, Maxwell-Gunter Air Force Base, Montgomery, AL," April 15, 2009, www.defense.gov/Transcripts/Transcript.aspx?TranscriptID=4403.

58. Author private interview, February 18, 2009.

59. Reuben E. Brigety, II, "On the Military's Role in Development Assistance," Testimony to the Senate Committee on Foreign Relations, 110th Congress, July 29, 2008, http://foreign.senate.gov/testimony/2008/BrigetyTestimony080731p.pdf.

60. Robert Gates, "Remarks as Delivered by Secretary of Defense Robert M. Gates," Landon Lecture (Kansas State University), November 26, 2007. Reprinted in *Military Review* (January–February 2008) and available at www.defense.gov/speeches/speech.aspx?speechid=1199.

61. "National Defense Strategy of the United States," June 2008, www.defense.gov/news/2008%20National%20Defense%20Strategy.pdf, 17.

62. Joseph Biden, "Military's Expanding Role in U.S. Foreign Policy," Hearing before the Committee on Foreign Relations, United States Senate, 110th Congress, Second Session, July 31, 2008.

63. "National Defense Strategy," 7.

64. Dana Dillon, "The Civilian Side of the War on Terror," *Policy Review*, no. 145 (October–November 2007), www.hoover.org/publications/policyreview/10185936.html.

65. Mackubin Thomas Owens, "Reflections on Future War," *Naval War College Review* 61, no. 3 (Summer 2008): 61–76.

66. Department of Defense, "Transformation Planning Guidance," April 2003, www.defense.gov/brac/docs/transformationplanningapr03.pdf, 3.

67. For example, see Michael Vickers and Robert Martinage, *The Revolution in War* (Washington, DC: Center for Strategic and Budgetary Assessments, 2005).

68. Max Boot, "The New American Way of War," *Foreign Affairs* 82, no. 4 (July–August, 2003): 42.

69. Ariel E. Levite and Elizabeth Sherwood-Randall, "The Case for Discriminate Force," *Survival* 44, no. 4 (Winter 2002–3): 81–98.

70. Quoted in "Battle Plan under Fire," PBS Nova, www.pbs.org/wgbh/nova/wartech/transform.html.

71. William Owens, "System-of-Systems: U.S.' Emerging Dominant Battlefield Awareness Promises to Dissipate 'Fog of War,'" *Armed Forces Journal International*, January 1996.

72. Arthur K. Cebrowski, "New Rules, New Era," *Defense News*, October 21–27, 2002: 28.

73. The new rules of information age warfare included information superiority, shared awareness, self-synchronization, dispersed forces, demassed forces, deep sensor reach, compressed operations, speed of command, and alter initial conditions at increased rates of change. Department of Defense, "Military Transformation: A Strategic Approach" (Washington, DC: Office of Force Transformation, 2003), 32.

74. Charles Dunlap, "America's Asymetric Advantage," *Armed Forces Journal*, September 2006.

75. National Research Council, *Avoiding Surprise in an Era of Global Technological Advances* (Washington, DC: National Academies Press, 2005).

76. Stephen Biddle challenged the view that the Afghanistan war was fought in a revolutionary way. See Stephen Biddle, "Afghanistan and the Future of Warfare," *Foreign Affairs* (March–April 2003): 31–39.

77. Boot, "New American Way of War," 44.

78. Ralph Peters, "A New Age of Warfare," *New York Post*, April 10, 2003.

79. Quoted in "Battle Plan under Fire."

80. Robert Scales, "Transformation," *Armed Forces Journal*, March 2005: 24.

81. H. R. McMaster, "Learning from Contemporary Conflicts to Prepare for Future War," in *Defense Strategy and Forces: Setting Future Directions*, ed. Richmond M. Lloyd (Newport, RI: Naval War College Press, 2008), 72.

82. John Nagl, *Counterinsurgency Lessons from Malaya and Vietnam: Learning to Eat Soup with a Knife* (Westport, CT: Praeger, 2002).

83. John Nagl, "Let's Win the Wars We're In," *Joint Force Quarterly*, no. 52 (1st Quarter 2009): 25.

84. Thomas Hammes, "Fourth-Generation Warfare: Our Enemies Play to Their Strengths," *Armed Forces Journal*, November 2004: 40–44.

85. Tim Benbow, "Talking 'Bout Our Generation? Assessing the Concept of 'Fourth-Generation Warfare,'" *Comparative Strategy* 27 (2008): 148–63.

86. Field Manual 3-07, "Stability Operations" (Washington, DC: Headquarters Department of the Army, 2008).

87. Scales, "Transformation," 25.

88. Nadia Schadlow, "War and the Art of Governance," *Parameters* 33 (Autumn 2003): 85–94.

89. Fred Kagan, "War and Aftermath," *Policy Review*, no. 120 (August–September 2003).

90. Nagl, "Let's Win the Wars We're In," 21.

91. Boot, "Struggle to Transform the Military."

92. Nagl, "Let's Win the Wars We're In," 22.

93. U.S. House of Representatives, Committee on Armed Services, Subcommittee on Oversight and Investigations, "Agency Stovepipes vs. Strategic Agility: Lessons We Need to Learn from Provincial Reconstruction Teams in Iraq and Afghanistan" (April 2008), http://armedservices.house.gov/pdfs/Reports/PRT_Report.pdf, 51.

94. I'm grateful to Nick Gvosdev for this construction.

95. David Galula, *Counterinsurgency Warfare: Theory and Practice* (Westport, CT: Praeger, 2006), 4–5.

96. Ibid., 72.

97. Petraeus letter to the troops, September 15, 2008, http://graphics8.nytimes .com/images/2008/09/15/world/20080915petraeus-letter.pdf.

98. Michael Vlahos, *Culture's Mask: War and Change after Iraq* (Laurel, MD: Applied Physics Lab, 2004), 2.

99. Frank G. Hoffman, *Conflict in the 21st Century: The Rise of Hybrid Wars* (Arlington, VA: Potomac Institute for Policy Studies, December 2007), 28.

100. "An Interview with Charles Krulak," *Newshour with Jim Lehrer,* June 25, 1999. www.pbs.org/newshour/bb/military/jan-june99/krulak_6-25.html.

101. Ibid.

102. Michael Evans, "From Kadesh to Kandahar: Military Theory and the Future of War," *Naval War College Review* 56, no. 3 (Summer 2003): 132–50.

103. Gates, "Remarks as Delivered, Maxwell-Gunter Air Force Base."

104. Department of Defense, "Capstone Concept for Joint Operations," ver. 3.0, January 15, 2009, www.afcea.org/events/east/09/documents/CCJO_2009_001.pdf, 14.

105. Quoted in Tom Ricks, "Tom Ricks's Inbox," February 1, 2009, www .washingtonpost.com/wp-dyn/content/article/2009/01/30/AR2009013002773.html.

106. John J. Kruzel, "U.S. Must Prepare for 'Hybrid' Warfare, General Says," American Forces Press Service, February 13, 2009, www.defense.gov/news/newsarticle .aspx?id=53089.

107. "Marine Corps Vision and Strategy 2025" (Washington, DC: Office of Naval Research, 2008), www.onr.navy.mil/en/~/media/Files/About%20ONR/usmc_ vision_strategy_2025_0809.ashx, 6.

108. FY 2007 Defense Authorization Act, Sec 1222, paragraph a2, http://frwebgate .access.gpo.gov/cgi-bin/getdoc.cgi?dbname=109_cong_bills&docid=f:s2766pp .txt.pdf.

109. Barack Obama, "Renewing American Leadership," *Foreign Affairs,* July–August 2007, www.foreignaffairs.org/20070701faessay86401/barack-obama/renewing-american-leadership.html?mode=print.

4

Demilitarizing Combatant Commands

IN CONTRAST TO POPULAR PERCEPTION, the real power in the U.S. military is not headquartered at the Pentagon. Instead, it is located at six geographic combatant commands located in Florida, Hawaii, Colorado, and Germany. With numerous changes in law, policy, and the perceptions of the security environment during the last half century, combatant commands have replaced the military services in prominence. Based on the president's Unified Command Plan, these combatant commands are responsible for planning and executing all military operations from major war to security assistance. Consequently, the officers who serve as combatant commanders have emerged as key leaders within the U.S. military and within the government's national security bureaucracy.

With major war a relative rarity today, combatant commands are changing to focus on security assistance and are incorporating civilian capabilities into their command structures. Key to this strategic approach is the need to build partners' security capacity to confront local challenges before these challenges create national or regional instability. For Adm. James Stavridis, who has commanded forces in the Western Hemisphere and now commands U.S. and NATO forces in Europe, "The security of the United States and that of our partners depends largely on our capacity to leverage joint, international, interagency, and public-private cooperation, all reinforced by focused messaging and strategic communication."[1] Chile's former president Michelle Bachelet agrees, "The U.S. can make an enormous contribution in this new stage of global development by helping deepen hemispheric cooperation and political dialogue. If successful, this will lead to a better future for our peoples."[2]

Stavridis and Bachelet make clear that national security can no longer be guaranteed by preparation for military confrontation with other countries. Instead, international cooperation is at the root of national and international security. The shift from confrontation to cooperation represents a profound change in the use of the military. This chapter explores the implications of this change by analyzing how the structure and function of combatant commands are changing, and it analyzes nonkinetic engagement programs designed to confront precursors to instability. Also examined is a new model for promoting national security that links defense, diplomacy, and development. This chapter addresses how the military is changing to meet the needs of national leaders who direct the military to fill a gap in the national government's and the international community's ability to respond to a security environment dominated by nonstate threats. The change is not simply the militarization of foreign policy. Rather, the change has resulted in incorporating civilian capabilities within military commands.

The Unified Command Plan

Issued every two years, the Unified Command Plan (UCP) is the overall blueprint for America's military commands.[3] First issued by President Harry Truman in 1946, the UCP delineates geographic areas of responsibility and substantive areas of focus.[4] As of 2010, there are six geographic commands (European, African, Pacific, North, Southern, and Central) and four functional commands (transportation, special operations, joint forces, and strategic).[5] The missions and responsibilities are defined in the UCP, but it is important to understand that U.S. military forces are employed through these commands and not through the military services located at the Pentagon. For example, the chief of naval operations (CNO) does not direct naval operations. Instead, the CNO trains and equips naval forces that are employed by component commanders reporting directly to a joint combatant command responsible for all U.S. military activities within a given region. The only exception to this is for forces assigned to carry out organizing, recruiting, training, supplying, and other functions of the military departments assigned in law or assigned to multinational peacekeeping organizations. What is true for the Navy is also true for the Marine Corps, Army, and Air Force. Today the job of service chiefs is to train and equip military forces, which are then employed by combatant commands such as Africa Command, or by the relevant component commands such as Naval Forces Africa.

Because the Unified Command Plan is written in the executive branch and approved under the president's commander-in-chief authority, the plan is relatively responsive to changes in the security environment and U.S. national strategy. Prior to 2002, for example, no single command had responsibility for protecting the continental United States. But the 9/11 terrorist attacks gave rise to the Northern Command to fill in the homeland defense gap, during the year needed for Congress to create the Department of Homeland Security. Likewise, Africa Command was established in 2008 to support the president's initiatives in Africa by providing focused security assistance. In contrast to the pre-2008 arrangement in which three military commands engaged in Africa, the newest

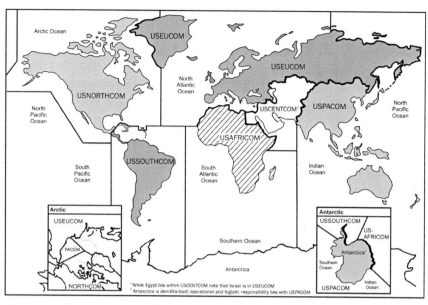

Figure 4.1 U.S. Department of Defense Combatant Command Boundaries.
Map by Jeffrey Stevenson Murer

combatant command serves as a single point of entry for defense matters.[6] In 2010 the importance of cyberspace to the military should be reflected in the UCP with formal assignment to U.S. Strategic Command.

In accordance with the 2008 UCP, each combatant commander is assigned missions and areas of responsibility. In general, the missions for all six geographic combatant commanders are the same and include[7]

- Detecting, deterring, and preventing attacks against the United States, its territories, possessions, and bases, and employing appropriate force to defend the nation should deterrence fail.
- Carrying out assigned missions and tasks, and planning for and executing military operations as directed.
- Assigning tasks to, and directing coordination among, subordinate commands to ensure unified action.
- Maintaining the security of and carrying out force protection responsibilities for the command, including assigned or attached commands, forces, and assets. The commander is also responsible for exercising force protection responsibilities for all U.S. military forces within the area of responsibility (except Department of Defense personnel for whom the chiefs of U.S. diplomatic missions have security responsibilities by law or interagency agreement).

- Certifying the readiness of assigned headquarters staffs designated to perform as a joint task force or functional component headquarters staff.
- Providing, as directed, trained and ready joint forces to other combatant commands.
- Planning, conducting, and assessing security cooperation activities.
- Planning and, as appropriate, conducting the evacuation and protection of U.S. citizens and nationals and, in connection therewith, designated other persons, in support of their evacuation from threatened areas; and reviewing emergency action plans.
- Providing U.S. military representation to international and U.S. national agencies unless otherwise directed.
- Providing advice and assistance to chiefs of U.S. diplomatic missions in negotiation of rights, authorizations, and facility arrangements required in support of U.S. military operations.
- Providing the single point of contact on military matters within the area of responsibility.
- Assuming combatant command of security assistance organizations in the event of war or an emergency that prevents control through normal channels or as directed.
- When directed, commanding U.S. forces conducting peace or humanitarian relief operations, whether as a unilateral U.S. action or as part of a multinational organization, or supporting U.S. forces that have been placed under the authority, direction, or control of a multinational organization.
- Establishing and maintaining a standing joint force headquarters core element.
- Planning for and conducting military support for [security, stabilization, transition, and reconstruction] operations, humanitarian assistance, and disaster relief, as directed.
- Planning for, supporting, and conducting the recovery of astronauts, space vehicles, space payloads, and objects, as directed.

In addition to the general missions assigned, some geographic combatant commanders have specific responsibilities. For example, Southern Command is responsible for defending the Panama Canal and the surrounding area. Northern Command is responsible for homeland defense, supporting civil authorities, planning for responses to pandemic influenza, and providing support to partner countries in the event of a catastrophic attack. And Africa Command is focused on building partners' operational and institutional capacity with no emphasis placed on fighting wars in Africa. Evident in the sixteen assigned responsibilities and specific missions listed above is that combatant commands do much more than fight wars. Instead, military commands support broader U.S. government efforts during peacetime through security cooperation. This is a major effort and requires high levels of cooperation among the military services, U.S. government departments, nongovernmental organizations, other governments, and international organizations. Generating unified action is not easy, but there are lessons from the military services' efforts to create jointness that are informing those efforts.

Overcoming Interservice Rivalry

For combatant commands to conduct operations and exercises, cooperation among the Air Force, Army, Navy, and Marine Corps is essential. This has taken sixty years to achieve. In fact, the seeds of joint warfare and the UCP were sown in the military service rivalries of World War II. Fighting a global war from 1941–45 emphasized the importance of multiservice cooperation. For example, the Navy had to provide transport, logistics, and gunfire support for Army forces. Yet rivalries among the Army and Navy over priorities and resources led to clashes among the war's principal warfighters, Gen. Douglas MacArthur, Gen. George Patton, Adm. Chester Nimitz, and Gen. Dwight Eisenhower. At the time, there was no secretary of defense or joint chiefs of staff to coordinate defense policy to ensure unity of command.[8]

The World War II rivalries exposed shortcomings in the military, which led to the creation of a postwar system of unified command culminating with the 1947 National Security Act. However, law could not overcome culture, and service rivalries persisted throughout the Cold War. In 1984 Samuel Huntington observed, "Each service continues to exercise great autonomy. . . . Unified commands are not really commands, and they certainly aren't unified."[9] James Schlesinger testified, "In all of our military institutions, the time-honored principle of 'unity of command' is inculcated. Yet at the national level it is firmly resisted and flagrantly violated. Unity of command is endorsed if and only if it applies at the service level. The inevitable consequence is both the duplication of effort and the ultimate ambiguity of command."[10]

Consequently, instilling "jointness" was the most significant military bureaucratic challenge since the 1947 National Security Act. During the Cold War, the services evaded jointness and simply divided functions or geographic space instead of working together. An example of this was the 1983 military operation in Grenada, which was then the largest U.S. military operation since Vietnam. The Army focused on the southern part of the island and the Marine Corps focused on the northern part of the island. Although both were American military forces, they had major interoperability problems and lacked the radio capability to communicate directly to one another. In many respects, the shortcomings of this military operation paved the way for massive defense reforms mandated by the Goldwater–Nichols Act (PL 99-433) in 1986.

Goldwater–Nichols was viewed as essential to "fixing" the Defense Department. Chairman of the Joint Chiefs of Staff Gen. David Jones testified before the law was passed: "The system is broken. I have tried to reform it from inside, but I cannot. Congress is going to have to mandate necessary reforms."[11] In response to this plea and the problems revealed by military operations in Vietnam, Iran, Lebanon, and Grenada, Sen. Sam Nunn, Sen. Barry Goldwater, and Rep. William Nichols led a bipartisan effort to strengthen unity of command and repair the flawed military structure. If the military were to improve its effectiveness, it was essential that the military services give way to joint commanders who could coordinate military action for the best effect on the battlefield and not the political field.

Overcoming Bureaucratic Challenges

Over the last twenty years, the service-centric bureaucratic challenge has been largely overcome. As the operations in Iraq and Afghanistan illustrate, it is not unusual for a Navy attack aircraft to get fuel from an Air Force tanker or to provide close air support for an Army unit. Implicit in this joint example is a Navy aircraft having a refueling probe and communication system that are compatible with the Air Force tanker. The Navy pilot also has the ability to communicate with a forward air controller on the ground who directs the munitions. And the Navy pilot has an appreciation for the appropriate sized weapon necessary to support a ground unit without causing fratricide or collateral damage that would impact national reconciliation efforts. The Navy has come a long way since former chairman of the Joint Chiefs of Staff Adm. William Crowe criticized his own service's culture, which was rooted in the idea of independent command at sea. "Ever since then [1949] the Navy has been the least eager among the services to endorse any move toward unification; anything that might give someone outside the Navy control over maritime forces is instinctively opposed. The Navy has traditionally opposed anything that looked, sounded, or smelled joint."[12] Like it or not, jointness is an important dimension of the U.S. military today, which gives it a critical edge to succeed. And to Admiral Crowe's surprise, the Navy has even embraced jointness and is taking joint education and staff assignments more seriously.

Warfare undoubtedly underscores how, why, and when to integrate service capabilities. But various mandated actions and fiscal realities truly institutionalized jointness. As jointness was gradually realized in the Department of Defense, military operations of the 1990s highlighted a new bureaucratic challenge—multinational or combined warfare. With combined operations in the Balkans, the U.S. military needed the ability to operate and communicate with a range of traditional and nontraditional partners. For example, when the Stabilization Force (SFOR) deployed to Bosnia-Herzegovina, thirty-five countries participated.[13] This group of countries included traditional NATO partners such as the United Kingdom but also included nontraditional partners under NATO command such as Russia and Morocco. With the diversity of languages, equipment, doctrine, and intelligence sharing relationships, there were serious bureaucratic challenges to overcome to ensure the overall goal of contributing to a safe and secure environment necessary for the consolidation of Bosnia-Herzegovina.[14]

The operational nature of the mission forced the resolution of the problems encountered. When there is risk to personnel involved, withholding information or resources is not acceptable in a conflict zone. To improve coalition operations, non-NATO countries have adopted NATO standards and doctrine, which have become the lingua franca of defense interoperability. Four years after operations in Bosnia-Herzegovina began, interoperability was tested once again in the Balkans with a 1999 deployment of fifty thousand troops to Kosovo. This deployment again included a diversity of countries ranging from Belgium to Ukraine.[15] Similar interoperability problems were encountered, but solutions could be found in SFOR's lessons and the similarity of the missions.

Both of NATO's deployments were designed to separate former warring parties and facilitate postconflict reconciliation and reconstruction. In Kosovo, NATO was tasked to deter renewed hostility and threats against Kosovo by Yugoslav and Serb forces; to establish a secure environment and ensure public safety and order; to demilitarize the Kosovo Liberation Army; to support the international humanitarian effort; and to coordinate with and support the international civil presence.[16] The latter objective highlighted a new bureaucratic challenge—integrating civilian agencies into the NATO-controlled battlespace. With military objectives largely achieved within the first eighteen months of these operations, this challenge became acute as social, economic, and political conditions kept NATO forces there for years. While the military had the capacity to deploy large numbers of personnel, it did not have the capability or culture to create social harmony and promote economic development. For example, when Serb women in Kosovo asked a U.S. Army commander for sewing machines to start a work cooperative, the battalion commander replied, "We don't do sewing machines."[17] Yet restarting the local economy was viewed as essential to bringing normalcy to Kosovo, reducing the threat of future violence, and allowing military units to redeploy to their home stations. (Just six years later in Iraq, a similar battalion commander would have the budget and attitude to support such requests.)

The challenge of integrating civilian capabilities into military-led operations was further highlighted by operations in Iraq and Afghanistan where military success did not translate into political success. The infamous banner, "Mission Accomplished," on the aircraft carrier USS *Abraham Lincoln* in May 2003 exemplified the gap between military victory and strategic success. The ensuing collapse of social order and the economic system in Iraq forced careful examination of the required capabilities to meet strategic goals. Furthermore, the nonpermissive nature of Iraq prevented private individuals or companies, nonmilitary elements of the U.S. government, and the international community from operating there to facilitate postconflict reconstruction. When groups tried, tragedy resulted. For example, UN efforts ended abruptly when UN envoy Sérgio Vieira de Mello was killed in August 2003. The risk of being killed or kidnapped was very real, and projects that were completed became instant targets for insurgent forces bent on keeping Iraq unstable. Consequently, the military adapted and filled roles and missions normally reserved for civilian agencies or private actors. It led major civil reconstruction projects, provided support for electoral processes, and funded community projects. When he commanded military forces there, Gen. Peter Chiarelli institutionalized these non-warfighting programs as the "SWEAT model" among his forces to focus on schools, water, electricity, academics, and trash removal. Programs such as SWEAT became formalized as the Commander's Emergency Response Program (CERP), which was about a $1.5 billion program in 2010.[18]

The previous discussion highlights the disconnect among warfighting, achieving military objectives, creating stability, and accomplishing national objectives. Made clear by flawed military operations such as the failed hostage rescue attempt in 1979 or military operations that failed to meet broader political objectives such as the 2003 Iraq War, the Defense Department has been responding to improve its effectiveness.[19] The examples here are largely taken from combat zones, but these lessons were not lost on those commands engaged in permissive environments such as Africa, the Western Hemisphere, Europe, and parts of Asia. Noting the major absence of civilian agencies, jointness was redefined more broadly to include agencies and departments across the government, international, intergovernmental, and nongovernmental communities. Now when the military talks of joint operations, there is an inherent civilian component that cannot be separated from the military component. This definitional change serves as a reminder for officers to integrate all elements of power in their strategies and plans.

Products of this new jointness are combatant commands that do not have core warfighting missions such as Southern Command and Africa Command. For Southern Command, with a focus on Latin America and the Caribbean, it is not about "launching Tomahawk missiles . . . [but about] launching ideas."[20] For

Africa Command, Gen. Carl Fulford hoped that the new command will "move us from an era of crisis-response relationships to a more mature partnership in order to foster stronger relationships on the continent and a more stable, secure environment for African citizens."[21] Accordingly, the Defense Department conceived Africa Command as an end in itself with a focus on "preparation for insecurity through building African military capacity rather than to default to mere crisis management."[22] In this case, Africa Command was conceived as a civilianized military command, and it launched the Defense Department on a path to overcome the latest bureaucratic challenge, civilianizing its activities. Its initial guidance called for developing an organizational structure that integrated military and civilian personnel, establishing focus areas of civil–military activities and military plans, increasing command presence in U.S. embassy country teams, and establishing a presence on the continent to facilitate cooperation with African organizations.[23]

Adapting to the Interagency Problem and the New Security Landscape

Recognizing the importance of civilian capabilities to counter transnational threats and reacting to a changed media environment required new organizational structures not predicated on traditional notions of war and peace. The old model, wherein the State Department offers a "carrot" in time of peace while the Defense Department threatens the "stick" in time of war, provides solutions only when peace and war are readily distinguishable. This worked well when interstate conflict was the primary national security concern, but today war and peace are not neatly divided. Likewise, civilian and military missions are not mutually exclusive. With this in mind, President Obama's national security advisor, Jim Jones, directed the Obama cabinet to be more agile saying, "The United States must navigate an environment in which traditional organizations and means of response to local challenges may be inadequate or deficient."[24] In practice, Admiral Stavridis, head of U.S. Southern Command at the time, said "our efforts are significantly influenced by our understanding of the complexities of the hemisphere and our ability to foster cooperation with—and among—willing and capable partners. We are certain that our security will involve deeper cooperation with multinational, interagency, and public-private partners."[25] Thus his job was "to build cooperative security relationships and to promote U.S. military-to-military interests in the region."[26] His command vision was unintelligible to traditional warfighters. "USSOUTHCOM seeks to evolve into an interagency-oriented organization seeking to support security and stability in the Americas."[27]

Gen. Kip Ward of Africa Command interpreted the national security advisor's guidance to mean creating "a joint command with significant interagency and intergovernmental involvement, which will become an effective multidimensional instrument in pursuit of our national interests and the shared interests of our global partners."[28] Just as with Southern Command, partnership is paramount for Africa Command. The primary mission of Africa Command is "to promote African security by building the capacity of partner nations and organizations."[29] Consequently, Africa Command's theater strategy includes mitigating violent conflicts; promoting stability, security, and reconstruction efforts; turning the tide of HIV/AIDS and malaria; strengthening democratic principles by fostering respect for the rule of law, civilian control of the military, and budget transparency; and fostering the conditions that lead to a peaceful, stable, and economically strong Africa.[30] By design, Africa Command is meant to be a different kind of military structure that places a premium on its ability to assist other countries as they confront their own security challenges, which may or may not be military in nature.

Leaders of Southern Command and Africa Command recognize the importance of transnational challenges and the importance of good governance. Furthermore, both commands see working with partners as essential to regional stability and U.S. security interests. Human security issues predominate over security concerns; health care, poverty alleviation, and development are important issues. While many critics misinterpret interest in human security issues as militarizing development, Africa Command addresses AIDS relief in a military context to prevent loss of readiness levels among African militaries. And all military commands supplement traditional development assistance by using development capabilities organic to the military such as medical, engineering, and construction personnel. (The Navy has twice as many construction personnel as the State Department has diplomats.) In spite of this, there is a deep skepticism about the military focusing on human security issues that comes from Congress, the State Department, and development NGOs who fear that traditional aid and diplomacy will be marginalized by the military and be directed away from the development community (see chapter 3).

The military's role in human security issues and development also extends to regions where traditional warfare is taking place. Lessons from Iraq and Afghanistan are being translated into programs in Yemen, Jordan, and Egypt. "With national and international partners, U.S. Central Command promotes cooperation among nations, responds to crises, and deters or defeats state and non-state aggression, and supports development and, when necessary, reconstruction in order to establish the conditions for regional security, stability, and prosperity."[31] Central Command has learned in Afghanistan that victory will not come from battlefield success alone but through defense, diplomacy, and development.

Regarding development, a former commander said: "Four strategic priorities support the counterinsurgency effort. These include embracing free market economic policy, enhancing government resources, addressing inflation and implementing structural reforms. Staying the free market course means resisting costly new subsidies, which serve to reduce resources for other more constructive expenditures in areas like infrastructure, education and health care. . . . Our Provincial Reconstruction Teams (PRTs) are key elements in these endeavors, and they have brought real improvement directly to the populace."[32]

These new economic mission sets for combatant commands have forced significant change across the Defense Department. One commander told me that future forms of military operations require unique organizations. Admiral Stavridis captured this in a speech:

> Given an environment of unceasing micro-conflict and constant ideological communication, "carrot and stick" must work not merely hand-in-hand, but hand-in-glove ("mano en mano" versus "mano en guante"). We cannot expect clear transitions between peace and war, and, thus, we need to explore a new standing organization chartered to operate within today's dynamic and changing international environment.
>
> The geographically focused Military Commands of today, like Southern Command, appropriately seek to maintain a vital regional perspective on security issues. However, enabling truly joint and interagency activities will require additional modalities to help improve synchronization of various U.S. government agencies' resources. We need better integration across the entire government of the USA, and better coalition integration. We also need stronger connections to the private sector.
>
> We need to "test drive" a new model that truly melds joint, interagency, international, and private-public cooperation. We plan to transition over a relatively short period to a more integrated posture that expands its strong interagency perspective and capacity.[33]

While the military often spoke of jointness in a pejorative way, the term interagency is used very differently today. Simultaneously, interagency connotes the complexity of a national security problem, the unity within the U.S. government required to be successful, and the partnerships the military needs to translate military success into strategic success. To be sure, interagency is a new mantra, but the military is also embracing it, welcoming nonmilitary personnel into its commands, and reorganizing to better reflect the security environment. General Petraeus testified to this point: "To effectively carry out these [military] plans, the military elements must be coordinated carefully with the corresponding State Department envoy or ambassador."[34] Defense cannot go it alone.

This change also includes international partners and nongovernmental organizations. For example, "achieving U.S. national goals and objectives in the CENTCOM AOR [Central Command area of responsibility] involves more than just the traditional application of military power. In many cases, a unified government approach is required, one that integrates all tools available [such as] international and interagency partners to secure host-nation populations, to conduct comprehensive counterinsurgency and security operations, to help reform, and in some cases build, governmental and institutional capacity, and to promote economic development."[35] What is true in Central Command is true throughout the Defense Department, and change is evident in combatant commands' organizational structures.

Changing Structure for New Missions

Perhaps the most significant change to a military command structure has been the creation of the deputy to the commander for civil–military activities (DCMA) position at U.S. Southern Command and U.S. Africa Command. Formerly, military officers planned and executed civil–military activities with limited advice from a political advisor. Now the commands are integrated; a senior foreign service or development officer can bring a differentiated perspective within the commander's group. In Africa Command's case, the first DCMA was a State Department officer. In theory, the increased interagency presence at these commands should help to link strategic goals and resources for regional engagement activities. And the DCMA, in Africa Command at least, is responsible for policy development, resourcing, and program assessment in support of security cooperation. Furthermore, the DCMA should provide the nonmilitary departments of the government better access to military planning and resources to unify development and diplomacy activities.

While the idea to have a civilian deputy logically flows from the interagency nature of military commands, legal execution was initially fraught with some problems. The original concept called for the command's deputy to be a non-military officer, but the law governing the military (Title 10) requires a military officer to lead forces when the position of the combatant commander is vacant or the commander is unable to fulfill his duties. Consequently, a foreign service officer or development specialist could not be a true second-in-command. To overcome this legal challenge, nonmilitary officers serve as deputies to the commander. In spite of this, creating the DCMA position was a legal way to insert a senior nonmilitary officer into the highest level of a military command. At the same time, a deputy to the commander for military operations was created to fulfill the statutory role of directing military operations in the absence of the commander. In addition to the DCMA, senior civilians lead other directorates within these commands to include U.S. Agency for International Development, Commerce, and Treasury. Nonmilitary advice is now embedded at senior levels of these commands. This is designed to enrich military planning of civil activities with civilian advice and to create a conduit between the combatant command headquarters and the State Department.

In addition to the command-level leadership change, commands are also moving beyond the Napoleonic J-code system and are being restructured to look less militaristic. For example, U.S. Southern Command experimented with combining an operations (J-3) directorate with an intelligence directorate (J-2) called the security and intelligence directorate. While the resemblance to the past structure exists, another new dimension is that the directorate head in 2009 was a non-DOD officer in the form of a Coast Guard admiral, and his deputy was an intelligence officer with the authority for operational forces, which is normally taboo within the military. Other attempted organizational changes include the enterprise directorate (formerly J6), policy and strategy directorate (formerly J-5), resources and assessments (formerly J-8), the partnering directorate, and the stability directorate. The latter two are new creations with little resemblance to preexisting command structures. As of this writing, it is unclear if General Fraser will continue Admiral Stavridis's efforts to move beyond J-codes. Challenges with this approach were revealed during Haitian earthquake relief operations. Apparently other military commands had a difficult time knowing who to talk to in the matrix organization. Nonetheless, change is constant.

The attempt to create new directorates is inconceivable to someone with a traditional military focus. For example, the partnering directorate is charged to engage the public and private sector to coordinate and integrate with interagency, nongovernmental organizations, and partner nations to facilitate good governance, the strengthening of economies, and a favorable investment climate in order to support economic independence, sustainable development, and prosperity throughout the region.[36] Because gangs, smugglers, and drug trafficking organizations are major causes of insecurity, outreach also extends to law enforcement agencies throughout the world. This stresses the legal limit of Title 10, but it relies on the embassy country team to implement the programs. To ease implementation, Southern Command attempts to infuse its organization with representatives from Treasury, Justice, Agriculture, Energy, and Homeland Security.

What is most striking about development activities is the nonmilitary nature of them. When asked why the military is involved in ensuring "a favorable investment climate" in Latin America and the Caribbean, a senior officer told me that poverty underlies most of the region's security issues. Consequently, the military is working with NGOs, business, and other U.S. government actors to construct meaningful antipoverty programs. For example, the coordinator for public–private cooperation coordinates theater security cooperation initiatives with the hope that donated goods can be delivered in a timely manner taking advantage of private groups' abilities to accept donations and the military's ability to deliver through its robust logistics capabilities. It seems that old barriers between the military and NGOs are breaking down as NGOs see a ready and willing resource-rich partner in the military and the military appreciates NGO skills and expertise in promoting development.[37] It is not unusual for NGO representatives to embark on Navy ships to conduct joint programs (see chapter 6).

Another innovative change to the military staff structure is the creation of a stability directorate, which has a specific focus on security cooperation activities (discussed in chapter 5). These activities are designed to build a partner nation's capabilities to neutralize internal threats and control its territory. In the past, these activities would have been planned by the J-5 and executed by the J-3. Now neither of those successor directorates is involved, which illustrates the high-profile nature of these non-warfighting activities. Instead, the Stability Directorate focuses on improving partners' capacity through exercises and operations; integrates military engagement projects with other interagency, partner nation, and regional organizations; builds humanitarian assistance and disaster preparedness capabilities; and oversees and coordinates State Partnership Program initiatives. Given the high deployment rates of the active duty forces, the State Partnership Program brings National Guard resources to bear by connecting citizen soldiers with partner countries' militaries.

Similar initiatives are under way at U.S. Africa Command. Beginning with a non-warfighting focus since its formal inception in 2008, the command structure does resemble a military organization with some differences. Instead of the standard J-codes found at most military organizations, Africa Command uses a scheme similar to Southern Command. There are directors for outreach, strategy, plans, and programs (resembles J-5); intelligence and knowledge development (resembles J-2); command, control, communications, and computers (resembles J-6); operations and logistics (resembles J-3 and J-4); and resources (resembles J1 and J-8). Of the directorates, the director of outreach is the most innovative of the functions. This directorate is headed by a civilian and is charged with strategic communication, which is woven into the fabric of combatant commands. Learned in Iraq, communications proactively promote partner political, economic, and security progress; refute inaccurate and misleading media coverage; and help a partner develop strategic communication capabilities for itself.[38] Web 2.0 tools are being used; you can follow military activities on Twitter, read the commander's blog, and connect with military leaders through Facebook. For the once insular military organization, the military is wading into social media to reduce suspicions.

In addition to warfighting directorates becoming interagency directorates, other changes are occurring to allay concerns about the increased role the military plays in U.S. foreign policy. One change is how the commands think of their areas of activity. Traditionally, commands have had areas of responsibility with defined geographic boundaries contained in the Unified Command Plan. But the imperial-looking map and paternalistic language is changing from "area of responsibility" to "area of focus" or "joint operating areas." Additionally, the term combatant command is giving way to unified command to illustrate that the military often does much more than combat; the military brings U.S. government unity of action to a particular security problem. For example, counterdrug programs encompass military commands, law enforcement agencies, and diplomatic posts.

The logical next step in evolving combatant commands is incorporating other countries' personnel more directly into U.S. or international command structures. This already occurs at the joint task force level. For example, the Combined Joint Task Force Horn of Africa, which is based in Djibouti, has non-U.S. officers at all levels in the command (albeit less than 5 percent). At sea, Central Command's Combined Task Forces 150 and 151 are frequently led by non-U.S. officers (French and Turkish in 2009). For a military that culturally resists being commanded by a non-American officer, these task forces illustrate that times are changing. But change is rooted in the past. The Navy has had for many years a ship rider program that embeds naval officers and sailors from other countries to qualify them on U.S. warships.

The necessary reorganization of military combatant commands, incorporation of civilians and non-American officers, and changing the lexicon is to ensure form follows function. That is, with coalition operations the norm today and nonstate actors challenging international security, the primary mission of the U.S. military in many regions of the world is security cooperation. The next chapter examines this in detail, but first it is essential to understand the underlying approach defined by defense, development, and diplomacy, or 3D.

Defense, Development, and Diplomacy

The Department of Defense, Department of State, and U.S. Agency for International Development are collaborating to fuse defense, development, and diplomacy to address security challenges.[39] Also characterized as whole-of-government, whole-of-community, or smart power, a 3D approach to U.S. foreign and defense policy places greater emphasis on development and diplomacy efforts to prevent crises before a military defense effort is needed.[40] Although cautious that budgetary imbalances can be overcome, Lisa Schirch and Aaron Kishbaugh think that "at its best, 3D security links to a broader analysis of current threats, a richer set of responses to security challenges, and a stronger role for local communities around the world to work in partnership with international actors in building global security."[41] Security is a precondition for development, and too often development resources are wasted when destroyed by conflict.[42] And when the military uses its construction assets for development, it lacks sufficient connections to local civil society groups. Thus, a diverse range of actors is coming together under the 3D banner with a common goal of creating capable and accountable governments.

The Alliance for Peacebuilding believes that 3D activities use a common approach of analysis, planning, training, and operations.[43] This approach asks

- How can government entities, military, local and international civil society organizations (CSOs), engage in joint assessment of the local context, conflict analysis, and research on early warning indicators in crisis regions?
- How can government entities, military, and local and international CSOs cooperate in policy planning for interventions in crisis regions, including identifying a clear division of CSO and government roles and developing flexible strategies that permit adjustments as contexts shift?
- What are the potential modes of joint training for civil society, government, and military leaders to build relationships with each other while enhancing capacities in stabilization and conflict prevention?
- How can government entities, military, and local and international CSOs operating in the same crisis regions interact at the field level?
- How can so-called host national governments be encouraged to adopt broader consultation strategies with civil society leaders throughout their region?

Not everyone in the U.S. government agrees with the 3D approach, and there is significant opposition to linking defense with diplomacy and development (see chapter 3). Yet the 3D approach to security is nothing new. Military infrastructure, such as highways, airfields, and ports, has always had an obvious role in facilitating development. Coercive diplomacy implicitly includes the threat of military action. And military hearts and minds campaigns usually encompass development projects and community outreach. What is new, however, is the breadth of these activities and incorporating nonmilitary personnel into military command structures. The military also wants a civilian face leading efforts. By doing this, the Defense Department attempts to infuse a 3D perspective on security issues instead of treating each tool separately. The goal is for defense, development, and diplomacy to be integrated and become a part of military commands' philosophies to change the way it approaches security assistance. Since all programs take place in defined sovereign territory, the U.S. ambassador is charged with implementing 3D solutions.

More broadly speaking, the 3D approach focuses on the prevention of insecurity. Anne-Marie Slaughter and others argue: "Prevention must become a central part of strategic doctrine, organizational structure, and decision-making. The difficulties of prevention must not be underestimated, but neither should its necessity. In so many areas such as civil conflicts, the global environment, global public health, democracy building, terrorism, and weapons proliferation, U.S. policies have been reactive rather than preventive for too long, leaving the United States with fewer and worse options, higher financial and human costs, and lower probabilities of success."[44] This extends to the military services in which Army doctrine now defines peacetime military engagement as one of its five operational themes.[45] The Navy sees humanitarian assistance as one its six elements of maritime power. In practice, a 3D approach is visible in Mozambique, which is clearly off the core national security agenda. Through the U.S. Embassy there, the 3D approach was used to minimize the impact of seasonal flooding of the Zambezi River. The U.S. government with its international partners led a multiyear program that created the Mozambique Integrated Information Network for Decision-Making, which strengthened early warning systems, improved disaster management, and educated communities about disaster preparedness. At the same time that civilian agencies were promoting these activities, the U.S. Army Corps of Engineers helped Mozambique channel flood waters to reduce flooding, develop more rational land management practices, and move hazardous materials from flood plains. Military medical teams trained first responders, civil engineers built hospitals and clinics, and logisticians working with aid organizations designed better ways to deliver supplies to disaster-stricken areas.[46] At the same time, NGOs provided fuel to Mozambique's military to reduce illegal animal poaching.

Prevention is clearly the goal, and it is reflected in how leaders of combatant commands define their roles in global security. For Gen. Kip Ward, "the creation of AFRICOM acknowledges that, with relatively modest theater security cooperation and capacity building resources, much can be done to help prevent crises from occurring if those resources are applied in a sustained and consistent manner."[47] Or for Gen. David Petraeus, "improving the overall effectiveness of our security efforts requires strengthening each country's ability to maintain security inside its own borders and to participate in joint endeavors. This capacity building includes collective and individual training programs, educational exchanges, and the development of security-related facilities and infrastructure, as well as equipment modernization efforts."[48]

Conclusion

This chapter highlighted how the Defense Department is adding civilian capabilities to warfighting commands and adapting for a security landscape defined by threats without borders. To be effective in this security environment, the military is relying on preventive measures through security assistance and cooperation. This is most visible in military commands without an identifiable combat mission such as in Africa and the Western Hemisphere. The other commands have similar programs, but European Command, Central Command, and Pacific Command retain at least a warfighting structure. Not to be forgotten, Adm. Tim Keating reminded Congress that his Pacific Command is "a warfighting command committed to maintaining preeminence across the full spectrum of operations. We are ready to fight and win, and to dominate any scenario, in all environments, without exception."[49] Given Pacific Command's concerns about Chinese military modernization, obligations under the Taiwan Relations Act, five mutual defense treaties, and an erratic North Korea with nuclear weapons, the statement is not too surprising. However, security assistance is also a key way that Pacific Command postures to be effective in the event of war. Allies in the Pacific receive U.S. equipment and training and participate in U.S.-led international military exercises. And countries that face humanitarian or natural disasters receive U.S. military assistance in the form of medical relief and construction projects.

While there has been much symbolic resistance to demilitarizing combatant commands, such resistance is not based on a critique of ongoing U.S. military security assistance activities or an understanding of how U.S. military power is shifting from a force designed for confrontation to one being redesigned for cooperation. Instead, criticism is based on outdated thinking about U.S. foreign policy or fear that the United States will displace particular regional powers or upset the development community. To overcome this, military commands will have to reassure key states that it seeks to serve as a catalyst for national security improvements and not necessarily to fill the security void with a large U.S. presence. Incorporating personnel from other government agencies, officers from other countries, and civilians from private organizations will be key to this. Critics must understand there is no political will or national interest for a U.S. hegemonic presence, nor the necessary resources to establish such hegemony. Instead, the changed face of the military accepts the limits of external actors (especially the U.S. military) and relies on partner countries to improve their own security and stability. Helping others solve their security problems appeals both to the American culture of giving but also to the strategic culture of burden sharing. The next chapter explores in detail how these programs operate.

Notes

1. James Stavridis, "U.S. Southern Command 2009 Posture Statement" (Miami, FL: SOUTHCOM, 2009), 1, www.southcom.mil/AppsSC/files/0UI0I1237496303.pdf.

2. Quoted in ibid., 4.

3. Title 10 of the U.S. Code requires that the chairman of the Joint Chiefs of Staff, at intervals not to exceed two years, "review the missions, responsibilities (including geographic boundaries), and force structure of each combatant command" and make recommendations to the president, through the secretary of defense, any changes that may be necessary. U.S. Code, Title 10, Subtitle A, Part I, Chapter 6, Sec 161(b), http://uscode.house.gov/uscode-cgi/fastweb.exe?getdoc+uscview+t09t12+116+13++%28%29%20%20A.

4. See William C. Story, "Military Changes to the Unified Command Plan: Background and Issues for Congress," Congressional Research Service Report Rl30245, June 21, 1999, https://www.policyarchive.org/bitstream/handle/10207/941/RL30245_19990621.pdf?sequence=1.

5. Transportation Command is located at Scott Air Force Base, Illinois; Special Operations Command is located at McDill Air Force Base, Florida; Joint Forces Command is located in Norfolk, Virginia; and Strategic Command is located at Offutt Air Force Base, Nebraska.

6. Far from being a peculiarity of the Bush administration, Congress, led by Senator Russ Feingold (D-WI), directed the military to conduct the feasibility study in 2006 legislation, which ultimately led to the command's creation a year later. It did so to meet the demands that presidents place on it for cooperative security missions. It also allows the three other geographic commands that had previous activities in Africa to focus on their cores areas of Europe, the Middle East, and the Pacific.

7. Department of Defense, Unified Command Plan 2008, signed October 3, 2008.

8. National Defense University Joint Forces Staff College, "Joint Forces Staff College Pub 1" (Norfolk, VA: JFSC, 2000), www.au.af.mil/au/awc/awcgate/pub1/introduction.pdf, 1–2.

9. Samuel P. Huntington, "Defense Organization and Military Strategy," *Public Interest* (Spring 1984): 24.

10. Quoted in U.S. Congress, Senate, Committee on Armed Services, *Organization, Structure and Decisionmaking Procedures of the Department of Defense*, Hearings before the Committee on Armed Services, 98th Cong., 1st Sess. (Washington, DC: Government Printing Office, 1983–84), Part 5, 187.

11. Quoted in James Locher III, "Has It Worked? The Goldwater–Nichols Reorganization Act," *Naval War College Review* 54, no. 4 (Autumn 2001): 101.

12. William J. Crowe, *The Line of Fire: From Washington to the Gulf, the Politics and Battles of the New Military* (New York: Simon & Schuster, 1993), 150.

13. NATO nations included Belgium, Canada, Czech Republic, Denmark, France, Germany, Greece, Hungary, Iceland, Italy, Netherlands, Norway, Poland, Portugal, Spain,

Turkey, the United Kingdom, and the United States. Non-NATO countries included Albania, Argentina, Australia, Austria, Bulgaria, Estonia, Finland, Ireland, Latvia, Lithuania, Morocco, New Zealand, Romania, Russia, Slovakia, Slovenia, and Sweden.

14. NATO, "History of the NATO-led Stabilisation Force (SFOR) in Bosnia and Herzegovina," www.nato.int/sfor/docu/d981116a.htm.

15. In 2008 NATO nations included Belgium, Bulgaria, Czech Republic, Denmark, Estonia, France, Germany, Greece, Hungary, Italy, Latvia, Lithuania, Luxembourg, the Netherlands, Norway, Poland, Portugal, Romania, Slovakia, Slovenia, Spain, Turkey, the United Kingdom, and the United States. Non-NATO countries included Armenia, Austria, Finland, Ireland, Morocco, Sweden, Switzerland, and Ukraine.

16. NATO, "NATO's Role in Kosovo," www.nato.int/issues/kfor/index.html.

17. Dana Priest, *The Mission: Waging War and Keeping Peace with America's Military,* (New York: Norton, 2003), 17.

18. CERP funds military commanders' projects related to water and sanitation; food production and distribution; agriculture; electricity production and distribution; healthcare; education; telecommunications; transportation; irrigation; civic cleanup; repair of civic and cultural facilities; economic, financial, and management improvements; efforts to improve rule of law and governance; condolence payments and former detainee payments; reimbursement for losses incurred as a result of U.S., coalition, or supporting military operations; protective measures to ensure the viability and survivability of critical infrastructure sites; and other urgent humanitarian or reconstruction projects. See U.S. Department of Defense, "Fiscal year 2010 Budget Request Summary Justification" (2009), www.defenselink.mil/comptroller/defbudget/fy2010/fy2010_SSJ.pdf.

19. Col. James Kyle, U.S. Air Force, who was the senior commander at Desert One, would recall that there were "four commanders at the scene without visible identification, incompatible radios, and no agreed-upon plan, not even a designated location for the commander." Quoted in Locher, "Has It Worked?" 100.

20. James Stavridis, "The Last Hour . . . Or the First?" Remarks by Admiral James G. Stavridis at *Americas Quarterly* Launch, Center on Media, Crime, and Justice, John Jay College, New York, October 22, 2007. http://coa.counciloftheamericas.org/article.php?id=729.

21. Carlton W. Fulford Jr., "Thinking through U.S. Strategic Options for Africa," *Naval War College Review* 62, no. 1 (Winter 2009): 31–32.

22. Jonathan Stevenson, "The U.S. Navy into Africa," *Naval War College Review* 62, no. 1 (Winter 2009), 60.

23. Robert T. Moeller and Mary C. Yates, "The Road to a New Unified Command," *Joint Force Quarterly*, no. 51 (4th Quarter 2008).

24. Jim Jones, "Memorandum: The 21st Century Interagency Process" (Washington, DC: The White House, March 18, 2009).

25. Stavridis, "U.S. Southern Command 2009 Posture Statement," 1.

26. Ibid, 18.

27. U.S. Southern Command, "Command Strategy 2018," January 6, 2009. Available at www.southcom.mil.

28. William E. Ward, "Statement before the Senate Armed Services Committee," March 13, 2008, 3.

29. Ibid., 14.

30. Ibid., 8.

31. U.S. Central Command, "Our Mission," www.centcom.mil/en/about-centcom/our-mission/.

32. "Statement of Admiral William J. Fallon, U.S. Navy, Commander, U.S. Central Command before the Senate Armed Services Committee," March 4, 2008, 11.

33. Stavridis, "The Last Hour."

34. David Petraeus, "Senate Armed Services Committee Statement of General David H. Petraeus, U.S. Army, Commander U.S. Central Command before the Senate Armed Services Committee on the Afghanistan-Pakistan Strategic Review and the Posture of U.S. Central Command," April 1, 2009.

35. Ibid.

36. U.S. Southern Command, Partnering Directorate, available at www.southcom.mil.

37. The implications for officer education are startling: "The joint commander of today needs to be able to integrate the efforts of a wider and more disparate set of organizations than ever before—from national intelligence services to charitable giving organizations." James Stavridis and Mark Hagerott, "The Heart of an Officer: Joint, Interagency, International Operations and Navy Career Development," *Naval War College Review* 62, no. 2 (Spring 2009): 27.

38. Bradford Baylor, "Multi-National Force Iraq Strategic Communication Best Practices 2007–2008" (Suffolk, VA: Joint Forces Command, March 10, 2009).

39. Donna L. Hopkins, "The Interagency Counterinsurgency Initiative," Ruger Workshop Proceedings (Newport, RI: U.S. Naval War College, 2007), 281–85.

40. Alliance for Peacebuilding, "Building Whole of Community Conflict Prevention Conference Report," October 30, 2008, available at www.3dsecurity.org/.

41. Lisa Schirch and Aaron Kishbaugh, "Leveraging '3D' Security: From Rhetoric to Reality," *Foreign Policy in Focus*, Policy Brief 11, no. 2 (November 15, 2006).

42. Alliance for Peacebuilding, "Building Bridges and Preventing Conflict: A Memo to the Obama Administration," December 28, 2008, available at www.3dsecurity.org/.

43. Alliance for Peacebuilding, "Building Whole of Community Conflict Prevention."

44. Michael A. McFaul, Anne-Marie Slaughter, Bruce W. Jentleson, et al., "Strategic Leadership: Framework for a 21st Century National Security Strategy," Center for a New American Security, July 2008, http://iis-db.stanford.edu/pubs/22204/StrategicLeadership.pdf.

45. FM 3-0, "Operations," defines five major operational themes: peacetime military engagement, limited intervention, peace operations, irregular warfare, and major combat operations.

46. William E. Ward and Thomas P. Galvin, "U.S. Africa Command and the Principle of Active Security," *Joint Force Quarterly*, no. 51 (4th Quarter 2008): 61.

47. Ward, "Statement before the Senate," 14.

48. Petraeus, "Senate Armed Services Committee Statement."

49. U.S. Pacific Command, "USPACOM Strategy," November 2008, www.pacom
.mil/about/PACOM_STRATEGY_14NOV08.pdf.

5

Security Cooperation

A NEW COOPERATIVE SECURITY APPROACH is replacing traditional notions of national defense, which is driven by an increase in preventive and humanitarian military interventions. This has been occurring for complex strategic reasons.[1] Benjamin Fordham has shown that concerns about the welfare of allies have an immediate impact on the decision for the United States to intervene.[2] Stephen Saideman sees domestic political concerns and public opinion driving intervention.[3] Logically, democratic will should be reflected in policy, which includes decisions to use the military for security assistance and to relieve human suffering.[4] Since World War II, the majority of American adults have consistently indicated that the United States should be a world power actively engaged in international affairs.[5] While there was a clear case to be made for supporting allies and advancing other interests during the Cold War, public support for an internationalist role did not diminish when fears about great power war disappeared in 1991. In 2006 (after two very difficult years in Iraq), 69 percent of Americans thought the United States should be active in international affairs, which is just one point higher than in 1947 and two points below 1956.[6] Unexpectedly, mixed outcomes in Iraq did not undermine the interventionist strain of U.S. foreign policy but instead were met with calls for escalation in Afghanistan, the Horn of Africa, and Southeast Asia. To be sure, "active" does not necessarily mean military intervention, but given how presidents use the military in non-warfighting ways, U.S. foreign policy has an important security assistance component.

While Americans do support an activist foreign policy, survey data suggest that the United States should not behave as the world's sheriff. Instead, 60 percent of Americans agree that the United States should be more willing to make decisions within the United Nations.[7] The Iraq experience certainly colors perceptions of U.S. intervention, but this finding is consistent with concerns about transnational threats that require multilateral solutions. In today's security environment, it seems that terrorism, rogue states, disease, and other concerns associated with weak states impact Americans' thinking about security. This is reflected in the percentage of people who fear a terrorist attack, which is much higher than the 36 percent of Americans who fear China will emerge as a world power or the 34 percent that fear Russia's military.[8] These concerns also lend support to the "civilian activities" the military conducts. In 2009, for example, 64 percent of Americans wanted the U.S. government to make efforts to improve health for people in developing countries. Due to health insecurity generated by the H1N1 pandemic, 85 percent endorsed the view that global "programs are important for the health of Americans as well as people abroad."[9] To be effective against challenges such as these, the United States embraced the notion of working with and through partners. This chapter looks more closely at global programs and the various forms of security assistance, and analyzes current cooperative security programs funded through the international assistance program. First it is essential to understand the intervention lessons of the last decade and the relationship between the Department of Defense and the Department of State.

Intervention Lessons

While this book does not directly address operations in Iraq or Afghanistan, some important lessons emerging from those conflicts are reshaping the military outside of counterinsurgency operations. First is the impact of intervention itself; forced democratization tends to produce semidemocratic governments with political instability and internal conflict.[10] Second, to bring stability to postconflict zones requires new ways of using military forces. For example, Gen. Barry McCaffrey noted that success in Afghanistan would be achieved when there are Afghan police units in every district, a greatly expanded Afghan National Army, and significant agricultural reform.[11] Absent from this solution is stepped-up lethal operations. A Navy SEAL (well known as a lethal actor) remarked that crop substitution from opium to foodstuffs is the key to bringing stability to Afghanistan and to alleviating food security concerns in the region.[12] Combat operations have taught the military that lethality cannot solve security problems. Instead, training and equipping indigenous forces to protect and control their territory is essential for long-term stability.[13] Security and development go hand in hand.

These lessons have gained traction and have been extended to weak states in more permissive environments. Paul Collier argues that the role for advanced militaries of the world is "to supply the global public good of peace in territories that otherwise have the potential for nightmare."[14] The National Security and the Threat of Climate Change committee, which is composed of distinguished retired senior military officers, noted, "the U.S. should commit to global partnerships that help less developed nations build the capacity and resiliency to better manage climate impacts."[15] One example of this is taking place in East Africa.

Rear Adm. Anthony M. Kurta, commander of Combined Joint Task Force Horn of Africa, said, "What we're doing here is the indirect approach to countering violent extremism" by deploying military construction and engineering personnel to East Africa.[16] The underlying assumption of this approach is clear. If national governments cannot create economic opportunities and improve their citizens' lives, then they are susceptible to recruitment by organized crime or terrorist organizations. Consequently, the U.S. military is employing its medical, construction, and civil affairs personnel to permissive environments throughout the world. Key to all of these activities is using the 3D (defense, development, and diplomacy) approach discussed in the last chapter and placing security assistance within the broader context of U.S. foreign policy.

Operationalizing the 3D Approach

The State Department is the lead foreign policy organization in the United States. It plays a critical role in security assistance through the Bureau of Political-Military Affairs, which is a direct link to the Department of Defense.[17] The Bureau focuses its activities on managing and regulating defense trade and arms transfers to reinforce the military capabilities of friends, allies, and coalition partners, and to ensure that the transfer of U.S.-origin defense equipment and technology supports U.S. national security interests. It promotes regional security through bilateral and multilateral cooperation and dialogue, as well as through the provision of security assistance to friendly countries and international peacekeeping efforts. The bureau also provides diplomatic support to U.S. military operations including the negotiation of status of forces agreements, defense cooperation, base access, cost sharing, and Article 98/International Criminal Court nonsurrender agreements. It also works with the Department of Defense on strategic and contingency planning to include counterinsurgency policy, and reinforcing partners' humanitarian capabilities. Additionally, the bureau promotes American values of democracy, respect for human rights, and civilian control of military forces by funding training that exposes the armed forces and civilian personnel of other countries to these values and to the professionalism of the U.S. military.

Given the bureau's broad mandate in international security affairs, active cooperation with the Defense Department is required. If done well, security assistance activities are coordinated with other interagency activities beginning at the national level where both the State Department and the Office of the Secretary of Defense derive priorities and guidance from the National Security Strategy, which in turn drives the military's theater campaign plans and embassies' mission strategic plans.[18] Because programs always take place in particular countries, ambassadors are at the forefront of security assistance. Under National

Security Decision Directive 38, the U.S. ambassador has absolute authority over all U.S. personnel and operations within a country, which means that all military programs are subject to ambassadorial approval. Given that embassies tend to be understaffed and lack adequate resources, chiefs of a mission often see security assistance programs as critical to promoting U.S. objectives and often welcome the programs.[19] Yet an ambassador's focus on one country and a combatant commander's focus on an entire region necessitate coordination.

A combatant command can serve as a regional hub for coordination as well as for interagency and combined planning. To coordinate activities, ambassadors communicate directly with the combatant command or provide direction to the military through the embassy-assigned military personnel. (The changes discussed in chapter 4 facilitate this cooperation.) At the same time, combatant commanders work extremely closely with their State Department political advisor and the country teams where their engagement programs occur. With time-limited tours of duty, combatant commanders need support from outside their military staffs. Political advisors, in particular, promote integration of political, economic, and military considerations during planning. Both combatant commands and ambassador-led country teams see their cooperation as essential to advancing national interests using the defense-development-diplomacy model.

While preparation for war is the military's traditional mission, security assistance has emerged as a key mission over the last twenty years. As Title 10 makes clear, "the Secretary of Defense may conduct military-to-military contacts and comparable activities that are designed to encourage a democratic orientation of defense establishments and military forces of other countries."[20] Security assistance programs are part of a combatant commander's theater campaign plan, which serves as the primary blueprint for regional military engagement. To ensure that other federal assistance is synchronized with theater security cooperation, the country team prepares a mission strategic plan (MSP) that communicates to senior State Department officials in Washington how the mission will contribute to achieving the primary goals of American foreign policy and development assistance in that country. In coordination with the senior defense representative, the MSP recommends cooperative defense activities and program funding within the State Department budget, such as international military education and training (IMET), foreign military sales, or economic support funds, which are critical elements of theater security cooperation.

Defining Security Cooperation

Security cooperation refers to all Department of Defense interactions that are carried out with foreign militaries and defense establishments.[21] Security cooperation is "the ability for DOD to interact with foreign defense establishments to build defense relationships that promote specific U.S. security interests, develop allied and friendly military capabilities for self-defense and coalition operations, including allied transformation, improve information exchange, and intelligence sharing to help harmonize views on security challenges, and provide U.S. forces with peacetime and contingency access and en route infrastructure."[22] Security cooperation falls under the purview of the overall geographic combatant commander, but his strategy and activities are executed at the country level through his security assistance officer, who is the combatant commanders' direct in-country representative and is a member of the country team at the U.S. Embassy working for the U.S. ambassador. Although not in all countries, the security assistance officer is one of the ambassador's favorite staff members since military assistance programs can create secure environments for development programs.

The overall goals of security assistance include creating favorable military balances of power (e.g., selling weapons and training to Saudi Arabia to balance Iran), advancing areas of mutual defense or security arrangements (e.g., collaborating with Japan on missile defense technology), building allied and friendly military capabilities for self-defense and multinational operations (e.g., training Georgian forces, the third-largest troop contributor in Iraq in 2008), and preventing crisis and conflict (e.g., facilitating Colombia's success against the decades-old Revolutionary Armed Forces of Colombia [FARC] insurgency). As noted in doctrine, there are six categories of security cooperation activity: military contacts, including senior official visits, counterpart visits, conferences, staff talks, and personnel and unit exchange programs; nation assistance, including foreign internal defense, security assistance programs, and planned humanitarian and civic assistance activities; multinational training; multinational exercises; multinational education; and arms control and treaty monitoring activities.[23] Underlying all of these activities is the clear intent to achieve U.S. national security objectives. It is important to remember that states must manage the risks of abandonment and entrapment by its friends and allies.[24] The United States does this by building a partner country's military and developing professional relationships across militaries.

These activities are increasingly enshrined in doctrine and are defined as "the ability to improve the military capabilities of our allies and partners to help them transform and optimize their forces to provide regional security, disaster preparedness and niche capabilities in a coalition."[25] For example, Commander Naval Forces Europe has been developing a capability for maritime domain awareness throughout Europe and Africa and has been working with NATO allies and African partners to develop a regional capability to protect trade, natural resources, and economic development. This work includes establishing maritime domain awareness through the automated identification system, an array of coastal radar systems, and through improved command and control of a naval reaction force.

Inherent in these activities is the need to develop enduring relationships. In the Near East, for example, long-term relationships have produced trust and access for the United States to have forward operating bases in Qatar, Kuwait, United Arab Emirates, and Bahrain. Additionally, weapons are prepositioned in other countries, including Oman. While partners benefit from these programs, programs like these also support broader U.S. foreign policy objectives of global influence.

Security cooperation also includes security sector reform, which is an area of increasing importance. It focuses on improving civil–military relations, promoting collaboration among regional partners, and fostering cooperation within partners' governments. The United States has learned that contemporary security challenges often require whole-of-government solutions and regional cooperation. Consequently, it seeks to foster this same approach around the world. Programs support legislative reform (e.g., providing legal advice used to write laws to seize assets from drug traffickers in Colombia), enhancing cooperation between police and defense forces (e.g., building bridges among bureaucratic rivals in Jamaica), and managing the legacy of past human rights abuses by militaries (e.g., integrating human rights training in programs in Latin America and Africa). Further, it considers the internal health and welfare of partners' military forces by combating HIV/AIDS in militaries, promoting noncommissioned officer development, and providing educational opportunities for officers.

The Department of Defense traditionally implements these international military assistance programs funded through the Department of State. Financed under Title 22 (Account 150), the international assistance budget was $27.3 billion in FY2009 (see table 5.1). Fifteen different programs are included in the Account 150, but only six programs can be considered related to security.

Table 5.1 U.S. International Assistance (Account 150) by Region, FY2009

Region	Nonsecurity ($ billion) Assistance	Security ($ billion) Assistance	Total
Africa	5.09	.20	5.30
East Asia and the Pacific	.47	.09	.54
Europe and Eurasia	.56	.17	.73
Near East	1.13	4.39	5.52
South and Central Asia	1.55	.66	2.22
Western Hemisphere	.912	1.13	2.05
Other/Global	10.38	.61	11.00
Total	20.10	7.26	27.37

Note: Derived from Department of State, FY2009 International Assistance Summary Tables. These data do not include supplemental funds or programs funded outside the Department of State. Regional designations are based on the Department of State's regional boundaries, which vary slightly from the Defense Department's boundaries.

These include foreign military financing (FMF), international military education and training (IMET), international narcotics control and law enforcement (INCLE), peacekeeping operations, the Andean Counterdrug Program, and Nonproliferation, Anti-Terrorism, Demining and related programs. While security assistance programs are substantial, nonsecurity assistance programs exceed them by at least two to one. And there are substantial differences across regions too. In Africa, for example, nonsecurity programs are the dominant approach to international assistance. In the Near East, however, the opposite is true because of military assistance to Egypt and Israel.

Although the United States has security assistance programs with 149 countries, it does privilege several others (see table 5.2). Historically, Israel has been the largest recipient of security assistance, and its neighbor Egypt benefited from Egypt's recognition of Israel and its control of the Suez Canal. Because of its proximity to the United States and challenges with drug trafficking organizations, Mexico has recently emerged as a top recipient of security assistance. Given the history of American military interventions in Mexico, this has required new efforts to build trust to reassure the Mexican government that the United States seeks to strengthen Mexico, not undermine it. One reason the United States focuses assistance on just a few countries is to promote particular countries as regional leaders. In practice, this means that Jordan hosts an international special operations exercise, peace operations training center, and an international police–training center. In Latin America, Colombia provides helicopter training for regional militaries, and El Salvador hosts a regional peacekeeping institute that attracts military personnel from countries throughout the Western

Table 5.2 Top Recipients of U.S. International Assistance (Account 150), FY2009

Overall	Nonsecurity Assistance	Security Assistance
Israel	Afghanistan	Israel
Egypt	Kenya	Egypt
Afghanistan	Nigeria	Mexico
Pakistan	Pakistan	Colombia
Kenya	Ethiopia	Pakistan
Colombia	Iraq	Afghanistan
Jordan	Mozambique	Jordan
Mexico	Jordan	Iraq
Nigeria	Haiti	Lebanon
Ethiopia	Egypt	Liberia

Note: Derived from Department of State, FY2009 International Assistance Summary Tables. These data do not include supplemental funds or programs funded outside the Department of State. Regional designations are based on the Department of State's regional boundaries, which vary slightly from the Defense Department's boundaries.

Hemisphere. This approach strengthens key partners and reduces both the need for American presence and the negative attention it sometimes generates.

Engagement Tools

Security assistance comprises about 27 percent of normal international assistance, which is implemented by a variety of government and nongovernmental actors. (Excluded from normal are those activities funded by supplemental budgets that largely benefit Iraq and Afghanistan.) From the Defense Department's perspective, combatant commanders have a broad array of security assistance tools at their disposal. For its part of the Account 150, security assistance often takes the form of IMET and FMF. Additionally, the Defense Department directly funds security assistance through section 1206/7 and other command funds, but this only makes up about $1 billion annually, which is less than 15 percent of security assistance funded by the State Department. Thus, the Department of State exerts considerable control of programs at both budgetary and implementation levels through the embassy country team.

In addition to those programs, combatant commands offer direct military assistance using Joint Combined Exchange Training. Using special operations personnel, military training teams teach foreign militaries how to combat insurgencies, interdict drug traffickers, and rescue hostages. The American military benefits through training in new environments and building relations with their foreign counterparts. The international participants benefit through receiving American training and financial assistance.

The FMF program that supplies grants and loans to finance American weapons and military equipment purchases augments the military training and education. The State Department oversees the FMF program, but combatant commands manage the program on a day-to-day basis. In addition to uniforms and small arms, the United States also provides cargo aircraft, land vehicles, and helicopters. Partners have come to rely on this equipment and do not necessarily want American values. As Admiral Crowe noted decades ago, Filipino president Marcos cared more about American arms transfers than he did about American concerns for human rights abuses by the Philippine military. Admiral Crowe recounted a typical Marcos' response on living conditions in the Philippines, "I appreciate your thoughts, Admiral. I know your heart's in the right place. But what's of more significance, I think, is when you are going to deliver those helicopters you promised us."[26] In contrast to the 1980s, when "fighting communism" was the overriding priority, congressional oversight is now substantial to prevent current or future Marcos-like leaders from receiving security assistance for repression. In the last several years, military coups have resulted in a near-immediate suspension of security assistance.

Concurrently with IMET and FMF, combatant commands also operate military "colleges." The George C. Marshall Center in Europe, for example, is designed to promote defense reform among countries in Central and Eastern Europe. Situated in the Bavarian Alps, the Marshall Center teaches primarily European military personnel, but its student cohorts are becoming more global. In Honolulu, Pacific Command operates the Asia-Pacific Center, which brings together military representatives from the Pacific Rim to focus on defense reform, economic development, and regional security issues. In addition to the educational opportunities these centers provide, they also afford the United States an opportunity to explain its intentions and ameliorate the animosity that U.S. foreign policy sometimes creates. The National Defense University in Washington, D.C., also hosts academic centers focused on the Western Hemisphere, the Near East, and Africa. In addition to the coursework, officer networking is a key outcome of these educational programs. Combatant commands tap into the military's senior service schools, such as the U.S. Naval War College, to run symposia, provide lectures, and help countries develop national strategies. After one conference, a senior officer told me, "I think we have exceeded the objectives. I would have been happy if all that we achieved was to allow persons from different organizations, different countries, to get together and create some common basis for operating. I think we have exceeded that, because we looked at the actual national security strategies that were implemented, and the participants came up with excellent ideas as to how we could make a few modifications to them, and also some ideas in moving forward."[27]

International Military Education and Training Program

Created by the International Security Assistance and Arms Export Control Act of 1976, Congress intended for IMET to accomplish three principal goals: to foster increased understanding between the United States and foreign countries in order to enhance international peace and security, for participating countries to become more self-reliant by improving their ability to utilize defense resources obtained through FMF, and to increase the awareness of internationally recognized human rights issues.[28] Thirty years later the objectives of the program remain fundamentally unchanged. Through the IMET programs, combatant commands train about 8,000 international military officers from 125 countries a year. By comparison, the Fulbright program run by the Department of State awards grants to about 4,000 international participants per year.[29] When other programs are included, the Defense Department reaches an international audience of at least 55,000 every year.[30]

The IMET program provides partner countries grant financial assistance for training at U.S. military schools to select foreign military and civilian personnel. From 1997 to 2004, IMET has funded 66,000 participants, with a notable threefold increase from 1997, when there were just 3,454 students, compared to 11,832 in 2004. Programs include English-language training at the Defense Language Institute, training activities such as the basic infantry officer's course, and attendance at U.S. professional military education institutions such as the Army War College. Regarding the latter, officers from other countries increasingly compose about 15 percent of the graduating class and it is a priority to increase representation.

While the training is often well received, "it is tougher to quantify how such relationships can impact policy issues and ties between the international community and the United States."[31] Nevertheless, Gen. Bantz Craddock, former head of U.S. European Command, testified that "IMET remains our most powerful security cooperation tool and proves its long-term value every day."[32] And IMET advances U.S. objectives on a global scale at a relatively small cost.[33] IMET programs build personal and professional relationships with people likely to rise to senior levels within their countries. In Botswana, for example, eleven of fourteen serving general officers are graduates of IMET programs. Furthermore, having a core group of well-trained, professional leaders with first-hand knowledge of the United States contributes to the professionalization of armed forces, winning access and influence for diplomatic and military representatives. As a testament to the quality of selections for the Naval War College's Naval Staff College, for example, 236 participants have attained flag rank, 102 later served as chiefs of service, 5 became cabinet ministers, and 1 became his nation's president.[34] Thus, in theory, a relatively small amount of IMET funding will provide a large return for the U.S. policy goal of global influence.[35]

In FY2000, IMET programs were budgeted at $49.8 million. The budget more than doubled by the end of the Bush years to $90.5 million in FY2009. As table 5.3 depicts, countries in Europe and Eurasia received the most funding

Table 5.3 International Military Education and Training Funding by Region, FY2009

Region	Amount ($ million)
Africa	13.8
East Asia and Pacific	7.9
Europe and Eurasia	25.5
Near East	16.3
South and Central Asia	9.5
Western Hemisphere	12.6
Other	4.9
Total	90.5

Note: Derived from Department of State, FY2009 International Assistance Summary Tables. These data do not include supplemental funds or programs funded outside the Department of State. Regional designations are based on the Department of State's regional boundaries that vary slightly from the Defense Department's boundaries.

while countries in East Asia and Pacific received the least amount of funding. Underlying the preference for training and educating military personnel from Europe and Eurasia is NATO integration. Since NATO expanded from sixteen countries in 1999 to twenty-eight countries in 2009, it is essential for the United States to train its new allies to facilitate the integration process. This also ensures that European officers network with other NATO officers.

Taken by region, IMET has global impact. In Africa, every country but Somalia and Zimbabwe received some type of IMET assistance in 2009. The top recipient countries are Senegal ($1 million), South Africa ($850,000), Nigeria ($800,000), Kenya ($750,000), and Ethiopia ($700,000). In East Asia and the Pacific, the top recipient countries are the Philippines ($1.7 million), Indonesia ($1.5 million), Thailand ($1.4 million), Mongolia ($970,000), and Malaysia ($750,000). In Europe and Eurasia, the top recipient countries are Turkey ($3 million), Poland ($2.2 million), Ukraine ($1.75 million), Romania ($1.6 million), and Czech Republic ($1.55 million). In the Near East, the top recipient countries are Jordan ($3.1 million), Lebanon ($2.1 million), Iraq ($2 million), Morocco ($1.72 million), and Tunisia ($1.7 million). In South and Central Asia, the top recipient countries are Pakistan ($1.95 million), Afghanistan ($1.4 million), India ($1.2 million), Kyrgyz Republic ($1 million), Bangladesh ($800,000), and Nepal ($800 million). In the Western Hemisphere, the top recipient countries are El Salvador ($1.6 million), Colombia ($1.4 million), Argentina ($900,000), Mexico ($834,000), and Dominican Republic ($800,000).

Although IMET is a relatively modest program in terms of cost, both the president and Congress attach significant importance to the program. Recipient countries, likewise, are heavily reliant on this grant program. In many cases the IMET program serves as the only method for partner militaries to receive advanced training from their U.S. counterparts. Without opportunities from countries such as the United States, there is little indigenous capacity to professionalize militaries through military colleges and training programs. To foster the independence and sustainability of these programs, the United States also assists many countries in developing their own professional military education network and educational programs. The United States does this through exchanging faculty, sharing curriculum ideas, and providing books and professional journals.

Foreign Military Financing Program

Augmenting military education and training is FMF, which supplies grants and loans to finance purchases of American weapons and military equipment. The State Department oversees the program, but combatant commands manage it on a day-to-day basis. In FY2009 the FMF budget was the largest program in the

Table 5.4 Foreign Military Financing by Region, FY2009

Region	Amount ($ billion)
Africa	.01
East Asia and Pacific	.04
Europe and Eurasia	.13
Near East	4.19
South and Central Asia	.31
Western Hemisphere	.09
Other	.06
Total	4.83

Note: Derived from Department of State, FY2009 International Assistance Summary Tables. These data do not include supplemental funds or programs funded outside the Department of State. Regional designations are based on the Department of State's regional boundaries, which vary slightly from the Defense Department's boundaries.

State Department's international assistance account, consuming nearly $4.8 billion.[36] Countries in the Near East are the top recipients, and countries in Africa receive the least amount of U.S. weapons and equipment. Because of the high cost of U.S. weapons and different needs by region, FMF is unevenly distributed.

Nearly 80 percent of FMF goes to Israel ($2.55 billion) and Egypt ($1.3 billion). Of the remaining 20 percent, just a few countries receive substantial assistance: Pakistan ($300 million), Jordan ($235 million), and Colombia ($66 million). Seventy countries share the remaining $300 million. Of note, only nine countries in Africa received FMF in 2009, compared to forty-five African countries that received IMET. This suggests that there is a deliberate policy to focus on professionalizing African militaries instead of arming them, which is a contrast from the past. The top recipients in Africa are Ethiopia ($4 million), Djibouti ($2.8 million), and Nigeria ($1.35 million). The limited sale of U.S. weapons also indicates the different levels of development among militaries. The United States tends to produce sophisticated (and expensive weapons), which have the greatest demand in the Near East and East Asia.

In contrast to Africa, nearly every country in Europe and Eurasia receives FMF. The top recipient countries are Poland ($27 million), Romania ($15 million), Turkey ($12 million), Georgia ($11 million), and Bulgaria ($9 million). In fact, Poland receives more than twice the amount of FMF as all of the countries in sub-Saharan Africa combined. NATO integration and U.S. missile defense programs largely explain this. In East Asia and the Pacific, the top recipient countries are Indonesia ($15.7 million), Philippines ($15 million), Mongolia ($2 million), Thailand ($800,000), and Cambodia ($750,000). Mongolia stands out, given its steady contribution to the U.S.-led military coalition in Iraq. In the Near East, the top recipients are Israel ($2.55 billion), Egypt ($1.3 billion),

Jordan ($235 million), Lebanon ($62.3 billion), and Bahrain ($19.5 million). In South and Central Asia, the top recipient countries are Pakistan ($300 million), Kazakhstan ($2 million), Bangladesh ($1 million), Sri Lanka ($900k), and Tajikistan ($675k). Pakistan stands out given its proximity to Afghanistan, the internal challenges it faces, and fears that it could become a radicalized nuclear power. In the Western Hemisphere, the top recipient countries are Colombia ($66 million), El Salvador ($4.8 million), Panama ($2.25 million), Haiti ($1.6 million), and Peru ($900,000). Over the last decade, U.S. assistance to Colombia has been several billion dollars as it wages a counterinsurgency and combats drug trafficking organizations. El Salvador has largely benefited from post–civil war activities and its contributions to the U.S.-led military coalition in Iraq. Based on discussion with several partner countries in the Western Hemisphere, there are serious concerns that efforts to support Mexico's counterdrug efforts will siphon off valuable resources and redirect the drug flow to the Caribbean, which causes security concerns there.

A program such as FMF advances U.S. interests in many ways. When countries buy U.S. military equipment through FMF (and through direct commercial sales), the basis for a relationship is formed. The countries typically secure long-term commitments for training in how to maintain and operate the equipment. As table 5.5 illustrates, the top recipient countries are long-time U.S. allies and partners: Saudi Arabia, Egypt, and Israel. The relationships are sustained through military sales. Additionally, providing spare and replacement parts ensures that competitor countries do not interfere with the relationship. Combined exercises build personal bonds between U.S. and partner countries' personnel.

Table 5.5 Foreign Military Sales Top Recipient Countries, FY1950–2008

Country	FY2008 ($ billion)	FY1950–2008 ($ billion)
Saudi Arabia	6.07	76.64
Egypt	2.32	31.61
Israel	1.32	30.22
Taiwan	.61	18.90
Turkey	.37	17.69
Australia	1.14	17.68
South Korea	1.13	17.83
Japan	.84	16.88
United Kingdom	1.10	17.12
Germany	.17	15.25
Greece	.23	12.93

Adapted from Defense Security Cooperation Agency, *Historical Facts Book* (Washington, DC: Department of Defense, 2008). Total dollar value of defense articles and defense services purchased with cash, credit, and military assistance program merger funds by a foreign government or international organization in any fiscal year.

Global Peacekeeping Operations Initiative

Outside of IMET and FMF, the Department of State operates integrated security assistance programs such as the Global Peacekeeping Operations Initiative (GPOI). The precursor programs to GPOI were created to respond to the need for peacekeepers in Africa.[37] With a shortage of peacekeepers, the UN Security Council found it difficult to separate former warring parties or deploy as a buffer to prevent the outbreak of war. The demand for trained and capable peacekeepers has grown from ten thousand in the 1980s to nearly one hundred thousand by early 2007, and it is expected to grow by at least fifty thousand in the coming years.[38]

Although the United States does not participate in peacekeeping missions wearing blue berets, it is responsible for about 25 percent of the UN peacekeeping budget and has many bilateral programs to train, equip, and deploy peacekeepers. In FY2009 the peacekeeping programs were valued at $395 million. In 2010 the peacekeeping program focuses on supporting African Union operations in Somalia, transforming the Sudanese People's Liberation Army into a conventional military force, and supporting militaries in Liberia, the Trans-Sahara, and East Africa. Although resources are substantial, General Ward testified before the Senate Armed Services Committee that "the equipment needs of troop-contributing countries for peace support operations in Darfur and other anticipated operations dwarfs GPOI's ability to provide the magnitude of equipment required to satisfy United Nations contingent-owned equipment requirements."[39]

There are seven core objectives of GPOI:

1. Train and equip at least 75,000 peacekeepers worldwide, with an emphasis on Africa, to increase global capacity to participate in peace operations.
2. Enhance the capacity of regional and sub-regional organizations to train for, plan, prepare for, manage, conduct, and obtain and sustain lessons-learned from peace operations by providing technical assistance, training, and material support; and, support institutions and activities which offer these capabilities to a regional audience.
3. Create a "clearinghouse" function to exchange information and coordinate G8 efforts to enhance peace operations training and exercises in Africa; continue to provide support for such clearinghouse initiatives throughout the life of the G8's Action Plan for Expanding Global Capability for Peace Support Operations.
4. Work with other G8 members to develop a globally oriented transportation and logistics support arrangement to help provide transportation for deploying peacekeepers and logistics support to sustain units in the field.
5. Develop a cached equipment program to procure and warehouse equipment for use in peace operations anywhere around the globe.

6. Provide support to the international Center of Excellence for Stability Police Units (COESPU) in Italy to increase the capabilities and interoperability of stability police to participate in peace operations.

7. Conduct sustainment/self-sufficiency activities in support of the objectives above with a focus on assisting partners to sustain proficiencies gained in training programs.[40]

GPOI now includes fifty-one partner countries and organizations throughout the world, although the emphasis is still on Africa (see table 5.6).[41] With increased capacity gained through GPOI, Africa's military contribution to U.N. peacekeeping doubled from 2000 to 2004.[42]

The training was initially conducted by the U.S. military, but demand for military personnel in Iraq and Afghanistan largely shifted responsibility to government contractors. However, a major goal is to reduce dependency on external actors such as the United States, so GPOI supports peace operations training centers in dozens of countries including Ghana, Kenya, Mali, Nigeria, South Africa, Bangladesh, Cambodia, Indonesia, Mongolia, Thailand, Belize, Dominican Republic, Guatemala, Honduras, Nicaragua, Paraguay, Peru, Uruguay, Albania, Bosnia, Ukraine, and Jordan. When the program concludes, it will be critical to see how well partners sustain momentum and participate in peacekeeping operations.

A New Model: 1206/1207

Created during the Cold War, IMET and FMF are long-term programs and are slow to respond to changes in the security environment. Thus, when the United States wanted to assist Kosovo, a new country, in formalizing its military structures or to help Afghanistan, a postwar country, build an army, it could not do so under traditional foreign assistance programs such as IMET and FMF. The military con-

Table 5.6 Global Peacekeeping Operations Initiative Participant by Region, FY2005–FY2009

Region	Peacekeepers Trained	Trainers Trained	Total
Africa	49,254	2,856	52,110
East Asia and Pacific	2,550	343	2,893
Europe and Eurasia	297	26	323
Near East	3	0	3
South and Central Asia	333	59	392
Western Hemisphere	1,806	66	1,872

Source: Adapted from Nina M. Serafino, "Global Peacekeeping Operations Initiative: Background and Issues for Congress" (Washington, DC: Congressional Research Service, 2009), table 2.

tended that traditional security assistance took three to four years from concept to execution, and a new model was needed.[43] In an effort to overcome lengthy program delays, Congress granted the Defense Department "global train and equip" authority under section 1206 of the 2006 National Defense Authorization Act.[44]

Section 1206 provides funds to build the capacity of foreign military forces. This is used primarily for counterterrorism, but it also gives combatant commands unprecedented levels of discretion and streamlines project development. As General Craddock testified before Congress, "Section 1206 capacity building authority allows Combatant Commanders, working jointly with Ambassadors, to rapidly train and equip partner nation forces for urgent or emergent counter-terrorism or security cooperation missions."[45] It is more flexible and is faster than the normal two-year budget cycle that FMF follows. Furthermore, the programs tend to be regional.

Under section 1207 the Defense Department also gained the authority to support stability operations in U.S.-led coalitions. Congress limited this assistance to a country's military forces (excluding police forces) and stipulated that no nation should receive assistance if otherwise prohibited from receiving foreign military assistance through other sources.[46] This caveat was included to ensure that the Defense Department did not undermine the State Department. A year later, oversight was strengthened when the 2007 National Defense Authorization Act delegated approval authority for section 1206 spending from the president to the secretary of defense but stipulated that the secretary of state must concur on all programs.[47]

In terms of fiscal scope, the Defense Department's security assistance programs are dwarfed by traditional military assistance funded by the State Department. In 2007 Congress increased section 1206 funding from $200 million to $300 million.[48] However, the military only used $100 million in FY2006 and $279 million in FY2007 for global train-and-equip projects. In FY2010 the request was for $700 million, which would effectively double the FMF account that is not earmarked for Israel and Egypt. The Defense Department in its budget justification reasoned that building partnership capacity programs reduces stress on U.S. forces by helping partners solve problems before they become crises; multiplies the global force by allowing partners to manage their own security problems; and improves the effectiveness of U.S. forces by teaming with foreign partners who know the local language, culture, and political terrain.[49]

To create secure regions and allow governments and populations to be safe from disease, terrorists, or pirates, security cooperation programs are increasingly focused at the regional level, which are funded through 1206 or 1207. Pacific Command, for example, developed programs to improve information sharing in the region and hosted the first-ever Asia-Pacific intelligence chiefs conference in order to increase regional capacity to combat transnational crime and terrorism. Through 1206 funding, Pacific Command provided more than $64 million to improve the maritime security capacity in Malaysia, Indonesia, the Philippines, and Sri Lanka.[50] Using 1207 funds, Pacific Command spent $16.9 million to expand economic development in the Southeast Asia triborder area (Indonesia, Malaysia, and the Philippines) and improve the responsiveness of regional military and law enforcement there.[51] Central Command hosted a similar conference and gave the new chiefs of defense from Iraq and Afghanistan increased stature and a path to normalize relations with neighboring countries. (Information sharing is a key way to increase regional cooperation.) Naval Forces Europe promoted maritime safety and security by sponsoring the regional Maritime Safety and Security Information System. With $5.8 million of 1206 funds in FY08, the program trained and equipped sixteen African countries, thereby increasing their capabilities to monitor their territorial waters and their exclusive economic zones.

Sections 1206 and 1207 provide expedient authorities for military commanders to fund programs, but such programs are not without oversight. The law requires that any services, defense articles, or funds provided or transferred must comply with the authorities and limitations of the Foreign Assistance Act of 1961, the Arms Export Control Act, or any law that makes appropriations to carry out such act. Furthermore, the secretary of defense must notify congressional committees when the authority is exercised, and the notification must be prepared in coordination with the secretary of state.[52] At the time the law changed, Secretary of State Rice said, "In 1206, we have provided a dual key approach of delivering resources for emergent short-term military assistance needs and counterterrorism activities."[53]

Nevertheless, there are limits to oversight. For example, Chad received $6 million to establish a light infantry rapid reaction force in FY2007.[54] But in the same year, the Department of State criticized Chad's security forces for "engaging in extrajudicial killing, torture, beatings, rapes and human rights abuses."[55] When this was investigated, it appeared that European Command did not brief embassy personnel until after the proposal received 1206 funding, at which time the embassy expressed concern.[56] Additional research is needed to understand the limits of oversight, but—at least in the FY2006 request—European Command only coordinated with four out of fourteen embassy staffs prior to submitting its global train-and-equip requests.[57] The Government Accountability Office did note that coordination improved in fiscal year 2007, and a program with Thailand was cancelled after a coup occurred there in 2006.[58]

Out of Control?

Fears about the militarization of foreign policy stem from the question of who should be in charge. The State Department oversees the security assistance programs that the Defense Department implements, yet new models such as

1206/1207 and CERP give the Defense Department the authority to execute security assistance programs directly, which creates coordination challenges. In principle, coordination should occur through the embassy country team that has the best situational awareness of the country where programs occur. However, with multiple staffs involved across the region and Washington, D.C., there are bound to be missteps. This occurred after 9/11 when the military stepped up lethal special operations in certain countries. Tension grew over other concerns about the changing face of the military. Congress noted, "Left unclear, blurred lines of authority between the State Department and the Defense Department could lead to interagency turf wars that undermine the effectiveness of the overall U.S. effort against terrorism."[59] Yet Congress noted that the problem could be solved in the field. "It is in the embassies rather than in Washington where interagency differences on strategies, tactics, and divisions of labor are increasingly adjudicated."[60] As the Obama administration attempts to improve interagency coordination, it will be well served to study country teams at U.S. embassies as a model. Embassies are simultaneously engaged at the tactical, operational, and strategic levels of national security. Furthermore, U.S. ambassadors think and act on the whole in government ways.

Both U.S. ambassadors and combatant commanders understand they need each other's cooperation. There is wide-ranging agreement between Defense and State that programs should "marginalize the enemies of peace and prevent conflict, thereby enabling the growth of strong and just governments and legitimate institutions to support the development of civil societies."[61] Likewise, there is agreement that partner countries should have the ability to protect the civilian populations from man-made and natural disasters. Thus, strengthening weak states is a diplomatic priority and is primarily conducted by the Defense Department as security cooperation. The next chapter offers a focused maritime case of this.

Notes

1. Dylan Balch-Lindsay and Andrew J. Enterline, "Killing Time: The World Politics of Civil War Duration 1820–1992," *International Studies Quarterly* 44, no. 4 (2000): 615–42.

2. Benjamin O. Fordham, "Power or Plenty? Economic Interests, Security Concerns, and American Intervention," *International Studies Quarterly* 52, no. 4 (2008): 737–58.

3. Stephen M. Saideman, *The Ties That Divide: Ethnic Politics, Foreign Policy, and International Conflict* (New York: Columbia University Press, 2001).

4. Security assistance is a group of programs, authorized by law, that allows the transfer of military articles and services to friendly foreign governments. Security assistance transfers may be carried out via sales, grants, leases, or loans and are authorized under the premise that if these transfers are essential to the security and economic well-being of allied

governments and international organizations, they are equally vital to the security and economic well-being of the United States. See Defense Security Cooperation Agency, "Security Assistance Manual," DoD 5105.38-M, October 3, 2003, www.dsca.osd.mil/samm/.

5. See Lydia Saad, "Americans Support Active Role for U.S. in World Affairs but Don't View Ethnic Conflicts as Critical to U.S. Interests," Gallup News Service, 1999.

6. Respondents were asked, "Do you think it will be best for the future of the country if we take an active part in world affairs or if we stay out of world affairs?" See figure 1.2: "Active Part in World Affairs," in Chicago Council on Global Affairs, "Global Views 2006," www.thechicagocouncil.org/UserFiles/File/POS_Topline%20Reports/POS%202006/2006%20India%20Topline.pdf.

7. Chicago Council on Global Affairs, "Global Views 2006," 18.

8. Respondents were asked to mark any of the following that represented "critical threats" to the United States over the next ten years. Adapted from figure 1-4: "Critical Threats to U.S. Vital Interests," in Chicago Council on Global Affairs, "Global Views 2006."

9. World Public Opinion, "Americans Support U.S. Working to Improve Health in Developing Countries," May 20, 2009, www.worldpublicopinion.org/pipa/articles/brunitedstatescanadara/610.php.

10. Nils Petter Gleditsch, Lene S. Chritiansen, and Havard Hegre, "Democratic Jihad? Military Intervention and Democracy," World Bank Policy Research Working Paper No. 4242 (Washington, DC: World Bank, 2007).

11. Gen. Barry R. McCaffrey, USA (Ret.), "After Action Report, Visit NATO SHAPE Headquarters and Afghanistan 21–26 July 2008," July 30, 2008.

12. Author private interview, December 17, 2008.

13. Support occurs when new states are created. In 2008, when Kosovo declared its independence, European Command purchased uniforms for the 2,500-person Kosovo Security Force, assisted training a noncommissioned officer corps, and helped to create a ministry of defense for Kosovo.

14. Paul Collier, *The Bottom Billion: Why the Poorest Countries Are Failing and What Can Be Done about It* (New York: Oxford University Press, 2007), 125.

15. See "National Security and the Threat of Climate Change," www.securityandclimate.cna.org. The group is composed of Gen. Gordon Sullivan, Adm. Frank "Skip" Bowman, Lt. Gen. Lawrence P. Farrell Jr., Vice Adm. Paul G. Gaffney II, Gen. Paul J. Kern, Adm. T. Joseph Lopez, Adm. Donald L. Pilling, Adm. Joseph W. Prueher, Vice Adm. Richard H. Truly, Gen. Charles F. Wald, and Gen. Anthony C. Zinni.

16. Quoted in James Warden, "Approaching Djibouti Locals from the Humanitarian Side," *Stars and Stripes*, March 25, 2009.

17. See "Bureau of Political-Military Affairs" at www.state.gov/t/pm/.

18. Department of Defense, "Joint Publication 5-0: Joint Operation Planning" (Washington, DC: Joint Staff, 2005), II-8, www.dtic.mil/doctrine/new_pubs/jp5_0.pdf. In European Command, for example, U.S. Naval Forces Europe working with the U.S. Department of State, U.S. European Command, and the Africa Center for Strategic Studies, led a ministerial-level

conference on Maritime Safety and Security in the Gulf of Guinea. See Gen. Bantz Craddock, "Statement of General Bantz J. Craddock, USA Commander, United States European Command, before the House Armed Services Committee," March 15, 2007, http://armedservices .house.gov/pdfs/FCeucom031507/Craddock_Testimony031507.pdf.

19. John D. Finney and Alphonse F. LaPorta, "Integrating National Security Strategy at the Operational Level: The Role of State Department Political Advisors," in Gabriel Marcella, *Affairs of State: the Interagency and National Security* (Carlisle, PA: Strategic Studies Institute, 2008).

20. U.S. Code, Title 10, Subtitle A, Part I, Chapter 6, Section 168.

21. Chairman, U.S. Joint Chiefs of Staff, "Joint Publication 3-0: Joint Operations" (Washington, DC: Joint Staff, 2006), I-8.

22. "Joint Capability Areas Tier 1 and Supporting Tier 2 Lexicon, Post 24 August 2006 JROC," available at www.dtic.mil/futurejointwarfare/.

23. Chairman, U.S. Joint Chiefs of Staff, "Joint Publication 5-0: Joint Operations Planning" (Washington, DC: Joint Staff, 2006), I-3.

24. G. H. Snyder, *Alliance Politics* (Ithaca, NY: Cornell University Press, 1997).

25. "Joint Capability Areas Tier 1 and Supporting Tier 2."

26. William Crowe Jr., "U.S. Pacific Command: A Warrior-Diplomat Speaks," in *America's Viceroys: The Military and U.S. Foreign Policy*, ed. Derek S. Reveron (New York: Palgrave MacMillan, 2004), 89.

27. Author private interview.

28. Committee on International Relations and Committee on Foreign Relations, "Legislation on Foreign Relations through 2002," United States House of Representatives, chapter 5. Available at www.internationalrelations.house.gov/about.asp?sec=documents.

29. In fiscal year 2007, the Fulbright program was $198.8 million. Of the 7,000 participants a year, slightly more than half are not American. This includes 1,650 foreign graduate students, 850 foreign scholars, 175 Humphrey fellows, and several hundred others. For more information, see http://fulbright.state.gov.

30. Department of Defense, "Fiscal Year 2010 Budget Request: Summary Justification" (Washington, DC: Pentagon, May 2009), http://comptroller.defense.gov/ defbudget/fy2010/fy2010_SSJ.pdf, 5–37.

31. Ronald H. Reynolds, "Is Expanded International Military Education and Training Reaching the Right Audience?" *DISAM Journal of International Security Assistance Management* (Spring 2003): 94.

32. Craddock, "Statement before the House Armed Services Committee," 11.

33. Chairman, U.S. JCS, "Joint Publication 3-0," I-2.

34. Bill Daly, "Building Global Partnerships," U.S. Naval Institute *Proceedings* 133, no. 4 (April 2007): 44–47.

35. Chairman, U.S. JCS, "Joint Publication 3-0," I-3.

36. U.S. Department of State, "Foreign Military Financing Account Tables," available at www.state.gov. It is important to note that military assistance for Iraq and Afghanistan is not included in these account data.

37. According to a Congressional Research Service report, "In 1996, the Clinton Administration proposed the creation of an African Crisis Response Force (ACRF), an African standby force that would be trained and equipped by the United States and other donor nations. The initiative was not well received on the continent, and was later reintroduced as the African Crisis Response Initiative (ACRI), a bilateral training program designed to improve the capabilities of individual African countries' militaries to participate in multilateral peacekeeping operations. ACOTA [African Contingency Operations Training and Assistance], which replaced ACRI in 2002, aims to upgrade the peace-enforcement capabilities of African militaries. ACOTA provides Peace Support Operations training, including light infantry and small unit tactics, and focuses on training African troops who can in turn train other African units. In 2004 ACOTA became a part of GPOI." Lauren Ploch, "Africa Command: U.S. Strategic Interests and the Role of the U.S. Military in Africa" (Washington, DC: CRS, October 2, 2009), 22.

38. Alix J. Boucher and Victoria K. Holt, "U.S. Training, African Peacekeeping: The Global Peace Operations Initiative (GPOI)" Henry L. Stimson Center, *Issue Brief*, July 2007, www.stimson.org/fopo/pdf/Stimson_GPOIBrief_Aug07.pdf, citing the press conference of President George W. Bush after the G8 Summit, Summit International Media Centre, Savannah, June 10, 2004.

39. Gen. William E. "Kip" Ward, U.S. Army, "Advance Questions," Senate, Anticipated Confirmation Hearing, Senate Armed Services Committee, 110th Cong., 1st sess., 2007, www.africom.mil/fetchBinary.asp?pdfID=20071029142917.

40. U.S. Department of State, Global Peacekeeping Operations Initiative, www.state .gov/t/pm/ppa/gpoi/c20337.htm.

41. Congressional Research Service, "The Global Peace Operations Initiative: Background and Issues for Congress" (Washington, DC: CRS, June 11, 2009), http://opencrs .com/document/RL32773/.

42. Nina M. Serafino, "Global Peacekeeping Operations Initiative: Background and Issues for Congress" (Washington, DC: Congressional Research Service, 2009).

43. U.S. Department of Defense, "Fiscal Year 2009 Budget Request Summary Justification," February 4, 2008, http://comptroller.defense.gov/defbudget/fy2009/ FY2009_Budget_Request_Justification.pdf, 103.

44. CRS Report RS22855, "Section 1206 of the National Defense Authorization Act for FY2006: A Fact Sheet on Department of Defense Authority to Train and Equip Foreign Military Forces." Updated by Nina M. Serafino (June 3, 2008), 1. Authorities provided to DOD under Title 10 cannot be generally used for training or equipment programs, whereas Title 22 funds, which are controlled by the State Department but which include some DOD-implemented programs such as FMF and IMET, cannot be used to fund military operations.

45. Bantz Craddock, "Statement of General Bantz J. Craddock, USA Commander, United States European Command, before the House Armed Services Committee," March 13, 2008, 41, www.dod.gov/dodgc/olc/docs/testCraddock080313.pdf.

46. National Defense Authorization Act of 2006, Pub. L. No. 109-163. 119 Stat. 3456–58.

47. John Warner National Defense Authorization Act of 2007, Pub. L. No. 109-364. 120 Stat. 2083, 2418.

48. Ibid.

49. U.S. Department of Defense, "FY 2010 Budget Request Summary Justification," 2009.

50. Tim Keating, "Statement of Admiral Timothy J. Keating, U.S. Navy, Commander, U.S. Pacific Command, before the House Armed Services Committee on U.S. Pacific Command Posture," March 12, 2008, 9. www.pacom.mil/speeches/sst2008/2008%20 PACOM%20HASC%20Posture%20Statement_12%20Mar%2008.pdf.

51. Nina Serafino, "Department of Defense 'Section 1207' Security and Stabilization Assistance: A Fact Sheet" (Washington, DC: Congressional Research Service, May 7, 2008).

52. Ibid.

53. Condoleezza Rice, "Building Partnership Capacity and Development of the Interagency Process," Testimony before the House Armed Services Committee, April 15, 2008, http://2001-2009.state.gov/secretary/rm/2008/04/103589.htm.

54. CRS Report RS22855, 4.

55. U.S. Department of State, "Country Reports on Human Rights Practices: Chad," March 6, 2007, www.state.gov/g/drl/rls/hrrpt/2006/78726.htm.

56. Government Accountability Office, Letter to Senator Richard Lugar, "Section 1206 Security Assistance Program," February 28, 2007, www.gao.gov/new.items/d07416r.pdf.

57. See ibid. and CRS Report RS22855.

58. GAO, Letter to Richard Lugar.

59. "Embassies as Command Posts in the Anti-Terror Campaign," A Report to Members of the Committee on Foreign Relations, United States Senate, December 15, 2006, p. 2, www.fas.org/irp/congress/2006_rpt/embassies.html.

60. Ibid.

61. William E. Ward, "Statement of General William E. Ward, Commander, United States Africa Command, before the House Armed Services Committee," March 13, 2008, 7, http://armedservices.house.gov/pdfs/FC031308/Ward_Testimony031308.pdf.

6

Promoting Maritime Security

MUCH ATTENTION HAS BEEN GIVEN to the ways governments are changing the use of their ground forces, especially when it comes to conducting peacekeeping, stability operations, and counterinsurgency. This attention is no surprise given that NATO countries have more than 250,000 military personnel deployed in Iraq and Afghanistan. These ground forces have learned the hard lessons of stability operations and are reequipping with better-designed uniforms and with vehicles better suited for terrain and IED-defense, and are training for conducting non-warfighting missions. For ground forces, change is necessary not only for success but also for survival in nonpermissive environments. These lessons also inform how military forces are changing in permissive environments where the U.S. military does not conduct combat operations.

Ground forces are not the only ones changing to suit twenty-first century missions. Naval forces are changing too. NATO-, EU-, and U.S.-led naval coalitions around the world are providing port security, patrolling strategic lanes of communication, combating piracy, delivering humanitarian assistance, conducting medical diplomacy, and cooperating with NGOs to promote development. These are very different missions from those for which warships were designed. In particular, the U.S. Navy is adapting to build partners' coast guards and navies to localize maritime-borne threats before they impact freedom of navigation or exploit the maritime commons for illicit activities. Furthermore, navies provide logistics platforms for NGOs to conduct fisheries conservation, provide medical assistance, and deliver relief supplies.

Underlying the change in navies is an effort to export security to build defense relationships that promote specific security interests, develop allied and friendly military capabilities for self-defense and coalition operations, and provide foreign forces peacetime and contingency access. Given its shrinking fleet and global challenges, the U.S. Navy has embraced security cooperation to augment its own force to improve maritime security. Senior Navy strategists Vice Adm. John Morgan and Rear Adm. Charles Martogolio wrote in 2005, "policing the maritime commons will require substantially more capability than the United States or any individual nation can deliver."[1] They recognized that a superpower has limits, and transnational actors increasingly generate maritime insecurity by capitalizing on weak security structures. As such, the United States seeks partnerships with international navies to create the proverbial thousand-ship navy, which can respond to piracy, smuggling, and other illegal activities and can protect important sea-lanes. Where no able partners exist, the United States will help build national capabilities. To be sure, the concept does not anticipate one thousand ships or confine itself to navy vessels only. Instead, global maritime partnerships include coast guards, commercial shipping companies, and port operators. This is logically based on the importance of seaborne trade, the size of the world's oceans, and globalization.[2] Maritime activities cross the public–private and national–international divides, therefore any attempt to improve maritime security must be comprehensive.

Embracing Thomas Friedman's vision of a flat world, Adm. Michael Mullen, who served as chief of naval operations and chairman of the Joint Chiefs of Staff, said we need to rid ourselves "of the old notion—held by so many for so long—that maritime strategy exists solely to fight and win wars at sea, and the rest will take care of itself. In a globalized, *flat world* the rest matters a lot"[3] (emphasis added). Consequently, the U.S Navy has been cooperating with partners that exist and creating new partners capable of working alongside many navies of the world. Lt. Cdr. Jon Bartee argues that these activities should become more formalized as foreign maritime defense, which he defines as participation by "U.S. civilian and military agencies to assist a government in developing or asserting sovereignty within its own internationally recognized territorial waters."[4] While this is a very large endeavor, and it will take decades to judge its effect, the rest of this chapter examines the rationale for maritime cooperation and the concepts to confront maritime security challenges.

Maritime Security Challenges

A little more than 70 percent of the earth's surface is covered by water, 80 percent of the world's population lives on or near a coast, and 90 percent of international commerce travels by sea. These facts have been true throughout human history, but there is increasing awareness of the dangers to maritime security and the challenges posed by its absence. In 2005 the UN General Assembly was "concerned that marine pollution from all sources, including vessels and, in particular, land-based sources, constitutes a serious threat to human health and safety, endangers fish stocks, marine biodiversity and marine and coastal habitats and has significant costs to local and national economies."[5] Conventions such as the

International Ship and Port Security (ISPS Code) seeks to prevent security incidents on ships and in ports.[6] Programs such as the Container Security Initiative place U.S. customs inspectors in international ports to screen cargo. And international naval coalitions with countries as diverse as Russia, South Korea, and Denmark are sending warships to deter piracy in East Africa.

At the same time that governments are sending their navies to conduct non-warfighting missions, pro-environmental groups seek to reduce maritime insecurity too. For example, Greenpeace and the International Crisis Group identify overfishing as a root cause of piracy. Groups such as Friends of the Earth and the Basel Action Network attempt to limit maritime pollution by targeting destructive ship disposal practices that escape state regulation or provide fuel for cash-strapped militaries to increase patrols of ecologically important areas. Because navies provide presence and logistical capabilities, governments and nongovernmental groups are coming together to address the sources of maritime insecurity, which includes illegal, unreported, and underreported fishing; piracy; illicit trafficking; and maritime pollution.

Illegal, Unreported, and Underreported Fishing

Fish provide more than 2.9 billion people with at least 15 percent of their average per capita animal protein intake.[7] Yet illegal, unreported, and underreported (IUU) fishing devastates fish stocks and undermines developing countries' food supplies. In 2004 the UN General Assembly Resolution 62/177 deplored the fact that "illegal, unreported, and underreported fishing constitutes a serious threat to fish stocks and marine habitats and ecosystems, to the detriment of sustainable fisheries as well as the food security and the economies of many states, particularly developing states."[8] The UN Food and Agriculture Organization declared that IUU fishing constitutes a serious threat to (a) fisheries, especially those of high value that are already overfished (e.g., cod, tuna, redfish, and swordfish); (b) marine habitats, including vulnerable marine ecosystems; and (c) food security and the economies of developing countries.[9] Under UN resolutions, states are encouraged to take effective measures to deter illegal activities that undermine fisheries conservation and management practices.[10] Given the importance of fish protein, the scope of the problem is global, but it has a disproportionate effect on developing countries that do not have alternate food sources, the income to afford food imports, or the maritime security forces to reduce IUU fishing.

For example, case studies conducted in nine African countries show estimates of total financial losses in exclusive economic zones (EEZs) to illegal fishing reaching an estimated $335 million (U.S. dollars) per year.[11] When considering all of sub-Saharan Africa, the total estimated EEZ losses are estimated to be a staggering $937 million per year.[12] Losses to struggling societies have an immediate economic impact, but future fish stocks are jeopardized too. At the current rate of overfishing, forecasters predict that the ecological systems that support the fish population will collapse by 2045, eliminating the primary protein sources for African coastal nations.[13] Consequently, the UN Food and Agriculture Organization has been brokering a global treaty to combat IUU fishing. Since boats involved in illegal activities must bring their catch ashore, enforcement in ports is seen as the solution. To support this, the United States and other countries are using their navies to assist developing countries build capacity for fisheries management to include monitoring their EEZs, patrolling territorial waters, and securing their port facilities.[14] These mandates underlie the changing face of the military and explain why navies are attempting to reduce maritime insecurity.

Piracy

The other side of the illegal fishing coin in East Africa is piracy. Fishers made redundant by illegal fishing have used their seamanship skills and knowledge of the seas to partner with criminal groups to hijack ships in the Indian Ocean and Gulf of Aden.[15] While largely a nuisance to developed countries since the nineteenth century, piracy has once again captured international attention. The International Maritime Bureau defines piracy and armed robbery as "an act of boarding or attempting to board any ship with apparent intent to commit theft or any other crime and with apparent intent or capability to use force in the furtherance of that act."[16] Legally, piracy must occur in international waters.

Hijackings of a Ukrainian ship loaded with weapons and a Saudi oil tanker with $100 million worth of oil in 2008 pushed piracy into the headlines, but the world has lived with piracy for millennia (Julius Caesar was once a victim). When American commerce was threatened in the nineteenth century, presidents Jefferson and Madison sent the Navy and Marines to North Africa to stop the pirate attacks from the Barbary states and were mainly successful. The victory is enshrined in the "Marines' Hymn." What may be different two centuries later, however, is that merchant fleets are mainly private, piracy is not state-sponsored, and threats to sea-lanes are now thought of as a global threat rather than a national one.

Up until 1994, reports of piracy and armed robbery against ships were relatively equally distributed around the world. As global trade increased throughout the 1990s, piracy increased in key shipping lanes in the South China Sea, the Malacca Strait, and the Indian Ocean. Since 2004 there have been about 275 attacks around the world every year. But pirate waters have shifted away from

Southeast Asia to both coasts of Africa. The reduction of piracy in Southeast Asia is attributed to cooperation among the navies of Malaysia, Singapore, and Indonesia and to the 2004 tsunami, which had a devastating effect on the "pirate fleets." In West Africa, piracy is primarily armed robbery at sea that occurs close to shore. In cases such as these, criminals board ships at anchor in the middle of the night and steal valuables from the crew or ship. But in the Horn of Africa, hijackings occur hundreds of miles from the coast, and ships and crews are held until ransoms are paid, which often takes months and costs millions of dollars.

A pirated vessel can produce exceptional income for the generally poor perpetrators of piracy. Acts of piracy ranging from crimes of opportunity against anchored vessels in the Gulf of Guinea and the Nigerian delta to ship seizures orchestrated by organized gangs in the Gulf of Aden and Somali waters can earn anywhere from a few thousand dollars in stolen booty to millions of dollars in ransom paid to recover a merchant ship and her crew. In 2009 Somali pirates earned an estimated $100 million through ship hijackings. The reemergence of piracy not only poses a threat to the local land-based economies of African states where piracy exists but also negatively affects the global maritime economy through price increases.

As piracy developed in east Africa, pirates garnered world attention because their activities affected commerce in the waters of the Red Sea and the Gulf of Aden, which are a strategic link between Europe and Asia. The area is an essential oil transport route, with 30 percent of the world's oil passing through the Gulf of Aden. Although pirates do not routinely target the larger tankers transiting the area, pirates became increasingly bold in 2009. A significant attack against a large tanker in the Gulf of Aden could cause delays or closure of the traffic through Bab el-Mandeb Strait, thus preventing Persian Gulf tankers from reaching the Suez Canal and leading to greater energy costs and a disruption to European energy supplies.[17] To date, pirates have only expressed an interest in hijacking for ransom and have not engaged in terrorism. Piracy is more analogous to carjacking than it is to carbombing.

Piracy not only affects the commercial shipping industry, it also directly affects efforts of the World Food Program, which delivers 90 percent of its food aid to Somalia by sea.[18] The first U.S.-flagged ship that was almost hijacked was carrying food aid to alleviate starvation in Somalia.[19] So while east Africans generally show greater concern about illegal fishing instead of piracy, international relief efforts to those societies are directly threatened by piracy. To ensure that food does reach populations in East Africa, naval coalitions conduct convoy operations and serve as escorts.

Most experts agree that the problem of Somali piracy begins ashore. Martin Murphy explains that the seven basic factors that enable maritime piracy are basic elements of sanctuary.[20] Large ungoverned areas, poor governance, the inability of governments to adequately patrol their territorial waters or defend seaports, and the violence and chaos existing in large portions of the Horn of Africa offer pirates (and other criminal or terrorist organizations) this sanctuary of protection and freedom of operations. U.S. efforts to improve security in ungoverned spaces are driving the changing face of the military and are captured in the twenty-first century naval strategy.[21]

Drug Trafficking

Illegal fishing and piracy recaptured international attention in 2008, but illicit trafficking of drugs by sea has provoked a maritime security response for decades.[22] Criminal groups increasingly benefit from maritime insecurity by exploiting trade routes to traffic drugs, people, and weapons. They thrive in the vastness of the oceans and relative lack of maritime domain awareness or response capabilities within the developing world.

Noncommercial maritime vessels, such as go-fast and fishing boats, are the principal conveyances used by traffickers to move cocaine shipments through the eastern Pacific, while go-fast boats and private aircraft are the most common cocaine transport methods used by traffickers in the western Caribbean vector. The result is that Mexican and Colombian drug trafficking organizations generate, remove, and launder between $18 billion and $39 billion in wholesale drug proceeds annually.[23] These groups use the profits to equip themselves with the latest weapons, which are often more advanced than their national government's forces. For example, Colombian drug trafficking organizations increasingly use semisubmersible vehicles to evade detection. Resembling a small submarine, an estimated sixty semisubmersibles shipped more than 330 metric tons of cocaine or other illicit material in 2009.[24] Traffickers' increasing sophistication has warranted a military response to detect and interdict these vessels as police forces lack the capacity to detect submarine-like vehicles.

Since the 1980s maritime forces have attempted to reduce illicit trafficking by sea. During the last decade efforts increased as traffickers used better techniques to get the drugs to market in the United States and Europe. Building on a Clinton-era initiative, the Bush administration declared that the Caribbean is America's third border, which was strangely applauded in the Caribbean. At the time, the Caribbean Community and the Dominican Republic "recognize[d] our interdependence and the importance of close cooperation to combat new and emerging transnational threats that endanger the very fabric of our societies. By virtue of their small size and geographic configuration and lack of technical and financial resources, Caribbean States are particularly vulnerable and susceptible to these risks and threats, especially those posed by illicit trafficking in persons, drugs, and firearms, terrorism and other transnational criminal activities."[25] The Third Border Initiative is intended to focus U.S.-Caribbean engagement through targeted programs that comprise both new and ongoing activities designed to enhance cooperation in the diplomatic, security, economic, environmental, health, and education arenas. This includes programs to detect and interdict drug traffickers.

For the U.S. military in general, and U.S. Southern Command in particular, the global illicit drug trade is a significant transnational security threat that undermines democratic governments, terrorizes populations, impedes economic development, and hinders regional stability.[26] The UN Office of Drug Control and Crime Executive director Antonio Maria Costa warned that "states in the Caribbean, Central America and West Africa, as well as the border regions of Mexico, are caught in the crossfire between the world's biggest coca producers, the Andean countries, and the biggest consumers, North America and Europe."[27] This formulation places Caribbean countries as victimized bystanders to a Yankee drug problem, but the Department of State recognized that this view is changing.[28]

> Instead, too often, there was a perception that without demand, supply would end, and that transit countries need not worry about addiction among their domestic populations. We now know that the lure of such incredible profits, as the drug traffic generates, makes this a trade that circumvents such a simple formula. Those who want to supply drugs make it their business to encourage demand by paying transit state residents in drugs instead of money and manipulating prices to get and keep addicts. Drug abuse and addiction is widespread in most transit countries; at least to some extent, drug supply creates its own demand. We all face a thinking, well-financed enemy and we must all, every legitimate nation-state and international authority, work together to thwart this network.[29]

The international challenge of combating drug trafficking is slowly moving the region beyond the United States' interventionist past. Indeed, there is a shared insecurity enabling cooperation on shared challenges. But this has not been easy. Drug traffickers successfully exploit weak security institutions in the hemisphere and take advantage of political tension created by U.S. drug policy. The challenge for the United States, however, is to build renewed relationships without overwhelming these countries with its military and law enforcement efforts. The size of the U.S. military too easily scares partners. The U.S. Marine Corps, for example, is larger than the militaries of almost every country in the Western Hemisphere and Africa.[30] One way the U.S. Navy is reassuring its partners is through the global fleet station concept.

Global Fleet Station

Due to the forty-year life span of ships, most of the U.S. Navy's ships at sea today were designed to conduct major combat operations during the Cold War. There are limits to the usefulness of this type of fleet in today's security environment. Aircraft carriers, cruisers, destroyers, and submarines can be as effective against transnational threats as a horse is against flies. To be sure, these assets are still used for warfare (supporting ground forces in Iraq and Afghanistan), but the military is adapting the use of these multipurpose ships by conducting activities ashore to improve human security. From the Navy's perspective, "We can show up, provide training, provide resources, and then leave very little footprint behind. And they're [partner countries] looking for our help."[31] Most recently this was evidenced during Haitian earthquake relief operations, where an aircraft carrier and sixteen other warships provided food, water, helicopters, and manpower. Military forces can also use their capabilities to enable nonmilitary participants' efforts.[32]

In particular, amphibious ships are proving to be good platforms for providing humanitarian assistance. Their large deck space provides good staging areas for helicopters. Small boats designed for landing marines ashore are perfect for moving supplies into isolated areas where no adequate infrastructure exists. And their large medical bays, designed for treating battle casualties, can accommodate pediatricians, obstetricians, and family practice physicians to treat myriad illnesses. That it is not necessary to convert warships into hospital ships is being proven through the global fleet station concept, which the 2006 *Naval Operations Concept* describes:

> Like all sea bases, the composition of a GFS [global fleet station] depends on Combatant Commander requirements, the operating environment, and the mission. From its sea base, each GFS would serve as a self-contained headquarters for regional operations with the capacity to repair and service all ships, small craft, and aircraft assigned. Additionally, the GFS might provide classroom space, limited medical facilities, an information fusion center, and some combat service support capability. The GFS concept provides a leveraged, high-yield sea based option that achieves a persistent presence in support of national objectives.[33]

The global fleet station is part of maritime sector development, which focuses on improving maritime safety and security through greater awareness, military professionalism, technical capabilities, and infrastructure to support operations. In 2008 the global fleet station featured the deployments of USS *Fort McHenry* and HSV-2 *Swift* with an international staff composed of representatives from ten countries (United States, United Kingdom, France, Spain, Portugal, Germany, Equatorial Guinea, Ghana, Gabon, and Cameroon) that engaged fourteen West and Central Africa countries, conducted thirty-five port visits, and engaged more than seventeen hundred African maritime professionals in courses custom tailored to each nation's maritime governance needs. In 2009 the centerpiece of global fleet station engagement was the deployment of USS *Nashville*. The commodore described the mission as "solidifying friendships and building new ones to ensure safer ports and waterways for Africa and the world's commerce that travels them."[34] France, United Kingdom, Germany, Portugal, Spain, the Netherlands, Cameroon, Gabon, Senegal, Nigeria, and Ghana provided staff members and training teams complemented by participation or support from the U.S. Coast Guard and embarked Department of State political advisors and other governmental and nongovernmental organizations. The commodore embarked on the USS *Nashville* captured the interagency nature of the global fleet station:

> The Lagos Harbor survey that is being conducted jointly with the Nigerian Navy and Nigerian Ports Authority is well underway, the 3-day meteorology and oceanography seminar conducted with the Nigerian Meteorology Agency (NIMET) was completed, and the 7-day NOAA-facilitated ocean data analysis workshop with the Nigerian Institute of Oceanography and Marine Research (NIOMR) is in progress. The MCAG [maritime civil affairs group]-led community outreach programs are also in full swing, as are the medical and dental programs at the Obesian civil-military naval hospital, all of which were closely coordinated with the U.S. Embassy and consulate, and with the Nigerian Navy.[35]

Global fleet station is a good example not of how the government is militarizing foreign assistance but rather of how the government is using the military in civilian ways. By adapting warships to serve as a global fleet station, the Navy is providing humanitarian assistance, serving as a training platform, and filling needed logistics capabilities for nongovernmental organizations and intergovernmental organizations operating in developing countries.

Humanitarian Assistance

While the Navy seems motivated by Friedman's flat-world construction, development is uneven and the world is not flat but spiky, according to Richard Florida.[36] This is plainly revealed in the UN human development index, which highlights the staggering differences in life expectancy and child mortality around the world.[37] These facts fuel insecurity and conflict both domestically and regionally. As discussed in chapter 1, transnational economic and social developmental issues have the clear potential to stoke instability and conflict, which can pose threats to the United States. Consequently, naval assets are employed to provide humanitarian assistance and basic medical care to undeveloped countries in the world. For U.S. European Command, "humanitarian assistance helps stabilize and secure regions, generates positive public relations for DoD and the U.S. government . . . and serves as an example of what a professional military can accomplish."[38]

For example, in 2008 the USS *Boxer* conducted more than 65,000 total patient treatments, including performing 127 surgeries, treating 4,000 optometry patients, performing 14,000 dental procedures, and training thousands of medical and military personnel. The same year, the USS *Kearsarge* treated more than 145,000 patients in six countries, dispensed more than 81,000 prescriptions, and provided veterinary care to nearly 5,600 animals.[39] Using medical capabilities organic to the military also provides its personnel with missions when they are not needed in combat zones.

To conduct missions like these, the global fleet station also tests mechanisms to improve civil–military cooperation. Given the diversity of missions these ships conduct, the Navy has enlisted the support of nongovernmental organizations, industry, and other government departments. Al Shimkus, a retired U.S. Navy captain who commanded the medical treatment facility aboard the hospital ship USS *Comfort*, observed, "The civilian volunteers are often more familiar with the area of operation than their military counterparts, as they have often practiced in that host nation previously, can often speak the local language, and have established a professional network associated with the parent NGO."[40] Building relationships with NGOs is critical for the military to be effective.

Training Platform

In addition to serving as vehicles for humanitarian assistance, the global fleet station is also used as a training platform. In 2009, for example, the amphibious ship USS *Nashville* served as the "Africa Partnership Station." The overall goal was to "help coastal nations in West and Central Africa achieve safety and security in the Gulf of Guinea." With the motto "one boat can make a difference," *Nashville* trained with the militaries and coast guards of West Africa. The international crew of *Nashville* offered courses in ocean data analysis, oil platform security, martial arts, nonlethal crowd control, and military decision making.

During a given week, students studied meteorology and oceanography, the automated information system, illegal unreported and unregulated fishing, firefighting and pipe patching. Groups of international officers were also likely to observe a flight deck emergency drill as well as landing craft and well deck operations. Other training areas included deck fundamentals, sea and anchor detail, man-overboard procedures, air operations, weapons familiarization, and watchstanding. After its four-month deployment in 2009, Africa Partnership Station *Nashville* conducted training for 1,735 people from twenty countries.[41]

Key to these activities is the need for the U.S. Navy to impart skills that will make the partner coast guard and navies more capable. But it is not always easy. The visits are relatively short with programs spanning two hours to two weeks. And with a goal of visiting many countries during a particular deployment, there are real constraints on program depth. As these programs mature, global fleet station will be challenged to offer nonintroductory courses.

When it comes to working with other militaries, there are differences in expectations. The former commander of U.S. Naval Forces Europe had to disabuse African governments of grandiose visions of acquiring powerful warships and instead had to encourage them to develop maritime policing capabilities.[42] Some partners want to return to Cold War days of receiving U.S. military equipment with no strings attached. However, U.S. commanders are guided by different logic that underscores professionalization and the ability to absorb the training. A general lesson of these training missions is that there seems to be unlimited demand for it. African militaries seldom have the resources to conduct their own training programs, and when a U.S. ship pulls into port, new opportunities are created. While governments may publicly object to Africa Command, in principle, they welcome U.S. security assistance training.

Logistics Ship

Given the size of the ships used, a global fleet station also serves as a logistics ship capable of delivering supplies and equipment. In March 2009, for example, Africa Partnership Station delivered sixteen pallets to sites identified by the Liberian Ministry of Health and twelve pallets delivered to United Methodist Church of Liberia. For 2010, the government of Liberia requested the Navy's help to facilitate the shipment of twelve school buses donated by Fairfax, Virginia. One would expect that a commercial shipping company would transport buses, but instead Liberia's Minister of Education indicated he would make a formal request through the Office of Security Assistance.

Thinking about the global fleet station concept, Fourth Fleet chief of staff Capt. Alfred Collins said, "We've come pretty close to institutionalizing these missions."[43] Capt. Nick Holman, who led the first partnership station mission in East Africa emphasized the importance of relationships. "The U.S. government and our Navy are committed to helping all African nations and regions achieve stability and economic prosperity, and East Africa is looking for help."[44] These observations are reflected in current Navy strategic documents and have become conventional wisdom.

What should be clear by now is that the military, and Navy in particular, is filling a gap where nongovernmental organizations, intergovernmental organizations, and other government departments are absent.[45] All too often military efforts such as the global fleet station become caught up in ideological discussions of the military's proper role. The question is not whether the government is militarizing foreign policy. Rather, the question is how the government is using the civilian capacities of the military for foreign assistance. The Navy has about sixteen thousand construction personnel and engineers who can be used in soft missions. While I directly address criticism of this in chapter 3, it is important to understand that efforts such as global fleet station represent a critical link to partners that the United States seeks to promote and to sustain.

Global Maritime Partnerships

As the term implies, Adm. Mike Mullen has made clear that partnership "is purely voluntary and would have no legal or encumbering ties. It would be a free-form, self-organizing network of maritime partners—good neighbors interested in using the power of the sea to unite, rather than to divide. The barriers for entry are low. Respect for sovereignty is high."[46] The overall goal is to create partnerships, not dependencies.[47] By developing or improving global maritime security capacity, the U.S. Navy seeks partners that can suppress threats in their territorial waters before they become threats to international sea-lanes. Furthermore, by approaching threats far from U.S. shores, programs that rely on partners serve as the first line of defense for the United States. Vice Adm. Kevin J. Cosgriff, commander of the U.S. 5th Fleet, summed up what the United States and more than twenty of its allies are attempting to do: "Even as we struggle daily against violent extremism, our maritime security operations offer tangible benefits to all entities that use the seas—and need to be able use the seas—without risk of harassment or worse. Our power is in the capability and intent to safeguard peaceful use of waterways and the resources of the sea."[48]

Naval cooperation is not new. Yet in an era when major naval engagements are rare relative to transnational actors exploiting the maritime commons, "the ability for countries' warships to come together in a disciplined and controlled environment remains a valuable stepping-off point for follow-on diplomatic progress."[49] There are many examples since 2001—NATO in the Mediterranean and the Indian Ocean; Malaysia, Singapore, and Indonesia in the Strait of Malacca; and various coalitions in the Gulf of Aden and East Africa. Rear Adm. Terry

McKnight, who commanded a naval coalition in the Indian Ocean, commented on how a diverse set of countries are providing naval forces to improve maritime security. "CTF 151 is a coalition of the willing. I never thought that in my service I would be operating in the same water space as the Chinese and Russians and co-operating on an issue of mutual interest. This task force proves that piracy is an international problem requiring an international solution."[50]

Many of these countries, including the United States, recognize that naval forces can only have a limited effect on maritime security. In terms of piracy, navies can provide escorts for commercial ships, create a maritime transit safe passage zone, and respond to ships in distress. Yet the problem of piracy and other maritime challenges can be best addressed by the countries where these challenges originate. By improving the security capacity of states that inadvertently provide sanctuary for actors that exploit the maritime commons, the international community hopes to minimize the impact of transnational actors. One such program (albeit stalled) is the East Africa and Southwest Indian Ocean Initiative.

East Africa and Southwest Indian Ocean Initiative

Africa Command focuses its efforts in East Africa through the Combined Joint Task Force Horn of Africa (CJTF-HOA), which is located in Djibouti. Although many of the external impressions of CJTF-HOA were defined by its early focus on lethal military action, the command has evolved since 2002 and has decidedly focused on building partners' capacity and civil affairs. Part of the command philosophy is "do no harm."[51] Whereas most military commands have the ability to generate lethal force, CJTF-HOA's vision emphasizes the broader shift in U.S. strategic thinking from confrontation to cooperation: "CJTF-HOA is all about building friendships, forging relationships, and creating partnerships. The integration of Diplomacy, Development, and Defense efforts is essential to ensuring our success. With effective partnership, we will see increased Security, improved Stability, and strengthened Sovereignty in the Horn of Africa."[52] Although the commander has been a Navy flag officer, he has no operational surface naval forces under his command and the mission of combating piracy and other maritime challenges falls outside of his purview. (Note: CJTF-HOA shares a base with Special Forces, but it is not under CJTF-HOA's control.)

To be sure, CJTF-HOA does train land and maritime forces to be more effective, but it also builds schools, digs wells, and facilitates development through road building and other infrastructure projects. Since CJTF-HOA pursues a regional approach that covers thirteen countries, working with key national representatives is critical.[53] The "C" in CJTF-HOA refers to the multinational character of the command where the American commander's deputy may be

British, and directorate heads may come from any country in the region. While the number of African officers is modest, CJTF-HOA does integrate officers from Africa into its headquarters to generate African responses to African security challenges. One such program is the East African Southwest Indian Ocean (EASWIO), which is focused on improving maritime safety and security from the Gulf of Aden to the Mozambique Channel.

Arguably, piracy off the Somali coast and fears of seaborne terrorism has brought international attention to maritime issues in Africa. Yet, improving national maritime capabilities for economic reasons will keep international navies and coast guards engaged in the region for the foreseeable future. With 90 percent of the world's trade seaborne, maritime security is a key component of energy security, food security, and economic security.[54] Tangible benefits include reducing IUU fishing, which is estimated to cost African countries one billion dollars annually.[55] Other tangible benefits include improving countries' abilities to monitor their territorial waters and exclusive economic zones, developing capabilities to respond to crises at sea, and improving the state's ability to provide security. Commanders lack the ability to process and disseminate the broad spectrum of information and intelligence necessary to understand maritime activity in their area of responsibility. This shortcoming prevents early threat identification and effective response against these threats and, when appropriate, to enable partners to respond.[56] In addition to the tangible benefits of cooperation, a major focus includes increasing political will to effect change. Political will is lacking for four basic reasons: lack of awareness, limited vulnerability of national governments to maritime threats, immature domestic industry to develop maritime resources, and government apathy when it comes to corruption, enforcement of maritime laws, and implementing existing international regulations.[57]

Started in 2006, EASWIO brings together many of the region's countries to discuss maritime issues and synchronize planning with partner countries. By hosting conferences, CJTF-HOA intends to raise awareness of maritime security issues, provide grist for national and regional maritime strategies, and work with other regional partners to improve maritime safety and security.[58] For former CJTF-HOA commander Rear Adm. Phil Greene Jr., "The importance of maritime security and safety in this region is driven because of the economic challenges that the region faces. This is due to criminal activities at sea, trafficking of drugs, smuggling of illegal cargo, trafficking of people as well as armed robbery and piracy at sea."[59]

The 2006 and 2007 EASWIO Maritime Security conferences were the primary regional maritime engagements for CJTF-HOA. The first was hosted in Antananarivo, Madagascar, in 2006. Representation was mostly military, and the conference focused on the need to develop maritime strategies. The second conference was hosted in Mombasa, Kenya, and was attended by a mix of military personnel, civilian maritime, and port security authorities. The Kenya conference focused on several key issues raised during ESAWIO I, including the need to develop bilateral and multilateral collaboration on maritime security issues in the region. The 2008 conference was hosted in Djibouti and had the explicit goal of producing a maritime strategy document that could be used as a template for both national and regional development for subsequent endorsement at a planned subministerial meeting. Conference attendees left with a solid academic background in strategy and the methodologies necessary to conduct capabilities gap analysis and an analysis of policy stakeholders. From CJTF-HOA's perspective, EASWIO nations need to expand national strategies and remove perceived barriers to African-led solutions to security challenges in the region. Through the EASWIO process, formalizing a maritime strategy should assist in the more effective development of national-level regulatory and legal regimes. To date, however, little progress has actually been made in strategy development, which has more to do with the political environment in those countries than it has to do with a willingness among those navies to act. The growth of East African piracy prompted renewed efforts to promote maritime strategy in 2010.

The three conferences held to date have solidified this regional view and have brainstormed approaches to creating effective maritime capabilities. As a basic goal, EASWIO has the potential to lay the groundwork for a regional maritime organization that can facilitate information sharing, establish regional maritime domain awareness, and foster regional cooperation. Fundamental to this is enabling EASWIO countries to take the lead in maritime issues. International cooperation is key to the U.S. approach toward maritime safety and security. This was institutionalized at the second EASWIO conference, where it was decided to create a maritime center of excellence. The center would fill many roles to include serving as a regional forum for development of policy and doctrine, hosting operational and tactical training, and promoting maritime standards and safety procedures. With the desired outcome of creating a self-sustaining institution with African instructors and administration, the center would service many countries from the region.[60] As of this writing, the center is running in Kenya with U.S. military funds and serves as a regional hub for military and civilians involved in maritime safety and security issues. Academic content was developed by the U.S. Naval War College and the Global Maritime and Transportation System center at King's Point. The Kenyan center has a limited capacity and trains fewer than one hundred people per year spread across a dozen countries. Given fiscal challenges, the program has not become self-sustaining and may be remembered as another good idea that did not survive.

In spite of this, there are individual benefits of this approach that were obvious during discussions with participants. At the 2008 conference, a participant from landlocked Uganda saw the importance of the international approach: "It is about partnership, it is about cooperation, it is about countries pooling their resources, sharing information, and all of this is for the economic benefit for the people in this region of Africa."[61] While bilateral assistance efforts must undergird the regional approach, the regional approach sets the course and speed for countries to reach. From a U.S. perspective, assistance is not about harking back to the Cold War practice of buying influence or building infrastructure for its own sake.[62] In fact, participants were disappointed that the lack of resources was the largest obstacle to achieving maritime safety and security. The obstacle was not as much a function of training, one African officer told me. Rather, the obstacle is the lack of equipment and the facilities required to maintain them. This key shortcoming is where the officer thinks Africa Command can make the biggest contribution— supporting maritime domain awareness through automated identification system receivers and coastal radar sites. Instead, the programs are about creating sustainable maritime services to improve countries' ability to control their territory. In an increasingly globalized political space, the United States and its European partners can no longer ignore instability far from its shores that produces illegal trafficking of people, drugs, and other contraband. However, decades of development efforts in Africa have also taught donors not to push beyond national limits. And with no cold war dynamic at play and an emphasis on linking results to strategy, programs can be cancelled if they fail to meet objectives. Partners do not fully appreciate this and sometimes play China against the United States, but this rarely works.

Promoting cooperation also extends to national governments. One tangible benefit of U.S. military–hosted conferences such as EASWIO is increasing the dialogue between civilian and military agencies on national maritime strategies and port security operations.[63] Because security issues are no longer the exclusive realm of militaries, a major security cooperation goal is to bring together personnel from law enforcement, port authorities, think tanks, and other relevant civilian government ministries such as natural resources, customs, and finance.[64] These conferences have an explicit goal of improving interagency cooperation within respective countries and sharing knowledge across countries. For example, at the 2008 EASWIO conference a civilian port operator from Mauritius was able to share his port's best practices with representatives from ten other countries. He explained the steps his port used to become certified under the International Ship and Port Facility Security Code (ISPS) and the international impact of becoming ISPS compliant. The example also highlights that maritime security is no longer defined at the water's edge but begins ashore in ports, customs facilities, and warehouses.

Having experts from the region present material has reinforced that the United States does not monopolize solutions to security problems. In fact, as the director of Strategy, Plans, and Policy said during the 2008 conference, "Seeing the issues each nation is up against sets a framework for finding solutions in the future. Because of the limited resources involved, and the overlapping challenges the countries in the region encounter, if they can start thinking about working together to improve the overall security situation, this region in Africa will be one step closer to achieving the goals of the working group."[65] Unfortunately, there was no EASWIO conference in 2009, and the future of the program is in doubt due to the changes taking place within AFRICOM.

Conclusion

The new security environment has forced militaries to improve their relevance and effectiveness in non-warfighting missions. Much attention is focused on ground forces, which are more common among countries, as they conduct counterinsurgency in Iraq and Afghanistan and build partner's ground forces to control territory and respond to man-made and natural disasters. This chapter illustrates that navies are changing too. Piracy, illegal fishing, and illicit trafficking by sea have forced the U.S. Navy to adapt its mission and think beyond major warfare with another maritime power. Instead, maritime civil affairs, humanitarian assistance, and disaster relief are becoming core competencies.

Maritime forces can provide persistent presence with a very small footprint and are proving to be effective engagement platforms. This enables the Navy to contribute to the U.S. government's efforts by bolstering allies, friends, and new partners. Through the global fleet station concept in Africa and Latin America, the Navy has illustrated how it can improve security and train coast guards to patrol their territorial waters and monitor their exclusive economic zones. No longer done as a hobby or sideshow, the Navy created the N52 international engagement office in 2009 to better coordinate these activities. Its first director, Rear Adm. Jeffrey Lemmons, put this in a strategic context. "Now we have a maritime strategy that speaks about the tenets of a strong maritime nation, the things that a maritime nation needs to be able to do [including] forward presence and providing maritime security in partnership with other nations to support and sustain the maritime economy."[66] With an emphasis on partnership to fill security gaps, programs that strengthen the maritime capabilities of countries are likely to continue for the foreseeable future.

Notes

1. John G. Morgan Jr. and Charles W. Martoglio, "The 1,000-Ship Navy: Global Maritime Network," U.S. Naval Institute *Proceedings* 132, no. 11 (November 2005): 18.

2. This is a strong underlying premise in the 2007 "Cooperative Strategy for Twenty-First Century Seapower," www.navy.mil/maritime/MaritimeStrategy.pdf.

3. Michael Mullen, "Remarks as delivered by Admiral Mike Mullen, Current Strategy Forum," Naval War College, Newport, RI (June 14, 2006), 5.

4. Jon Bartee, "Teaching Navies How to Be Navies," U.S. Naval Institute *Proceedings* 135, no. 4 (April 2009): 71.

5. UN General Assembly, Resolution 59/24, "Oceans and the Law of the Sea," February 4, 2005, 12. http://daccess-dds-ny.un.org/doc/UNDOC/GEN/N04/477/64/PDF/N0447764.pdf?OpenElement.

6. ISPS is an amendment to the Safety of Life at Sea Convention (1974/1988). At least 110 countries are a party to this.

7. Food and Agriculture Organization of the United Nations, *The State of World Fisheries and Aquaculture* (New York: UN Press, 2008), www.fao.org/docrep/011/i0250e/i0250e00.HTM.

8. United Nations, "General Assembly, Concerned about World's Marine Ecosystems, Adopts Texts on Law of Sea, Sustainable Fisheries," November 17, 2004. www.un.org/News/Press/docs/2004/ga10299.doc.htm.

9. FAO of the UN, *State of World Fisheries and Aquaculture*.

10. UN General Assembly, Resolution 62/177, "Sustainable Fisheries, Including through the 1995 Agreement for the Implementation of the Provisions of the United Nations Convention on the Law of the Sea of 10 December 1982 Relating to the Conservation and Management of Straddling Fish Stocks and Highly Migratory Fish Stocks, and Related Instruments," February 28, 2008, http://daccess-dds-ny.un.org/doc/UNDOC/GEN/N07/474/39/PDF/N0747439.pdf?OpenElement.

11. Marine Resources Assessment Group (MRAG), "Review of Impacts of Illegal, Unreported and Unregulated Fishing on Developing Countries," Report to DFID, June 17, 2005, figure 2, www.imcsnet.org/imcs/docs/iuu_fishing_synthesis_report_mrag.pdf. MRAG conducted year-long case studies for ten countries; nine were African countries: Guinea, Somalia, Angola, Mozambique, Sierra Leone, Seychelles, Liberia, Kenya, and Namibia. Papua New Guinea was estimated at $40 million USD and subtracted from the $375 million USD estimate.

12. (MRAG Ltd 2005). P. 8, Table 3. The estimate from sub-Saharan EEZs is based on MRAG research estimating total losses for the region.

13. Kip Ward, "United States Africa Command 2009 Posture Statement" (Stuttgart, GM: Africa Command, 2009).

14. A long-term solution is viewed as reducing global fishing fleets, especially those that are artificially high due to government subsidies. With reduced capacity, IUU fishing is estimated to decline.

15. UN Convention on the Law of the Sea, part VII, "High Seas," 2001. www.un.org/Depts/los/convention_agreements/texts/unclos/part7.htm. Article 100: All states shall cooperate to the fullest possible extent to repress piracy. Article 101: Piracy consists of illegal acts or voluntary participation in acts of violence, detention or depredation committed for private ends by the crew or passengers of a private ship or aircraft on the high seas against another ship or aircraft outside the jurisdiction of any State. Article 102:

48. Quoted in "Maritime Security Operations Key to Regional Stability, Security." *Navy Newstand*, October 11, 2007.

49. Chuck Nygaard, "Reengaging the Navy, at Home and Abroad," U.S. Naval Institute *Proceedings* 135, no. 4 (April 2009): 61.

50. Quoted in Asma Salman, "Task Force Making Waves in Piracy War," *Gulf Weekly*, March 18, 2009.

51. United States Central Command, "Memorandum for Combined Joint Task Force–Horn of Africa, Strategic Guidance for 2008," March 10, 2008.

52. Combined Joint Task Force Horn of Africa, "Command Brief," May 2008, www .hoa.africom.mil.

53. This includes Comoros, Djibouti, Eritrea, Ethiopia, Kenya, Madagascar, Mauritius, Seychelles, Somalia, Sudan, Tanzania, Uganda, and Yemen.

54. "The National Strategy for Maritime Security," 1, Department of Homeland Security website, www.dhs.gov/xlibrary/assets/HSPD13_MaritimeSecurityStrategy.pdf.

55. Marine Resources Assessment Group Ltd, "Review of Impacts of Illegal, Unreported and Unregulated Fishing on Developing Countries Synthesis Report" (July 2005), www.dfid.gov.uk/pubs/files/illegal-fishing-mrag-synthesis-report.pdf.

56. Zachary M. Peterson, "Navy Creates New Offices to Better Align with Maritime Strategy: International Partnerships, MDA Eyed," *Inside the Navy*, March 23, 2009.

57. Combined Joint Task Force Horn of Africa, "Conference Report," East Africa and Southwest Indian Ocean Maritime Security Conference (EASWIO), Antananarivo, Madagascar, July 25–27, 2007.

58. It is important to pointout, however, that there are other national and international organizations pursuing similar goals, so it would be essential to understand the extent to which military activities are coordinated with nonmilitary activities.

59. Quoted in Scott Cohen, "African Nations Working for Maritime Security," June 23, 2008, www.defense.gov/news/newsarticle.aspx?id=50302.

60. CJTF-HOA Maritime Security Group, "Maritime Regional Center of Excellence Concept," East Africa and Southwest Indian Ocean (EASWIO) Maritime Security and Port Security Seminar, Mombasa, Kenya, September 4–7, 2007.

61. Cohen, "African Nations Working for Maritime Security." Although Uganda is landlocked, it has considerable maritime issues on Lake Victoria and plans to provide coastal patrol forces for a peacekeeping deployment off the Somali coast.

62. In fact, this can be frustrating for the partner countries that expect U.S. resources to make up for national shortfalls. The United States continues to balance resource requests against what is sustainable. It is very easy to provide boats to a country, but if there is insufficient infrastructure or trained personnel to maintain the boats, the investment will fall short of expectations.

63. This also holds true from a U.S. government perspective. Representatives from at least six other U.S. organizations, including the Department of State, Office of Secretary of Defense, and other non-CJTF-HOA DOD components, attended the 2008 EASWIO conference.

64. With the development of national-level and regional strategies, the EASWIO process gives way to civil–military discussions of strategy. Although military personnel are often better positioned than civilian personnel to develop strategy, tenuous civil–military relations can prevent the necessary dialogue. Through EASWIO, CJTF-HOA brings together personnel from across the government to ensure that dialogue can produce consensus on the ways and means required for improving maritime safety and security.

65. Author private interview.

66. Quoted in Peterson, "Navy Creates New Offices."

7

Implications for the Force

IN RESPONSE TO A SOLDIER'S QUESTION about lacking the appropriate training and equipment for counterinsurgency in Iraq, Secretary of Defense Donald Rumsfeld quipped, "you go to war with the army you have." That may be true, but the secretary of defense is responsible for determining the type of military the country needs. This is important not only when the military is engaged in warfare but also during peacetime missions such as security cooperation. Given that security assistance missions are so different from combat, it is imperative for the military to develop concepts and capabilities appropriate to work with partners outside of combat zones in permissive environments. Rumsfeld's successor, Robert Gates, wrestled with this: "The U.S. military's ability to kick down the door must be matched by its ability to clean up the mess and even rebuild the house afterward."[1] Thus Secretary Gates called for a balanced force structure that would prepare the military for future conflict but would also ensure that the military changes to incorporate the lessons of current operations that challenge the U.S. military in noncombat ways. This is represented not only in defense strategy but also in military concepts for development of the force.

As my discussion of the traditionalist, modernist, and irregular warfare schools in chapter 3 suggests, how force development is undertaken will have profound implications for getting the future military force right both in size and in scope. Four basic categories of military activity underlie force development: combat, security, engagement, and relief and reconstruction.[2] Combat remains a core mission for the military, but the last three categories reinforce that the Defense Department wants "to develop a stable environment in which civil society can be built and that the quality of life for the citizenry can be improved."[3] Talking about the new capstone concept for joint operations, retired Marine colonel Jerry Lynes said, "Things have changed significantly. We have taken our traditional principles of war and added to them."[4] Key among these is peacetime engagement in permissive environments. Since engagement is premised on preventing conflict by empowering partners to confront their own security challenges, it is arguably more important and more likely for the U.S. military than combat. This chapter explores how the U.S. military is developing concepts and capabilities to promote regional stability through building partners' capacity.

Concept for Force Development

One of the enduring changes to defense planning that secretary of Defense Donald Rumsfeld made was the introduction of capabilities-based planning.[5] In contrast to the Cold War–model of "be better than the Soviets" or the 1990s model of threat-based planning against Iraq and North Korea, capabilities-based planning broadens the scope. It asks the question, what type of capabilities does the military need? To identify the appropriate capabilities, the military first identifies strategic challenges, such as ungoverned maritime spaces. It identifies strategic objectives, such as assuring friends and allies, and it identifies the missions that it is likely to conduct in the future, such as combined maritime security operations in the Gulf of Aden. Planners set planning targets, such as enabling a partner to conduct maritime security operations within five years. Capabilities-based planning develops joint concepts, such as building partnerships, and it presents capability options, such as mobile training teams teaching port security. Finally, capabilities-based planning selects forces, such as a Navy explosive ordnance disposal unit embarked on a high-speed vessel. Defense programmers can use this approach to apply resources to deliver a capability or opt to assume risk by not funding the program and using existing assets.[6]

A key dimension in the capabilities-based planning model is developing joint concepts, which are the ways something might be done. Concepts are an end-to-end stream of activities that define how elements, systems, organizations, and tactics combine to accomplish national objectives or tasks.[7] By specifying ways or concepts, the military departments can then develop required capabilities and attempt to limit redundancies. For example, there are many ways for the military to conduct global strike operations: submarine launched missiles, precision weapons delivered by bombers, or sabotage missions conducted by Special Forces. The choice is ultimately the president's, but the Defense Department sees its role as developing options with various levels of risk involved. Similar logic can be applied to developing capabilities for security assistance.

Linking concepts to overall national objectives, the "Capstone Concept for Joint Operations" serves as a guide to future force development, characterizes the future operating environment for policymakers and others that employ military force, establishes a conceptual foundation for subordinate joint and service concepts, and guides the evaluation of concepts and supporting capabilities.[8] The document is intended to get the military departments to share a common vision of the future and imbue a common approach to defense planning by explicitly stating what the government expects it can do. In 2009 there were about twenty concepts that ranged from preparing for major combat operations to conducting security cooperation activities. Each concept is designed to fully appreciate the various missions the military may undertake and is used to identify excesses and gaps in military force structure. Before a detailed discussion of these requirements for engagement and building partnership capacity, it is important to understand where these activities fall in military operations.

Placing Engagement

Placing security assistance and cooperation in military operations is somewhat problematic, and the language to describe these activities has been changing. This illustrates not only the reluctance to enshrine these activities in doctrine but also that current vocabulary is somewhat deficient to properly describe these softer missions of the military. During the Clinton administration, the activities were simply called theater engagement with little distinction between port visits, joint exercises, or security assistance. President Bush did not like the notion of engaging for the sake of engagement and instead linked the activities to specific goals such as reducing the drivers of terrorism. These activities were included in joint doctrine and called "shaping" to imply the instrumental goals associated with the United States exerting its influence. They were further incorporated into military planning and were called "phase zero" operations (see figure 7.1).

Figure 7.1 Phasing Model of Military Operations

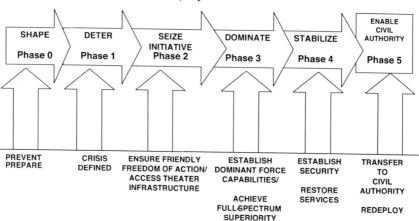

Source: Based on figure IV-9, Department of Defense, "Joint Publication 5-0: Joint Operation Planning," December 26, 2006, www.dtic.mil/doctrine/new_pubs/jp5_0.pdf.

As the phasing model depicts, current doctrine attempts to divide military operations across six distinct phases: shape, deter, seize initiative, dominate, stabilize, and enable civil authority. "Shape" includes various government activities performed to dissuade or deter potential adversaries and to ensure or solidify relationships with friends and allies. "Deter" includes efforts to prevent undesirable adversary action by demonstrating the capabilities and resolve of the joint force (e.g., military exercises). "Seizing the initiative" includes operations designed to gain access to theater infrastructure and to expand friendly freedom of action while degrading enemy capabilities with the intent of resolving the crisis at the earliest opportunity. The "dominate" phase focuses on breaking the enemy's will and depends on overmatching the adversary through force. The "stabilize" phase occurs where there is no operating civil authority and the military provides or facilitates delivery of basic services to a population. The final phase, "enabling civil authority," enables the military to redeploy from the operating area once a civilian government is created.

Phasing operations from 0 to 5 is a useful construct when thinking about combat operations with other states that have a clear beginning, middle, and end to fighting (e.g., Yugoslavia in 1999 or Iraq in 1991), but as chapter 3 suggests, postmodern conflict cannot be easily conducted in phases. Militaries more often find themselves being two-fisted fighters in three-block wars where combat, reconstruction, and humanitarian assistance occur simultaneously in relatively confined areas. And the same military finds itself in permissive environments training foreign militaries, building civil projects, and promoting public health. Thus there is a tension between shaping and stability operations, but both focus on reducing state fragility. They just differ on timing.

The phasing model detailed in joint doctrine is also in tension with the continuous nature of engagement activities. Conducting phase 0, or shaping activities, does not necessarily lead to the succeeding phases and has caused alarm among some partners.[9] However, it is up to the military commander whether campaigns include all six phases. In spite of this, there are increasing calls to rethink this construction and the terms to describe the activities.[10] First, partners do not appreciate the notion of being "shaped" when activities are supposed to fill both U.S. and partner country interests. Second, the term "shape" is often associated with precombat activities, such as bombing, as in the phrase "shape the battlespace." A related third point is by placing phase 0 operations in a larger construct of the six-phase model, engagement with a country implies that phase 0 can lead to phase 1, and so on, which is the path to war. While this is wrong, it is easy for partners to misinterpret this. Finally, some governments do not want American security assistance programs. This is especially true in regions where a coup is the historical path to political power; such governments are unsurprisingly afraid of their armies and do not want them to become better trained and equipped.[11] Fortunately, coups d'état are relatively rare; there was just one attempt in 2007, one success in 2008, and two successes in 2009.[12]

As the previous discussion suggests, the lexicon has not yet settled and new terms are emerging. The term "shaping" is yielding to "cooperative security," which is meant to emphasize cooperation on common security challenges. At the operational command level where these activities are planned, the term "active security" has emerged. For Africa Command, active security is "a persistent and sustained level of effort focused on security assistance programs that prevent conflict in order to contribute to an enhanced level of dialogue and development. The goal of active security is to enable our partner to marginalize the enemies of peace; minimize the potential for conflict; foster the growth of strong, just governments and legitimate institutions; and support the development of civil societies."[13]

In general, these activities are designed to address underlying conditions to prevent a situation that later requires coercive military intervention. In order to inform force development to do these activities, the joint operating concept cooperative security was developed.

Joint Operating Concept for Cooperative Security

Officially released in 2008, the 148-page operating concept was written to answer the challenging question, "How does a JFC [joint force commander] contribute to fostering a security environment favorable to U.S. interests as well as establish a solid base for effective crisis response given 1) it is difficult to anticipate where and in what types of situations the United States will be involved, 2) the willingness and ability of others to cooperate is not always readily apparent, and 3) the lack of definition in what will constitute success in a given situation?"[14]

Overall, the concept is focused on the indirect uses of military power, which are focused on crisis prevention. These security cooperation activities are integrated into a larger campaign plan that explains how the military will advance and defend national interests. The concept focuses on how military operations contribute to larger U.S. government activities in a region. This includes increasing cultural and political awareness of regions and subregions but also focuses on improving the receptivity of the United States among international audiences. Without public support in partner countries—and in the United States, for that matter—the programs are unlikely to succeed. Military commanders build trust and the habits of cooperation as part of wider U.S. efforts to achieve common security goals that prevent the rise of security threats and promote a constructive security environment.[15]

There are five core objectives to cooperative security activities.

1. Strengthen the U.S. security posture in the region.
2. Advance constructive security initiatives and build transnational and part-ner nation capacity and capabilities in the region.
3. Thwart the emergence of security threats (transnational and host nation) in the region.
4. Contribute to U.S. and international initiatives to alleviate the underlying conditions, motivators, and enablers of violent extremism and destabiliz-ing militancy.
5. Enable and improve cooperative security arrangements for improved mul-tinational operating performance.[16]

The core tenet of cooperative security is working with partner countries against common security challenges such as terrorism, piracy, and the illicit trafficking of weapons, drugs, and people. The concept, and the strategy that it supports, presumes that partners will naturally want to collaborate and confront these challenges. This is generally true, but there are also examples of foreign militaries explicitly involved in illegal activity. To guard against this, partner military personnel involved in these programs are subject to vetting under the Leahy amendment.[17]

The analysis in chapter 5 suggests that the United States discriminates in the type of aid (education versus equipment) and is cognizant of the importance of military professionalism, the promotion of human rights, and the installation of civilian control of the military throughout its programs. Additionally, gen-eral agreement may overlook specific challenges. For example, the United States and East African countries share a common goal of improving maritime secu-rity. But as discussed in chapter 6, African countries see illegal, unreported, and underreported (IUU) fishing as a greater challenge than piracy, which is a higher American concern. Yet improving the maritime capabilities of coast guards in that region is a common solution that can address both IUU fishing and piracy. Underlying cooperation is that many countries recognize that most threats no longer come from aggressive neighboring states but rather from new nonstate networks that pose military, political, economic, and social challenges, which can overwhelm the capacity of individual nations.[18]

Peacetime operations that respond to partners' security concerns or humani-tarian needs also sustain support for the United States. In the Middle East, for example, radicals have portrayed the United States as neocrusaders and support-ers of apostate regimes. In Latin America, opponents of the United States play up the history of "Yankee imperialism" and charge that the United States pursues a neoimperial agenda through its military and economic system. (Hugo Chavez of Venezuela characterized Haitian earthquake relief efforts in 2010 as a "gringo invasion.") In Africa, opponents cast the United States in neocolonial terms, which reflects the continent's troubled and recent colonial history. While international opinion of the United States was negatively affected during the Bush years, it is important to point out that governments continued and increased cooperation on security matters. For example, although Indonesia objected to the U.S. invasion of Iraq in 2003, it welcomed assistance after the tsunami in 2004. Pakistan has objected to the United States striking targets within its border at the same time it has received security assistance to better control its territory. Given the importance of legitimacy, military commanders are advised to portray themselves as defenders of national interests based on United Nations principles, advocates for international cooperation, and preservers of the human condition by alleviating disease, hunger, or other threats to life.[19] In an attempt to break historical stereotypes, commanders also increase transparency of their commands through peer exchanges, command visits, and even blogs and You-Tube videos. It is also common to see officers from dozens of countries embedded in U.S. military units and command headquarters.

The joint operating concept also acknowledges that the United States cannot solve contemporary security challenges alone. While Iraq stands out as a negative example, the United States seeks to strengthen sovereignty around the world through these cooperative security activities.[20] Such bilateral military ties that strengthen a partner's sovereignty are key. Since transnational actors occupy particular geographic spaces, governments and their security services are the first line of offense to confront these challenges. While partner countries certainly benefit from this approach, U.S. security is increasingly tied to global security. For example, Secretary of Defense Gates noted that "the most likely catastrophic threats to our homeland—for example, an American city poisoned or reduced to rubble by a terrorist attack—are more likely to emanate from failing states than from aggressor states." Accordingly, "through preventive investments, we can help shape the environment to reduce requirements for major U.S. interventions and their attendant costs."[21] Ideally, these investments are consistent with a partner country's national and defense strategies, if they exist, or national strategy implied by the partner country's law, culture, and politics.

Through this strategic approach, partner countries share responsibility for protecting the United States. There is some risk associated with this approach, but current thinking mitigates the risk by leveraging partners' knowledge of language, culture, and adversaries in ways that U.S. military forces cannot. The implications of this are obvious. The U.S. military must strengthen and expand alliances, partnerships, and coalitions. It does so by building the capabilities and capacity of foreign partners to combat internal threats and threats that spill over into the region. This includes providing assistance and persuading national audiences that the United States is the preferred partner of choice.

Assistance takes the form of providing humanitarian development assistance, conducting military exercises, and including partners' officers in U.S. training and educational institutions, military construction, and outreach teams. Chapter 5 provides detailed analysis and discussion of these objectives, but there are important implications for personnel and training. As the joint operating concept notes, a regional policy developed by the Department of State and funded by Congress would sustain relationships. But "more often, the JFC [joint force commander] will be working with U.S. ambassadors to construct ad hoc partnerships."[22] While we regularly hear that the interagency is broken, that is truer in Washington than in the field. At the embassy level, elements of the U.S. government coordinate activities under the direction of the U.S. ambassador.

Personnel and Training Implications

In contrast to the old model, cooperative security encompasses much of the military and is no longer the exclusive domain of Special Forces.[23] The effects of this for personnel and training include increasing language and cultural capabilities and capacities and improving the ability to integrate with other U.S. agencies and partners.[24] According to a Navy SEAL, his training "used to concentrate on core mission areas of counter-terrorism, direct action, and special reconnaissance. Today, SEALs must be skilled in foreign internal defense, which requires extensive cultural and language training to be effective."[25] The success of these missions is highly personality dependent and situation dependent. Mission success also requires warfighters to embrace their role in war prevention activities. Those who are successful have good intercultural skills and can translate their U.S. security perspective to the conditions and culture in the partner country.

It is increasingly common for analysts and leaders to reinforce these ideas among military personnel with statements such as the following:

- "Non-kinetic capabilities should be integrated with military assets at all levels, and we should seek to reform the military policies of targeted countries so that they incorporate unconventional warfare approaches."[26]
- "Interoperability goes well beyond joint and combined forces. We have to be able to bring in all effects that the interagency and the local governments bring to bear."[27]
- "We don't have to be in charge; other elements of the government ought to leverage that potential and that capability."[28]

Thus, one of the identified six core competencies for the Marine Corps now includes enabling interagency activities. The counterinsurgency manual also makes clear that "the organizing imperative is focusing on what needs to be done, not on who does it."[29]

Yet the key challenge when working with partners from the U.S. government, nongovernmental organizations (NGOs), or allies is achieving unity of effort without unity of command, which partly explains why the military is embracing noncombat missions. Consequently, the military finds itself facing recurring challenges as it fills programmatic voids and balances efforts to support partners without destabilizing organizational structures, mediating jurisdictional issues with other U.S. government departments, and assuming risk with technology and skill set transfers. As I argued elsewhere, military commanders are as much policy entrepreneurs as warfighters, which is made possible by policy voids on regional security challenges.[30] This creates tension within the government since critics would like to see a civilian face conducting foreign policy. To be sure, the Department of State does oversee security assistance programs, but it also relies on the Department of Defense to provide experts to train and equip partners' security forces. This creates a challenge for the military, which must implement policy that is often vague and ambiguous.

Personnel must be trained and educated in conducting assessments and advising on the proper materiel or services for partner countries. This includes identifying and supplying assistance that is consistent with goals and national interests. The defense attaché leads these efforts and acts as the in-country focal point for planning, coordinating, supporting, and executing U.S. defense activities in the partner country. These activities include theater security cooperation plans (embedded in theater campaign plans) conducted under the oversight of the combatant commander. The attaché also serves as the principal embassy liaison with partner country defense establishments and actively participates in national security and operational policy development and coordination. Furthermore, the attaché represents the secretary of defense and the Department of Defense (DOD) components to host-nation counterparts and foreign diplomats accredited to the host nation. Internal to the embassy, the attaché presents coordinated DOD views on all defense matters to the chief of mission and acts as the single DOD point of contact to the chief of mission.[31]

In many embassies, a security assistance officer (SAO) serves as the primary link between the host nation military and the wide variety of security assistance programs offered through the Department of Defense. Officers who fill these jobs in U.S. embassies around the world are charged with assessing the partner nation's strategic needs and developing effective acquisition and resourcing strategies to improve partners' security forces. The SAO assists host-nation security forces by planning and administering military aspects of the security assistance program. It also helps the U.S. country team communicate host-nation assistance needs to policy and budget officials in the federal government. In addition, the SAO oversees training and assistance teams temporarily assigned to the host nation, although the SAO is prohibited from providing direct training assistance. Instead, training is provided through special teams and organizations assigned to limited tasks for specific periods, such as mobile training and technical assistance teams. For example, the Naval War College regularly sends faculty teams around the world to assist other defense colleges develop and deliver curriculum.

In contrast to defense attachés that have open source reporting requirements, SAOs work closely with partner nation security forces and the U.S. embassy country team to promote the professionalization of the military through programs on training and education as well as equipment and technology acquisition. The goals are to promote interoperability with U.S. forces and to promote regional stability by enabling the partner military to confront threats before they exceed national borders. These programs fall broadly under the Foreign Military Financing and the International Military and Education and Training programs (see chapter 5). As such, SAOs coordinate security assistance programs that bring training teams into the country, transfer military equipment, and assist DOD in the selection and preparation of foreign officers attending education and training programs in the United States. To be effective, SAOs need both an understanding of the partner country and appropriate U.S. capabilities. In the best case, SAOs should underpromise and overdeliver.

People are the key element to being successful in cooperative security operations. It is easy to think of the military simply as a collection of warfighting platforms such as ships, tanks, and aircraft; more important are the people who use these platforms as tools for warfighting. When it comes to security assistance, people are the key platform that either facilitate or decimate cooperation with partner countries. Because these types of activities began in the Special Forces community, the Special Operations Command motto is relevant here. "Equip the people, don't man the equipment." With this in mind, it is essential to understand how the changing face of the military affects its most important asset—the 3 million active duty, reserve, and guard personnel in uniform today. David Galula's advice on counterinsurgency is equally relevant in security cooperation: "If the forces have to be adapted to their new missions, it is just as important that the minds of the leaders and men—and this includes the civilian as well as the military—be adapted to the special demands of counterinsurgency warfare. Reflexes and decisions that would be considered appropriate for the soldier in conventional warfare and for the civil servant in normal times are not necessarily the right ones in counterinsurgency situations."[32]

A common criticism of the military's role in non-warfighting activities is its lack of regional expertise or cultural tone deafness. This stereotype is certainly overblown with U.S. military officers, who work from U.S. embassies and often have more time in the region and experience than junior foreign service officers. In countries that are dominated or have been dominated by military elites, this is even truer. Julien Bryan's wisdom should be understood: "When you break bread with people and share their troubles and joys, the barriers of language, of politics, or religion soon vanish."[33]

The military sees language deficiency as a problem to correct. Working through interpreters creates barriers. Lt. Gen. Michael D. Rochelle said, "What has become clear is a critical need to expand our strategic capability in critical languages to help us fight global terrorism." Consequently, the Army launched a language incentive pay program to encourage its officer recruits to study Arabic, Farsi, and Mandarin.[34] Furthermore, all military personnel have access to online language programs such as Rosetta Stone or are given opportunities for language immersion programs. It is increasingly common to hear and speak languages other than English in American-led command centers, forward operating bases, and education institutions. The head of U.S. European Command reinforced language as a key capability. "Developing Navy leaders is an enduring priority. NAVEUR's [Naval Forces Europe] mission requires some skill sets not previously emphasized for U.S. Navy professional. . . . [These include] insight into the religion, economics, history, culture, and politics of countries [where it engages]."[35]

Training may not be enough to replicate the highly selective foreign service officer program to duplicate Department of State's capabilities, and I suggest there is no desire within the Department of Defense to do this. Yet we should also not assume that military officers are ill suited for these missions. There are many examples of military leaders rising outside its ranks to perform explicit functions as diplomats. A short list includes Gen. Colin Powell, who became America's chief diplomat as secretary of state; Adm. William J. Crowe, who was President Clinton's ambassador to the United Kingdom; Adm. Joseph Prueher, who was President Clinton's ambassador to China; and Gen. Tony Zinni, who served as President Bush's Middle East Envoy. Zinni understood the importance of cultural awareness and observed in the Middle East that not all American military professionals are up to the challenge.

> In the Arab world, they conduct business far more casually than we do at home—or in Europe, the Pacific, and other places where I'd served. In America or Europe, the meetings are structured. . . . That's not the way Arabs like to do business. . . . Personal relations and trust built out of friendship are more important than signing paper agreements. . . . Our way of conducting business just doesn't work there [Arab world]. When we try it, we're not well received. Yet politeness, graciousness, and hospitality are so inbred in Arabs that we may not recognize that they've turned off to us.[36]

With Tony Zinni's observations in mind, the Defense Department embarked on an ambitious program to instill cultural awareness and regional expertise in its officers. This shift is being done primarily through the military's educational institutions, which educate tens of thousands of officers a year. The chairman of the Joint Chiefs of Staff sets the priorities for education, which "entails ensuring that officers are properly prepared for their leadership roles at every level of activity and employment, and through this, ensure that the U.S. Armed forces remain capable of defeating today's threat and tomorrow's."[37] Specific learning objectives include comprehending how society, culture, and religion shape military planning; analyzing the impacts of military-to-military contacts; and providing officers an awareness of the culture, customs, and language of where they will operate.

Doctrine Implications

Much of the doctrinal implications of the changing face of the military are contained in the U.S. Army's stability operations and counterinsurgency manuals, which address military missions, tasks, and activities to maintain or reestablish a safe and secure environment, and which provide essential governmental services, emergency infrastructure reconstruction, and humanitarian relief.[38] It is worth highlighting here, however, that security sector reform may be replacing "train and equip" as a way of operating.[39] Security sector reform aims to provide an effective and legitimate public service that is transparent, accountable to civil authority, and responsive to the needs of the public. It may include integrated activities to support defense and armed forces reform; civilian management and oversight; justice, police, corrections, and intelligence reform; national security planning and strategy support; border management; disarmament, demobilization, and reintegration; and concurrent reduction of armed violence.[40]

The difference may be subtle, but security sector reform enlarges the recipients of security assistance from the military only to other relevant security actors within partner countries. These other actors include police, customs, coast guard, foreign ministry, foreign trade, first responders such as firefighters, and the judicial sector. Given the relative decline of interstate conflict, enlarging the scope beyond preparation for war is not only essential but also long overdue. The 2006 National Security Strategy made this clear: "The world has found through bitter experience that success often depends on early establishment of strong local institutions such as effective police forces and a functioning justice and penal system."[41] Yet policing is one of the most ill-used tools available to tackle extremism, and much of policing is delivered in an uncoordinated and ineffectual manner.[42] Andrew Legon argues that policing is essential: "Security is essential for socioeconomic development, while upholding the rule of law and contributing to the provision of justice engenders faith and legitimacy in national government institutions."[43] Therefore, military-to-civilian activities are likely to increase and push the legal limits of these programs.

The key principles guiding security sector reform include supporting partner country ownership, incorporating good governance and respect for human rights, balancing operational support with institutional reform, linking security and justice, and fostering transparency.[44] With these principles in mind, National Security Presidential Directive 44 (NSPD-44) attempted to bring to bear nonmilitary tools of power in security sector reform. The policy established that the United States should "work with other countries and organizations to anticipate state failure, avoid it whenever possible, and respond quickly and effectively when necessary to promote peace, security, development, democratic practices, market economies, and the rule of law."[45] After three years, NSPD-44 largely failed to bring non-DOD capabilities to bear as evidenced by the dominating role the U.S. military plays in security assistance. While the Obama administration expects to rebalance the tools of power, this will be the third attempt in as many administrations. Consequently, the military is not waiting to see whether this attempt will be successful but is transforming to meet nonmilitary challenges in South America, Southeast Asia, and Africa. In short, the military is attempting to "policize" its security assistance programs to help nonmilitary security services control organized crime, interdict illicit trafficking, and provide basic security for its citizens. Because the military has explosive ordnance disposal specialists, it teaches partners' police forces how to investigate bomb blasts and reconstruct forensic evidence. Likewise, the military has a robust corps of lawyers who teach partners about rules of evidence, chains of custody, and prosecutorial techniques.

In permissive environments, the military is learning to detect and disrupt the nexus between criminality, corruption, and transnational actors. These include developing capabilities to detect money laundering, prevent human smuggling, and protect against cyber attacks. Thus military commanders are increasingly concerned with criminal groups or syndicates that operate on national, regional, or a global scale. Adm. James Stavridis discussed these concerns in the Western Hemisphere:

> Security threats most often take forms that we more readily associate with crime than war. In the region's growing gang activity, we see criminals and the disenfranchised band together and combine traditional criminal activities in ways that threaten our regional partners as well our own national security. Kidnapping, counterfeiting, human trafficking, and drug trafficking—which leads to over 10,000 cocaine-related deaths annually in the USA—combine with extremist ideologies to create a dangerous blend.
>
> All of these conditions can undermine fragile democracies. Not to mention the devastating and destabilizing affects of ecological natural disasters.

These new threats—while ultimately not susceptible to traditional military operations—tend to operate at our intellectual seams, and thrive in our bureaucratic and cultural blind spots. Our system of legal, political, moral and conceptual boundaries defining what constitutes combat versus criminal activity; domestic vs. international jurisdiction; and governmental versus private interests all provide operational space for lethal opponents with no such boundaries to respect.[46]

To be effective against transnational challenges requires the military to refocus its situational awareness from the state level to the substate and even group levels. It is increasingly doing this by adopting an analytical framework to understand the interrelationship of political, military, economic, social, infrastructure, and information systems (PMESII). This is a key change when a typical intelligence requirement is to determine the readiness of a foreign warship. Now, the military attempts to understand how economic conditions may influence criminal groups' abilities to impact the global supply chain. Dubbed tag, track, and locate, or TTL, the military seeks to identify and monitor high-risk entities or high-value individuals such as organized crime leaders, nuclear scientists, or terrorists.

Focusing on nonstate actors also requires the ability to share information with a range of potential partners where there can be significant cultural, policy, technical, and legal impediments. Given the reflexive nature of classifying government information, such information sharing is no small feat. The 9/11 Commission's conclusions to intelligence sharing within the United States apply equally to intelligence sharing with partner countries: "current security requirements nurture over-classification and excessive compartmentalization of information among agencies. Each agency's incentive structure opposes sharing, with risks (criminal, civil, and internal administrative sanctions) but few rewards for sharing information."[47] The Department of Defense recognized this problem and issued a memorandum stating that the "incorrect use of the NOFORN [U.S.-only consumers] caveat on DoD information has impeded the sharing of classified national defense information allies and coalition partners."[48] Improving information sharing with international partners is a key dimension of exporting security.

Organizational Escape?

Given that a core function of the military is to build surrogate and partner country security force capacity, provide interim military government, or perform civil administration functions, new organizational models have been proposed. This includes creating specialized formations designed for stability operations, developing interagency teams, or segmenting the force. A small attempt at this is the provincial reconstruction team, which is used in Afghanistan and Iraq. Provincial reconstruction teams are eighty- to one-hundred-person teams composed of both civilians and military who can work directly with local populations developing economic opportunities and providing immediate assistance. The team typically includes a mix of security, development, and diplomacy experts. In many ways, provincial reconstruction teams resemble an expeditionary embassy country team.

A larger attempt was proposed by Andrew Krepinevich who argues that creating forward liaison and assistance groups composed of forty-five brigades (approximately two hundred thousand personnel); military assistance group headquarters of three hundred to three thousand personnel; security training and equipping groups of two thousand to three thousand personnel; and civil operations, reconstruction, and development support groups of four thousand to five thousand troops.[49] Similarly, the Congressional Research Service listed one organizational option to create five divisions optimized for reconstruction and stability operations. These divisions would contain military police, engineers, medical personnel, civil affairs, and psychological operations units.[50] John Nagl advocated creating a permanent twenty-thousand-member advisory corps to train and advise military and police forces, and Scott Wuestner argued for a five-thousand-person security assistance and advisory command to augment current efforts by country teams.[51]

Although the changed strategic focus and security challenges should consider the impact on organizations, history suggests that specializing security assistance and assigning it to specialized units, the reserves, allies, or private contractors will be insufficient to meet the global demand for security assistance. Breaking the engagement, stability, and reconstruction operations away from the core force risks exacerbating the high-demand, low-density problem that currently exists. For various reasons, the military services tend to subscribe to this view and do not favor dividing the force between those that break things and those that rebuild. One Army study noted that a traditional brigade combat team could execute 93 percent of its mission sets, including stability operations, and 100 percent of its major combat requirement whereas specialized units could execute only 68 percent of its total mission set and just 20 percent of its major combat requirements.[52] Thus, the traditional military is incorporating non-warfighting missions into its core mission set.

The Marine Corps commandant prescribes that his "Marines must be agile, capable of transitioning seamlessly between fighting, training, advising, and assisting—or performing all of these task simultaneously."[53] Marines can be warriors, diplomats, builders, and guardians. Much of this learning has come from experiences in nonpermissive environments in Iraq and Afghanistan. "An insurgency's complex diplomatic, informational, military, and economic context precludes military leaders from commanding all contributing organizations—and they should not try to do so. Interagency partners, NGOs, and private organizations have many interests and agendas that military forces cannot control."[54] However, these lessons are more relevant in permissive environments where security cooperation takes place, such as in Latin America, Africa, and Asia.

To fill voids, the military services are adapting. For example, the Navy partners with "Project Handclasp" to link the capacity of the private sector with the logistics capability of the military. Under this program the military facilitates delivery of donated materials such as ambulances, school supplies, high-nutrition meals, bicycles, and many other things donated by the U.S. private sector. During the 2009 Africa Partnership Station deployment, Project Handclasp delivered 235 pallets of medical, hygiene, and school supplies to seven countries.[55] Doctrine now prescribes that "commanders should know which companies are present in their AO [area of operations] and where those companies are conducting business."[56] The chief of staff of the Army put this in larger context: "The nature of war doesn't change, but the character of conflict can change, and as I look back at the character of the wars that I've prepared to fight in my career, it's fundamentally different now for young folks. They're dealing with non-state actors."[57] In this case nonstate actors includes both friendly and unfriendly groups.

To be successful, commanders work with embassy country teams and are guided by five ideas.[58]

1. Do no harm.
2. Help resolve local conflicts.
3. Assist at-risk host governments.
4. Align with well-liked partner country actors.
5. Pay particular attention to local populations.

Instrumental Rationale

As discussed in chapter 3, the objections to the changing face of the military emanate from many circles. Some see the military supplanting the role of development agencies. Others see disturbing irreversible moves away from the military's ability to wage major war. Yet building partners' capacity is not purely devoid of national interests. By design, certain U.S. military activities are implicitly and explicitly focused on international cooperation. Among these are developing headquarters for coalitions, coordinating security assistance activities, and participating in a multinational force. Coalition warfare has emerged as the norm over the last several decades, and partnerships before war smooth the logistics and interoperability challenges that naturally occur in an operational environment. Thus, building relationships with strategically important countries is an important reason for exporting security.

As the preceding chapters suggest, the United States has an expansive view of the security environment, a view too large for it to affect alone. The United States cannot command the commons; piracy in the Gulf of Aden, drug trafficking in Latin America, and terrorism in Europe suggest otherwise. Consequently, the United States has embraced the notion of operating indirectly through partners. Inherent to these activities is identifying partners' capabilities that complement or assist the United States as it furthers its national interests. The military is strengthening the capacity of key countries in the Caribbean and Central America to better control illicit trafficking of people, drugs, and weapons. The military views these partners as "friendly surrogates" that can conduct operations when using American forces is not feasible or objectionable. Thus, Jamaica, Dominican Republic, and Honduras provide the first defense of America's third border in the Caribbean.

There are further instrumental reasons underlying engagement activities. Each geographic combatant commander has specific responsibilities that necessitate running programs that have little to do with warfighting. These include stationing of U.S. forces, sustaining forward-deployed forces, obtaining multinational support against nonmilitary threats, supporting regional interagency activities, and coordinating planning with other government departments. Egypt, for example, expedites Navy ship transits through the Suez Canal. Developed states also offset defense costs by providing host-nation support. Singapore, for example, has developed port infrastructure to accommodate U.S. naval vessels and has purchased U.S. weapons systems, thereby reinforcing levels of cooperation. Japan provides about $4 billion annually to support U.S. forces on its territory, and Kuwait provides fuel, electricity, water, meals, and other allowances totaling $1 billion per year.[59]

Goodwill activities serve a greater purpose to sustain access. For example, when Navy ships make port visits, the crew regularly plans and conducts community relations programs such as rehabilitating schools. This allows the sailors to do good things and it builds good will among a population that will either welcome the next ship that visits or will protest and obstruct it. American disposition for charity certainly underlies cooperative security activities, but for basing rights or gaining access to resources from partner countries, quid pro quo is necessary. Training and equipping partners' security forces, conducting humanitarian activities, and facilitating military construction projects are just a cost of doing business.

Having U.S. forces forward deployed in regions facilitates the identification of emerging threats, which can be confronted before mass violence outbreaks. The uncertainty of where the military will operate in the future is counterbalanced through security relationships with 149 countries. When critics divorce cooperative security programs and sustained support for U.S. military presence, they risk undermining the ability for the military to conduct high-end operations if necessary. Trust cannot be surged during a crisis; presence during peacetime matters as much as attention matters during conflict. The cooperative security concept sees that "geographic access is not ours for the taking; instead, it is gained by negotiating within a framework of shared interests among sovereign states."[60] Regular military-to-military interactions keep communication going between the United States and its partners. Secretary of defense Gates noted this. "Convincing other countries and leaders to be a partner of the United States, often at political and physical risk, ultimately depends on proving that our own government is capable of being a reliable partner over time. To be blunt, that means we cannot cut off assistance and relationships every time a country does something we dislike or disagree with."[61]

Conclusion

The U.S. government has no good answer for what happens after major combat concludes. "By default, U.S. and multinational military forces often possess the only readily available capability to meet many of the local populace's fundamental needs."[62]

Likewise, the international community has no good response to prevent state failure, prevent or stop genocide, or counteract transnational actors that take advantage of weak security services. Thus, David Galula notes, "to confine soldiers to purely military functions while urgent and vital tasks have to be done, and nobody else is available to undertake them, would be senseless. The soldier must then be prepared to become . . . a social worker, a civil engineer, a schoolteacher, a nurse, a boy scout. But only for as long as he cannot be replaced, for it is better to entrust civilian tasks to civilians."[63] These two thoughts explain why the United States military is changing.

The military accepts Galula's idea as stated in the National Defense Strategy: "Our forces have stepped up to the task of long-term reconstruction, development, and governance. The U.S. Armed Forces will need to institutionalize and retain these capabilities."[64] At an institutional level, this occurs at Southern Command and Africa Command, which are focused on permissive environments. These lessons are proliferating to other commands that retain a focus on preparation for major war, but this is not without some peril. Risks include failure of the personnel system to develop and retain suitable talent, overreliance on partners, potentially training future adversaries, and loss of public support of the military.

When the military completely forgets what makes it unique for government or thinks that violence no longer is relevant to conflicts, it has the potential to do more harm than good. Along these lines, operations in Iraq and Afghanistan offer some important lessons. Gen. John Abizaid, who led Central Command during the most difficult years in Iraq and the best years in Afghanistan, once commented that observers characterized Iraq as the "bad war" and Afghanistan as the "good war." Iraq had limited international support, high casualty rates, and the greatest potential to destabilize an entire region and upset global energy markets. In contrast, Afghanistan had strong UN, NATO, and NGO presence; low casualty rates; and modest national reconciliation successes. Afghanistan was seen as the poster child for counterinsurgency efforts.

The "good war" and "bad war" traded places in 2006 for many reasons outside the scope of this book. The important point worth discussing is that violence is still important for militaries. During the bad years in Iraq, the United States was blamed for making the situation worse by being too lethal against terrorists and insurgents. British general Aylwin-Foster wrote in a prestigious U.S. military journal that the U.S. Army is fatally flawed, "always seeing itself as an instrument of national survival, over time the Army has developed a marked and uncompromising focus on conventional warfighting, leaving it ill-prepared for the unconventional operations" in Iraq.[65] Counterinsurgency expert David Kilkullen captured the British approach that some argued was superior, "Look at us, we're on the street in our soft caps and everyone loves us."[66] But when the British became targets, they could not adapt as the United States did, with better tactics and armor, so they hunkered down in their bases and let instability reign. In contrast, the U.S. stepped up its offensive operations, hired and trained Iraqis to protect their own neighborhoods, and trained and equipped Iraqi military forces. By 2009 the aggressive U.S. approach was validated, which enabled President Obama to reduce the U.S. presence in Iraq. This also led Warren Chin to declare British counterinsurgency doctrine obsolete.[67]

The relevant lessons of the good and bad wars come from the British. Attempting to apply templates across regions or situations can produce dangerous outcomes. The United States military must understand this both in counterinsurgency but also in permissive environments where it works with partners on common security challenges. Yet change creates winner and losers. While bureaucracies are slow to change, the central argument of this book has been that the U.S. military is changing. It is becoming less focused on training, equipping, and deploying for major war. Instead the military is being driven by national strategies and experiences in a new security environment that suggest isolating security challenges is paramount. Preemption is now focused on weak states. Warfighting skills will always be prerequisite for leading the military departments and the combatant commands, but officers who have an understanding of the new security environment will be more likely to succeed in a world characterized by threats without borders.

Notes

1. Robert M. Gates, "The National Defense Strategy: Striking the Right Balance," *Joint Force Quarterly*, no. 52 (1st Quarter 2009): 3.

2. Department of Defense, "Capstone Concept for Joint Operations," ver. 3.0, January 15, 2009, www.afcea.org/events/east/09/documents/CCJO_2009_001.pdf.

3. Department of Defense, "News Briefing with Mr. Henry and Lt. Gen. Sharp from the Pentagon," February 7, 2007, http://www.defense.gov/Transcripts/Transcript .aspx?TranscriptID=3882.

4. Quoted in Bryan Bender, "Pentagon Flexes Its Altruism Muscle: Aims to Win Trust with Soft Power," *Boston Globe*, July 28, 2008.

5. Rumsfeld wrote, "A central objective of the Quadrennial Defense Review was to shift the basis of defense planning from a 'threat-based' model that has dominated thinking in the past, to a 'capabilities-based' model for the future. This capabilities-based model focuses more on how adversaries might fight rather than specifically who the adversary might be or where a war might occur. It recognizes that it is not enough to plan for large conventional wars in distant theaters. Instead, the United States must identify the capabilities required to deter and defeat adversaries who will rely on surprise, deception, and asymmetric warfare to achieve their objectives." Department of Defense, "Quadrennial Defense Review Report," September 30, 2001, www.defense.gov/pubs/ pdfs/qdr2001.pdf.

6. Sean C. Sullivan, "Defense Resource Allocation: The Formal Processes in U.S. Defense Planning," unpublished manuscript, May 15, 2008, in author's possession.

7. Paul Wolfowitz, "Prepared Statement for the Senate Armed Services Committee Hearing on Military Transformation," April 9, 2002, www.defense.gov/speeches/ speech.aspx?speechid=202.

8. DoD, "Capstone Concept for Joint Operations."

9. Department of Defense, "Joint Operations," Joint Publication 3-0 (Washington, DC: Department of Defense, September 17, 2006), IV-27; Department of Defense, "Joint Publication 5-0: Joint Operations Planning" (Washington, DC: U.S. Joint Forces Command, December 2006), IV-35.

10. The "Capstone Concept for Joint Operations" makes clear that "shaping operations provide the joint force continuous opportunities to assess the structure and dynamics of potential adversaries and crisis locations to the extent practicable." Department of Defense, "Capstone Concept for Joint Operations," 9.

11. Paul Collier, *The Bottom Billion: Why the Poorest Countries Are Failing and What Can Be Done about It* (New York: Oxford University Press, 2007), 36.

12. This compares to more than twenty per year in the 1960s and 1980s. Heidelberg Institute for International Conflict, *Conflict Barometer 2008* (Heidelberg, GM: HIIK, 2008).

13. William E. Ward and Thomas P. Galvin, "U.S. Africa Command and the Principle of Active Security," *Joint Force Quarterly*, no. 51 (4th Quarter 2008): 62.

14. Joint Forces Command J-9, "Military Contribution to Cooperative Security," ver. 1.0 (Suffolk, VA: Department of Defense, 2008).

15. Ibid., 9.

16. Ibid., 10.

17. The 2001 Foreign Operations Appropriations Act (Sec. 563 of P.L. 106-429) states: "None of the funds made available by this Act may be provided to any unit of the security forces of a foreign country if the Secretary of State has credible evidence that such unit has committed gross violations of human rights, unless the Secretary determines and reports to the Committees on Appropriations that the government of such country is taking effective measures to bring the responsible members of the security forces unit to justice."

18. Joint Forces Command J-9, "Military Contribution to Cooperative Security," 23.

19. Ibid., 13.

20. Even though the United States withdrew recognition of Saddam Hussein as the sovereign in Iraq, it also created processes to allow a democratic successor government to assume sovereignty in relatively short order. In contrast to postwar Japan and Germany, there was not a long period of U.S. occupation.

21. Gates, "The National Defense Strategy," 3.

22. Joint Forces Command J-9, "Military Contribution to Cooperative Security," 13.

23. Robert Gates, "Remarks as Delivered by Secretary of Defense Robert M. Gates," Landon Lecture (Kansas State University), November 26, 2007. Reprinted in *Military Review* (January–February 2008) and available at www.defense.gov/speeches/speech .aspx?speechid=1199.

24. DoD, "Capstone Concept for Joint Operations."

25. Author private interview.

26. Dan Green, "Harnessing the Islamist Revolution: A Strategy to Win the War against Religious Extremism," *Strategic Studies Quarterly* (Fall 2008): 137.

27. "An Interview with George W. Casey, Jr." *Joint Force Quarterly*, no. 52 (1st Quarter 2009): 19.

28. Ibid.

29. U.S. Army and U.S. Marine Corps, *Counterinsurgency Field Manual* (Chicago: University of Chicago Press, 2007), 57.

30. Derek S. Reveron, ed., *America's Viceroys: the Military and U.S. Foreign Policy* (New York: Palgrave Macmillan, 2004).

31. Department of the Army, *FM 3-07: Stability Operations* (Leavenworth, KS: U.S. Army, 2008), appendix A, http://usacac.army.mil/cac2/repository/FM307/FM3-07.pdf.

32. David Galula, *Counterinsurgency Warfare: Theory and Practice* (Westport, CT: Praeger, 2006), 69.

33. Quoted in Green, "Harnessing the Islamist Revolution," 133.

34. "Army Announces Critical Language Incentive-pay Program," Army.mil, August 11, 2008, www.army.mil/-newsreleases/2008/08/13/11649-army-announces-critical-language-incentive-pay-program/.

35. Bantz J. Craddock, "United States European Command before the House Armed Services Committee," March 13, 2008, 25, www.dod.mil/dodgc/olc/docs/testCraddock080313.pdf.

36. Tony Zinni, *Battle Ready* (New York: Palgrave Macmillan, 2006), 308–9.

37. Chairman of the Joint Chiefs of Staff (J7), "Officer Professional Military Education Policy (OPMEP), CJCSI 1800.01C," December 2005, 1, http://www.au.af.mil/au/awc/awcgate/opmep/cjcsi1800_01c-cancelled.pdf.

38. The preface of the "Stability Operations Manual" acknowledges that the "manual also provides doctrine on how those capabilities are leveraged to support a partner nation as part of peacetime military engagement. Those activities, executed in a relatively benign security environment as an element of a combatant commander's theater security cooperation plans, share many of the same broad goals as stability operations conducted after a conflict or disaster. Such activities aim to build partner capacity, strengthen legitimate governance, maintain rule of law, foster economic growth, and help to forge a strong sense of national unity. Ideally, these are addressed before, rather than after, conflict. Conducted within the context of peacetime military engagement, they are essential to sustaining the long-term viability of host nations and provide the foundation for multinational cooperation that helps to maintain the global balance of power." U.S. Army, "FM 3-07: Stability Operations" (Leavenworth, KS: U.S. Army, 2008).

39. See ibid., chapter 6.

40. Ibid., 6-1.

41. "National Security Strategy of the United States of America" (Washington, DC: White House, 2006), 16.

42. Robert Templar, "Afghanistan/Pakistan: Call in the Police (But Please Help Them First)," *Foreign Policy*, March 27, 2009. http://experts.foreignpolicy.com/posts/2009/03/27/call_in_the_police_but_please_train_them_first.

43. Andrew Legon, "Ineffective, Unprofessional, and Corrupt: The Afghan National Police Challenge," Foreign Policy Research Institute E-Notes, June 5, 2009, www.fpri.org/enotes/200906.legon.afghannationalpolice.html.

44. U.S. Army, "FM 3-07: Stability Operations," 6-6.

45. George W. Bush, National Security Presidential Directive 44, "Management of Interagency Efforts Concerning Reconstruction and Stabilization," December 7, 2005. www.fas.org/irp/offdocs/nspd/nspd-44.pdf.

46. James Stavridis, "The Last Hour . . . or the First?" Center on Media, Crime, and Justice, John Jay College, New York, October 22, 2007. http://coa.counciloftheamericas.org/article.php?id=729.

47. National Commission on Terrorist Attacks upon the United States, *The 9/11 Commission Report* (New York: W.W. Norton, 2004), 417.

48. Stephen A. Cambone, "Memorandum: Use of the 'Not Releasable to Foreign Nationals' (NOFORN) Caveat on Department of Defense (DoD) Information," May 17, 2005, www.dtic.mil/whs/directives/corres/pdf/int050517noforn.pdf.

49. Discussed in Scott G. Wuestner, "Building Partner Capacity/Security Force Assistance: A New Structural Paradigm" (Carlisle, PA: U.S. Army War College, 2009), www.strategicstudiesinstitute.army.mil/pdffiles/PUB880.pdf.

50. Andrew Feickert, CRS Report for Congress, "Does the Army Need a Full-Spectrum Force or Specialized Units? Background and Issues for Congress" (Washington, DC: Congressional Research Service, 2008).

51. Wuestner, "Building Partner Capacity."

52. Robert D. Ramsey III, "Advising Indigenous Forces: American Advisors in Korea, Vietnam, El Salvador," Global War on Terror Occasional Paper #18 (Fort Leavenworth, KS: Combat Studies Institute Press, 2006).

53. U.S. Marine Corps, "Marine Corps Vision and Strategy 2025," 3, www.onr.navy.mil/~/media/Files/About%20ONR/usmc_vision_strategy_2025_0809.ashx.

54. U.S. Army and U.S. Marine Corps, Counterinsurgency Field Manual, 59.

55. Africa Partnership Station Nashville, "End of Deployment Fact Sheet," June 2009.

56. U.S. Army and U.S. Marine Corps, Counterinsurgency Field Manual, 65.

57. "An Interview with George W. Casey, Jr.," 19.

58. Joint Forces Command J-9, "Military Contribution to Cooperative Security," 35.

59. "Statement of Admiral William J. Fallon, U.S. Navy, Commander, U.S. Central Command before the Senate Armed Services Committee," March 4, 2008, 23.

60. Joint Forces Command J-9, "Military Contribution to Cooperative Security," D-3.

61. Robert Gates, "The Nixon Center's Distinguished Service Award: Remarks as Delivered by Secretary of Defense Robert M. Gates," The Nixon Center, Washington, D.C., February 24, 2010.

62. U.S. Army and U.S. Marine Corps, Counterinsurgency Field Manual, 68.

63. David Galula, Counterinsurgency Warfare, quoted in U.S. Army and U.S. Marine Corps, Counterinsurgency Field Manual, 2-9.

64. Department of Defense, "National Defense Strategy of the United States" (Washington, DC: Pentagon, 2008), 17, http://www.defense.gov/pubs/2008National DefenseStrategy.pdf.

65. Nigel Aylwin-Foster, "Changing the Army for Counterinsurgency Operations," Military Review (November–December 2005), 12, www.au.af.mil/au/awc/awcgate/milreview/aylwin.pdf.

66. Quoted in Sean D. Naylor, "Panel Gives U.K. Counterinsurgency Effort Poor Marks," Defense News, July 28, 2008, 12.

67. Warren Chin, "Why Did It All Go Wrong? Reassessing British Counterinsurgency in Iraq," Strategic Studies Quarterly 2, no. 4 (Winter 2008): 119–35.

8

From Confrontation to Cooperation

AS MANY SCHOLARS HAVE RECOGNIZED, the international system has changed substantially enough to merit reconsidering fundamental ideas about power and security. This book is an addition to that literature; I suggest that power cannot be measured in military terms alone, that militaries do more than fight wars, and that nonstate actors increasingly challenge traditional understanding of national security. Because of this, international cooperation has become essential to advance and defend national interests.

In opposition to this view, critics identify single cases of states defying international norms, such as the United States invasion of Iraq in 2003, Israel's invasion of Lebanon in 2006, and Russia's invasion of Georgia in 2008. But these wars are increasingly the exception. At the same time that international order was viewed as breaking down during the Bush years, states voluntarily submitted to strengthening international order as evidenced by the evolution of the World Trade Organization, the expansion of the European Union and NATO, and strengthening regional organizations such as the Caribbean Community and the Association of South East Asian States.

The United States has not used its power to slow international integration but in many cases has sponsored it. It views regional organizations as key partners and encourages the pluralization of international security issues. The emerging consensus on climate change, shared challenges of the global economic system, and dangers posed by transnational actors offer opportunities to improve interstate relations and international cooperation. The United States does not attempt to dictate resolution to these challenges but sees partnerships as prerequisites for international security. Admittedly, it did not get to this place easily. The change took failed bilateral attempts with North Korea, international outrage for U.S.-dominated military operations in Iraq, and success from humanitarian assistance and disaster relief operations around the world. Still changing, the United States is attempting to use its military power differently from previous great powers. With few exceptions, the United States bolsters sovereignty through security assistance.

The rationale for security assistance has been based on the assumption that instability breeds chaos, which would inevitably necessitate military intervention. Accordingly, the U.S. military should support other countries through military-to-military contacts, equipment transfers, and combined training activities to help foreign governments help themselves prevent tragedy. This book grounds the strategic rationale for these cooperative security activities in events of the last twenty years, but it is important to point out that the U.S. military did not get to this place easily. There was much organizational resistance both from uniformed and civilian defense personnel. Deborah Avant argued in 1996 that "until there is consensus about the conditions under which responding to low-level threats is important to American security, the military will not abandon its cautionary role."[1]

During the Clinton years, the lack of consensus was publicly acrimonious. Diplomats readily promoted military intervention to address concerns that ranged from human rights abuses to disaster relief. The military reluctantly agreed but often deployed allies, reservists, and the National Guard instead of front-line active duty forces. This perspective changed after the September 11 terrorist attacks as both military officers and civilians gained an appreciation for preventing crises. Chairman of the Joint Chiefs of Staff, Adm. Mike Mullen, said, "I believe if you have these kinds of relationships they would go a long way to ensuring that we don't get into a war or get into a fight with people that we're engaged with like this."[2] Secretary of Defense Robert Gates said, "our strategy is to employ indirect approaches—primarily through building the capacity of partner governments and their security forces—to prevent festering problems from turning into crises that require costly and controversial American military intervention."[3] As Mullen's and Gates's comments make clear, it appears that the consensus Avant sought has been reached. Combating low-level threats is now a core mission for the U.S. military; security assistance is the primary means to do this.

The criticisms of this change are substantial and include a concern with diluting the military's warfighting ethos, but these security assistance activities are not likely to end anytime soon. By law, "the President is authorized to furnish military assistance, on such terms and conditions as he may determine to any friendly country or international organization, the assisting of which the President finds will strengthen the security of the United States and promote world peace."[4] Presidents, both Democrat and Republican, have not exercised discretion in use of this authority. Instead, they find a ready tool in the military to respond to natural disasters, to bolster new diplomatic friendships or long-standing allies, and to use its latent civilian capabilities to meet the global demand for humanitarian and security assistance. Congress also sees security assistance as a key part of the international assistance account and funds programs at high levels.

In 2010 the Pentagon's reaction to security assistance is different from the reaction in the 1990s, when interventions in Somalia, Haiti, and Bosnia led to a "never again" syndrome and nation-building was declared incompatible with the character of a superpower. The military now seeks ways to do it better. By institutionalizing stability operations in 2005 and irregular warfare and cooperative security in 2008, the Pentagon raised the stature of non-warfighting missions to that of preparation for warfare. Consequently, the question is not whether the military should be engaged in security cooperation activities. Rather, the question is how to structure these operations to fully include government agencies and civilian organizations to ensure that broader national security objectives are attained. Robert Killbrew wrote: "Iraq and Afghanistan are worst-case examples of "enabling and empowering" allies. The secretary's real thrust—and the topic of debate in Washington, D.C., today—is how to merge military power with other government agencies to support allies in emerging states before events reach crisis proportions, and to help our friends manage their own affairs without U.S. conventional forces."[5]

The implications of these changes are important for civil–military relations theory. As Samuel Huntington wrote, "a military service may at times, of course, perform functions unrelated to external security such as internal policing, disaster relief, and citizenship training. There are, however, subordinate and collateral responsibilities. A military service does not exist to perform these functions; rather it performs these functions because it has already been called into existence to meet some threats."[6] If the military's warfighting function gives way to promoting internal security, albeit in other countries, then there are important implications for thinking about threats and the appropriate structures to respond to them. While not discounting failed policies in Afghanistan or the difficulty of creating a functioning state in Iraq, extended operations there also highlight that the United States currently does not have good answers to contemporary security challenges that occur at subnational and transnational levels. What is certain, however, is that the military is now embracing its role in non-warfighting missions and is developing concepts to be prepared for a certain future of providing security assistance. This was recognized in the 2010 Quadrennial Defense Review.

There are still calls for the State Department to do more, but that misses the point. Fundamentally, foreign service officers are diplomats, not urban planners, contract managers, or town councilors. Although diplomats are civilians, they are no more prepared to rebuild countries than are their counterparts in the military. For Secretary of Defense Gates, "For the most part, America's instruments of national power—military and civilian—were set up in a different era for a very different set of threats. Our military was designed to defeat other armies, navies and air forces, not to advise, train and equip them. Likewise, our civilian instruments were designed primarily to manage relationships between states, rather than to help build them from within."[7] But there is a demand for these skills, and the military is attempting to meet it. Too often the military meets these needs in an ad hoc way, but as the previous chapters suggests, personnel, education, and training are attempting to fill the void.

Adding Ploughshares

Because civilian leaders will always task their militaries to use violence to achieve national ends, this book does not suggest that defense establishments should be abolished or transform away from their core function of warfighting. While there is no great power struggle in the world today, regional conflicts and mutual defense agreements still require militaries to be prepared for war. And the types of transnational challenges facing many of the world's countries today still requires military forces to identify illicit transit routes, disrupt terrorist groups, and stop hijackings of commercial ships. Secretary of Defense Gates sees that conducting security assistance "is even more urgent in a global security environment where, unlike the Cold War, the most likely and lethal threats—an American city poisoned or reduced to rubble—will likely emanate from fractured or failing states, rather than aggressor states."[8]

The versatility of today's weapons systems has made the military multipurpose. Cargo aircraft can move both tanks and humanitarian supplies. Helicopters can be used in combat missions and search-and-rescue operations, and warships can secure sea-lanes, combat illegal fishing, interdict smuggling, and disrupt piracy. Furthermore, engineers can dig wells, doctors can conduct humanitarian assistance, and soldiers can build schools. Given the complex nature of security that crosses public–private, national–international, and civil–military boundaries, the government readily uses the military to improve global conditions.

These non-warfighting activities certainly frustrate some within the military and civilian agencies, but they also appeal to the charitable nature of American political culture and reinforce national objectives. Policymakers see a ready tool in military assistance because it offers immediate tangible actions. With interventions in unstable places likely to continue, governments still need people who can deploy in austere conditions and work with partners to create stability. Politicians need immediate answers to stopping genocide, providing famine relief, and preventing state collapse. To paraphrase what UN Secretary-General Dag Hammarskjöld once said about peacekeeping, it is not a soldier's job, but only a soldier can do it.[9] The challenge for defense leaders in and out of uniform is to balance training, doctrine, policy, and equipment for militaries to be competent in all areas of national service.

In the military's quest to operate in the civil–military space, it does have to be careful. Facilitating national dialogues, political reconciliation, and social harmony are things that external actors can only upset. Actors at local, regional, and national levels must drive these essential processes and work out the "best" form of government and economic system given their national conditions and political cultures. Yet external actors such as the U.S. military (and the international assistance community) do attempt to build governments, economies, and societies. The challenge for warrior-diplomats is to avoid upsetting national processes that can unfairly disadvantage the society it is supposed to be helping. This is accepted in current defense thinking. "While military power can contribute significantly to resolving some political problems, and sometimes is essential to doing so, it rarely will do so exactly as envisioned and without unintended and irreversible consequences."[10] This conclusion must be reconciled with the "can do" attitude in the military, which seeks solutions to the problems it sees.

For its part, the U.S. military does continue to be cautious about its extensive deployment in state-building operations, and it encourages the U.S. government to develop nonmilitary capabilities for state-building operations. Adm. William "Fox" Fallon of Central Command said, "There is clearly a need for better integration and more comprehensive application of all the elements of national power."[11] The head of Central Command argued that "enduring solutions require predominately non-military initiatives."[12] This is a lesson that is now ingrained in today's officer corps and is in contemporary national defense strategy.

> The use of force plays a role, yet military efforts to capture or kill terrorists are likely to be subordinate to measures to promote local participation in government and economic programs to spur development, as well as efforts to understand and address the grievances that often lie at the heart of insurgencies. For these reasons, arguably the most important military component of the struggle against violent extremists is not the fighting we do ourselves, but how well we help prepare our partners to defend and govern themselves.[13]

While there has not been a new Abrams or Weinberger doctrine emerge to constrain these activities, the lessons of Iraq and Afghanistan will not be lost on this current generation of military officers. Chairman of the Joint Chiefs of Staff Admiral Mullen came close to articulating a new doctrine, but given the importance of the U.S. military today, he could not. He did say that "in the future struggles of the asymmetric counterinsurgent variety, we ought to make it a precondition of committing our troops, that we will do so only if and when the other instruments of national power are ready to engage as well."[14]

Because of the diverse mission set and roles military personnel fill in security, engagement, and stability operations, traditional lines among defense, development, and diplomacy are breaking down. As discussed in chapter 7, the biggest changes occurring in the military are at the personnel level.[15] Retired U.S. ambassador Howard K. Walker observed the implications of this blending:

A new type of leader will be required to manage . . . crises in the 21st century: I call these hybrids soldier-diplomats and diplomat-warriors. There are soldiers who can also think like diplomats and diplomats who can think like soldiers. It is important for soldier-diplomats to understand why and how diplomacy operates to win international support and how domestic political considerations constrain the way force is used to achieve military objectives and what operational constraints the military faces in trying to achieve those objectives.[16]

If former secretary of state Condoleezza Rice is right that "the United States doesn't have permanent enemies,"[17] then the demand on soldier-diplomats and diplomat-warriors will be greater in the future. So far, generals and admirals tend to be welcomed in foreign capitals. Military diplomacy is increasingly accepted. One admiral in Africa told me, "4-stars are the best diplomats. They know how to build trust over time."[18] Yet there are limits to how political a four-star can be before the Defense Department reins him in. Thus, military commanders are embracing diplomats and development specialists in their commands and attempting to infuse command strategies with a 3D approach, defense, development, and diplomacy. Commanders are challenged to get enough nonmilitary people in their commands, but this is a top priority for the military.

Measuring Effectiveness

A logical consequence of adding ploughshares to the military's force structure is diversifying the way it measures goal attainment. In pure combat terms, it is relatively easy to measure whether the military disrupts, degrades, or destroys enemy forces. In permissive environments, the objectives are less clear and more broad than traditional military objectives. Joint Chiefs of Staff chairman Admiral Mullen noted that the effects may never by clearly measurable and cultural sensitivities might preclude measurement.[19] However, in a resource-constrained environment, it is important to understand which activities are more effective than others. President Obama's national security advisor echoed this in a memo to cabinet secretaries. "Once a decision has been made, it is incumbent on the NSC [National Security Council] to oversee the implementation process in such a manner that concrete results are achieved within the time that has been agreed upon."[20]

Security assistance programs have clearly measurable objectives beyond the good feeling generated by improving people's lives. These include the strength of regional security agreements, the types of regional cooperation (air, maritime, land, customs, etc.), and the relative receptivity of U.S. forces within the partner country. Internal to countries, one can measure how well partners combat security challenges, the strength of civil–military relations, and the levels of respect for human rights. Measurement can include the extent to which international commerce flows freely, levels of cooperation between military and international relief organizations, and support for international initiatives to combat disease, illicit activity, and weapons proliferation.

Military commands are attempting to understand how effective their activities are. In 2009, for example, Africa Command identified three strategic end states that allow measurement.[21] First, African countries and organizations are able to provide for their own security and contribute to security on the continent. This can be measured by examining the rate of participation in peacekeeping operations, the percentage of non-Africans serving on peacekeeping missions in Africa, and the relative ability of the government to combat threats. Second, African governments and regional security establishments have the capability to mitigate the threat from organizations committed to violent extremism. This can be measured by examining levels of internal violence, prevalence of transnational groups in the country, or levels of cooperation between national and subregional organizations on security issues. Third, African countries and organizations maintain professional militaries that respond to civilian authorities, respect the rule of law, and abide by international human rights norms. This can be measured by analyzing autonomy of the military, human rights abuses committed by the military, and the extent to which a military abstains from political disputes.

In addition to the measures listed above, the Army Field Manual on Stability Operations sees the following questions as guiding assessment:[22]

- Are the trained forces competent from the ministerial level to the individual soldier and police officer, across related fields of interest and functional specialties?
- Are trained forces capable in size and effective enough to accomplish missions, remain sustainable over time, and maintain resources within state capabilities?
- Are forces committed to the security and survival of the state, the preservation of the liberties and human rights of the citizens, and the peaceful transition of authority?
- Are trained forces confident in the ability to secure the country, earning the confidence of the citizenry, the government, and the international community?

In Africa, the impact of security assistance is evident in the effort to develop indigenous capability and capacity for peacekeeping operations. Using military mentors, advisors, and contractors to conduct the training in the host country,

Africa Contingency Operations Training and Assistance (ACOTA) trains members of African militaries to be trainers, and it equips their militaries to conduct peace support operations and humanitarian relief. Since 2004 ACOTA has trained approximately 68,000 African soldiers and 3,500 African trainers from twenty-one African partner countries.[23] U.S.-trained and -equipped forces are attempting to stabilize Darfur, Somalia, and the Democratic Republic of Congo. Without this training and equipment, there would be even fewer options for international negotiators to bring peace to parts of Africa that lack adequate security.

While the number of available African peacekeepers has increased, current efforts are deficient and fall short of the goal of Africans providing for African security. Of the seven UN peacekeeping missions in Africa in 2009, only the hybrid UN–African Union mission in Darfur is composed of an African majority (see table 8.1). Non-Africans primarily compose the other six UN operations. In addition to the shortfall on UN missions, there are open billets on African Union peacekeeping missions too. In sum, there is a shortfall of at least forty-five thousand African peacekeepers necessary to meet the African Union objective of Africans providing for their own security. Given standard deployment cycles, the number can be multiplied by three to account for forces that are training to deploy, are deployed, and recover from deployment.

In addition to the personnel shortfalls, there are significant operational limits. U.S. ambassador to the UN, Susan Rice, detailed shortfalls to Congress: "UNAMID is not alone in facing logistics challenges. . . . Beyond deployed strength, a peacekeeping force's capacity to operate effectively depends on several other factors, many of which are in short supply in the missions in Darfur,

Table 8.1 UN Peacekeepers in Africa

Mission	Total Number of Peacekeepers[a]	Number of Non-Africans[a]	Largest Contributor
MINURCAT (Central African Republic and Chad)	2,626	2,128 (81%)	France
UNAMID (Darfur)	15,686	2,210 (14%)	Nigeria
UNMIS (Sudan)	9,894	7,426 (75%)	India
UNOCI (Cote d'Ivoire)	9,010	5,937 (66%)	Bangladesh
UNMIL (Liberia)	11,242	7,646 (68%)	Pakistan
MONUC	18,398	13,295 (72%)	India
MINURSO (Western Sahara)	227	163 (72%)	Malaysia

[a] As of April 30, 2009. Totals include military, police, and observers.

Source: Derived from United Nations, "Background Note: United Nations Peacekeeping Operations," and UN peacekeeping totals available at the United Nations website, www.un.org/Depts/dpko.

Chad, and the Democratic Republic of Congo. These factors include . . . the capacity to rapidly deploy and move forces in theater; readily available medical, engineering, intelligence, and aviation—particularly helicopter-units."[24]

Risks

The U.S. military has embraced this mission of military engagement and security assistance, but there are some fundamental limits to what can be accomplished. As an external actor, security assistance can only have marginal impact on a country's security and stability. And as the data on African peacekeeping suggest, there still is much work to close the security deficits that exist. All of these programs clearly indicate that change in weak states must come primarily from within; external actors are limited in what they can accomplish.[25] Since most of these programs are military-to-military and not military-to–law enforcement or even law enforcement–to–law enforcement, the capabilities exported may not be immediately relevant to societies that struggle against transnational actors or are plagued by human security challenges.

Furthermore, security assistance programs are not entirely risk-free activities. While U.S. forces do not engage in combat or law enforcement activities in partner countries, some countries can misinterpret the meaning of U.S. military support. A 2008 example involves Georgia, Russia, and the United States. After a failed attempt to retake the territory of South Ossetia, Georgia expected more than moral support from the West in its conflict with Russia. Georgian president Mikheil Saakashvili wrote at the time, "Russia's invasion of Georgia strikes at the heart of Western values and our 21st century system of security. If the international community allows Russia to crush our democratic, independent state, it will be giving carte blanche to authoritarian governments everywhere."[26] Saakashvili's expectations were not that unrealistic. After all, U.S. forces had been training and equipping the Georgian military for years, President Bush lobbied allies to grant Georgia NATO membership and the sovereignty protection that goes with it, and Georgia had more than two thousand troops of its small army in Iraq with the United States. Yet the Georgian government appeared to misinterpret these acts and expected the United States to do more to prevent Russian domination of the South Ossetian crisis.

However, the United States could not risk direct confrontation with Russia over a decades-old conflict in Georgia. Russia refused to blink and called into question Washington's military assistance programs to Georgia. Russian foreign minister Sergei Lavrov directly asked, "Did Washington purposely encourage an irresponsible and unpredictable regime in this misadventure?"[27] Former Soviet general secretary Mikhail Gorbachev thought yes. "Western assistance in training Georgian troops and shipping large supplies of arms had been pushing the region toward war rather than peace."[28] Ioan Mircea Pascu sees acts such as this as Russia's attempt to counter what it interprets as U.S. hegemony: "With its invasion of Georgia, Russia demonstrated the determination to 'come back into the game' in style. Regenerated through the surge of energy prices, Russia's leaders want to make up their losses from the 1990s and get payback for the accompanying humiliation. Her aggressive policies, heralded by the political use of the energy weapon starting in 2006, have been beefed up now with a willingness to openly employ military might."[29]

Beyond Georgia, Russia has been strengthening relations with regimes considered unfriendly to the United States, including Venezuela. In addition to billions of dollars of weapons deals, Russia also conducted a very short deployment of two TU-160 Russian bombers to Venezuela in September 2008. Russia followed up with a naval deployment in November 2008 to the Caribbean. *Komsomolskaya Pravda's* headline captured the Russian meaning of this deployment: "Russia's Fist in America's Belly." The editorial saw "Russian naval and air forces approaching U.S. territory as an adequate response to U.S. and NATO military bases. . . . Russia is trying to achieve a strategic balance and is letting Washington know that Moscow is able to defend its interests."[30] In addition to causing a panic in Georgia, America's other key partner, Colombia, felt the pain too as it sought reassurances that Russia would not upset the balance of power with its Venezuelan neighbor.

This case does offer a good lesson for partner countries and security assistance officers about the meaning of U.S. security assistance programs. The United States is committed to partners' efforts to improve their security, but it is not agreeing to protect all partners from aggression. This is consistent with my argument that the United States is not an empire, and it would be foolish for the United States to commit itself to such a broad security agenda. After all, the United States maintains security cooperation relationships with more than 150 countries. It will certainly exercise discretion to avoid being pulled into a wider conflict where U.S. national interests would not be well served. The days of patron–client state relations are gone, and these security assistance programs do not resemble cold-war arrangements of the past. The United States appears willing to break with its security partners when political circumstances change and will deny certain capabilities that would upset domestic or regional balances of power. Furthermore, the United States seeks to foster independence and encourages partners to graduate from its security assistance programs and help other countries in the region.

Although the security assistance officers are fully committed to their jobs, their tour lengths do limit the impact they can have. In Iraq or Afghanistan, for example, tribal leaders, government officials, and other elites develop fatigue with American officers who show up to help for seven to fifteen months. In non-combat situations, being in-country for only two to three years is a real handicap to developing sustainable programs and can provoke backlash. For another country's officers that are fighting an insurgency, attempting to professionalize its military, or strengthening the government's control in feral regions, an American showing up to help for two years can be frustrating. After all, U.S. international partners have dedicated their lives to creating security and stability; they do not think of these activities as simply one tour. Consequently, American officers have to be careful not to overpromise, and they should align U.S. activities with the interests of its partner countries to ease the challenges of cooperation.

Partners Are Changing, Too

The focus of this book is on the United States, but exporting security is evident elsewhere. Lt. Gen. Freek Meulman, vice chief of defense of the Netherlands Armed Forces, noted similar trends in European militaries since 1990. "We understood rather quickly that the world would never be the same as before ... so we started the process of reorganizing, making it more agile, deployable, working our way toward what we called humanitarian operations."[31] At a broader level, NATO is taking steps to become more effective at integrating civil–military cooperation. This is evident in Afghanistan, where NATO forces focus on building functioning political and socioeconomic systems.

There is evidence that change is occurring in dozens of lesser-developed countries too. For example, Ugandan president Yoweri Museveni understood the non-warfighting roles that militaries now fill. "Our role in Somalia is to try to help the Somalis rebuild their state. We are there to help them defend the airport and the seaport and the government house. But more important, we'd like to see ourselves as a catalyst in building the Somali army and police."[32] In the Philippines, the military rebuilds markets, constructs schools, clinics, and community centers, and brings power to areas lacking electricity.[33] Brazil, through its military, is strengthening ties with other Portuguese-speaking countries. In 2009 Brazil's military sent the logistics vessel *Garcia de Avila* to Mozambique on a mission that resembled the U.S. Navy's global fleet station discussed in chapter 6, and Brazil is helping Namibia build a navy.[34]

Will Change Come to an End?

Those that fear the creeping militarization of U.S. foreign policy should take heart and understand that the government is using the military's civilian capabilities to support diplomatic and development goals. These capabilities include urban planning, civil engineering, and medicine. To best integrate these capabilities, both the military and civilian agencies are developing new ways to work together. Just as jointness was the primary bureaucratic problem of the 1990s, interagency and public–private partnerships remain contemporary bureaucratic challenges. The changes made at Southern Command and Africa Command point to the future of the U.S. military, but also the future of international assistance that is defined by the 3D approach. To date, the data suggest that increasing military-to-military contacts are positively and systematically associated with liberalizing trends throughout the world.[35] Because of this change, the military's willingness to provide logistics support, and the decline in donors, Kathi Sohn argues that "NGOs cannot alone foster the positive environment prescribed in post-9/11 strategies."[36] Instead, there is room for nontraditional development actors such as the military.

The Obama administration is attempting to rebalance the government, exercise "smart power," and institutionalize a whole-of-government or interagency approach to improve global security. This idea has permeated the national security bureaucracy and trickled down to a little-known intelligence document.

> No single person or organization can protect our Nation from the many and varied threats we face today. These threats, from looming terrorist plots, to pandemic disease, to the proliferation of weapons of mass destruction, require that we, as a government, work together. As we have articulated in the Intelligence Community (IC)'s Vision 2015, we must partner with intelligence consumers to meet the need for more timely and unique intelligence. In order to enhance our relationships, it is important for consumers to understand the mission, background, opportunities, and challenges facing the IC. We have published this handbook with this very thought in mind—to broaden your understanding of our work and to help us become stronger partners in protecting our Nation.[37]

Partnership is certainly a virtue in today's complex security environment. And ideas such as smart power are welcome relief from Bush foreign policy, but it has been obvious for decades that whole-of-government solutions are needed to address weak states. The Department of State observed in 1992: "Future U.S. military action abroad is most likely to involve relatively small local conflicts and to be in the context of a UN or other multilateral peacekeeping process. Consequently, political and diplomatic factors are likely to be even more important than in the past."[38] The Chairman of the Joint Chiefs General Hugh Shelton said similar things in 2000:

> Our experiences in Kosovo and elsewhere have demonstrated the necessity to ensure that all concerned government agencies conduct comprehensive planning to encompass the full range of instruments available to

decision makers. We all must move forward with our efforts to achieve increased levels of integrated interagency planning now. To better support other agencies, DOD needs to give greater consideration to political, diplomatic, economic, information, and other non-military activities in defense planning. In addition, the U.S. government must establish dedicated mechanisms and integrated planning processes to ensure rapid, effective, well-structured, multi-agency efforts in response to crises."[39]

The military certainly supports sharing the work with civilian agencies, but it has come to accept that "interagency" is an adjective to describe a process of bringing together elements from across the government and not a noun to describe an organization that brings solutions. As people continue to search for interagency solutions, the military is not waiting. As this book suggests, the military is incorporating civilian functions to ensure that it accomplishes national goals. Officers have learned from operational experiences that they cannot ignore civilian requirements and increasingly conduct civilian missions.

If reducing the military in non-warfighting activities is truly the Obama administration's goal, then congressional action is necessary to restrict use of the military and empower the rest of the U.S. government to meet the demands of America's partners. To be fair, the Department of State feels encroached upon not only by the military but also by the more than thirty agencies represented overseas. In many diplomatic posts, State Department personnel are in the minority, and this can create uncoordinated action. Ambassador Thomas A. Schweich noted this in Afghanistan:

> There is action, but without coordination. In looking into, for example, prosecutor training, I found that we had three separate sets of curriculum being done by different U.S. agencies. They were inconsistent. This was the kind of lack of coordination that was going on among the agencies in Afghanistan. In another situation, where we were trying to build courthouses, we had one agency that was providing computerized equipment and another that decided they could delay providing electricity to those buildings during this time. So there was all this equipment but no electricity.[40]

It is up to the U.S. ambassador in the partner country and the combatant command representatives to work things out and ensure that U.S. policies are consistent. As the discussion of section 1207 funding in chapter 5 suggests, piecemeal policies will not be enough. Experience to date suggests that achieving unity of effort without unity of command is difficult, which partly explains why the military embraces the 3D approach of defense, diplomacy, and development. While military commands on the ground are working through important interagency challenges, reality has not yet caught up in Washington where department budgets still restrict behavior. To overcome these challenges, the Defense Department continually seeks authority to transfer funds to the Department of State.

Secure, not Dominate, World Order

The overarching goal of the United States is to promote global stability, which is different from global domination. To be sure, the current international system speaks with an American accent, but the United States voluntarily submits to binding bilateral and multilateral agreements. If it were intent on dominating, it would not allow its "dependencies" to defect as they regularly do during routine diplomacy. Instead shared norms on the dangers posed by nonstate actors and certain countries pose threats to international instability, which serve to unite activities. While the UN system has had decades to learn how to manage interstate security challenges, the friction of the last decade illustrates that it is ill-equipped to confront intrastate and transnational challenges. Today security concerns cross private, international, and government lines. UN reform is certainly essential, but given how reform can be easily politicized, the United States prefers to empower friends, allies, and new partners to secure world order. Consequently, the U.S. military is changing from its single focus on major combat to building the security capacity of its partners. This book makes no normative judgment of this change but offers a framework to understand the change and to illustrate how the U.S. military is changing from a force of confrontation to one of cooperation. As Gen. Tony Zinni remarked, "The military is not the best answer . . . but if there is a gap, the military will fill it."[41]

Notes

1. Deborah Avant, "Are the Reluctant Warriors out of Control? Why the U.S. Military Is Averse to Responding to Post–Cold War Low-Level Threats," *Security Studies* 6, no. 2 (Winter 1996–97): 90.

2. Quoted in "CNO: Humanitarian Missions Essential to Relationships, Global War on Terrorism," *Navy Newsstand*, June 19, 2007.

3. Robert M. Gates, "The National Defense Strategy: Striking the Right Balance," *Joint Force Quarterly*, no. 52 (1st Quarter 2009): 3.

4. Committee on International Relations and Committee on Foreign Relations, "Legislation on Foreign Relations through 2002," July 2003, vol. 1A, chapter 2, Section 503, www.internationalrelations.house.gov/archives/108/87164.pdf.

5. Robert Killbrew, "SecDef Has Signaled a Turning Point in U.S. Defense Thinking," *Armed Forces Journal* 145, no. 7 (February 2008): 1.

6. Samuel Huntington, "National Policy and the Transoceanic Navy," U.S. Naval Institute *Proceedings* 80, no. 5 (March 1954): 483.

7. Robert Gates, "The Nixon Center's Distinguished Service Award Remarks as Delivered by Secretary of Defense Robert M. Gates," The Nixon Center, Washington, D.C., February 24, 2010.

8. Ibid.

9. Theo van den Doel, "Peacekeeping: Only a Soldier Can Do It," Geneva Centre for the Democratic Control of Armed Forces, www.dcaf.ch/lpag/ev_stpeter_031001_doel.pdf.

10. Department of Defense, "Capstone Concept for Joint Operations," ver. 3.0, January 15, 2009, www.afcea.org/events/east/09/documents/CCJO_2009_001.pdf, 1.

11. "Statement of Admiral William J. Fallon, U.S. Navy, Commander, U.S. Central Command before the Senate Armed Services Committee," March 4, 2008, 30, www.dod.mil/dodgc/olc/docs/testFallon080304.pdf.

12. Ibid., 3.

13. Department of Defense, "National Defense Strategy of the United States," June 2008, www.defense.gov/news/2008%20National%20Defense%20Strategy.pdf, 8.

14. Admiral Michael Mullen, "Landon Lecture Series Remarks," March 3, 2010. www.jcs.mil/speech.aspx?ID=1336.

15. Secretary Gates's efforts to rebalance the force is as much about reducing preparations for high-end combat as it is about cost overruns that plague next generation systems such as F-22, the Army's future combat system, or DDG-1000.

16. Howard K. Walker, "Diplomacy, Force and the Diplomat-Warrior," *Foreign Service Journal*, September 1998: 41.

17. Quoted in David Gollust, "Rice Says Enmity with North Korea, Iran, Syria Need Not Be Permanent," *VOA News*, December 21, 2007.

18. Author private interview.

19. DoD, "Capstone Concept for Joint Operations," 17.

20. Jim Jones, "Memorandum: The 21st Century Interagency Process" Washington, DC: The White House, March 18, 2009.

21. Kip Ward, "United States Africa Command 2009 Posture Statement" (Stuttgart, GM: Africa Command, 2009), 11.

22. U.S. Army, "FM 3-07: Stability Operations" (Leavenworth, KS: U.S. Army, 2008), 6–10.

23. Ward, "U.S. Africa Command 2009 Posture Statement," 14.

24. Susan Rice, "Africa: U.S. House Committee Hearing on Peacekeeping," allAfrica.com, July 29, 2009, http://allafrica.com/stories/printable/200907310813.html.

25. Paul Collier, *The Bottom Billion: Why the Poorest Countries Are Failing and What Can Be Done about It* (New York: Oxford University Press, 2007).

26. Mikheil Saakashvili, "Russia's War Is the West's Challenge," *Washington Post*, August 14, 2008.

27. Sergei Lavrov, "America Must Choose between Georgia and Russia," *Wall Street Journal*, August 20, 2008, 19.

28. Mikhail Gorbachev, "Russia Never Wanted a War," *New York Times*, August 20, 2008, 23.

29. Ioan Mircea Pascu, "Russia's Back in the Game," *New Atlanticist*, September 22, 2008. www.acus.org/new_atlanticist/russia-back-game-it%E2%80%99s-west%E2%80%99s-move.

30. Viktor Baranets, "Russia's Fist in America's Belly," *Komsomolskaya Pravada*, September 23, 2008. www.kp.ru/daily/24168/380592/.

31. Freek Meulman, interview with Antonie Boessenkool, *Defense News*, July 28, 2008.

32. Yoweri Musevani, "The Strategy of the Protracted Peoples' War," U.S. Army Command and General Staff College, Fort Leavenworth, KS, September 30, 2008. www.africom.mil/getArticle.asp?art=2144.

33. Tim Keating, "Statement of Admiral Timothy J. Keating, Commander, U.S. Pacific Command, before the Senate Armed Services Committee on U.S. Pacific Command Posture," March 11, 2008, 8, http://www.pacom.mil/web/pacom_resources/pdf/080311-keating-sasc.pdf.

34. "Mozambique: Brazilian Navy to Support Country," allAfrica.com, June 9, 2009.

35. Carol Atkinson, "Constructivist Implications of Material Power: Military Engagement and the Socialization of States, 1972–2000," *International Studies Quarterly* 50 (2006): 509–37.

36. Kathi Sohn, "The Global Fleet Station: A Powerful Tool for Preventing Conflict," *Naval War College Review* 62, no. 1 (Winter 2009): 46.

37. Office of Director of National Intelligence, "National Intelligence: A Consumer's Guide" (Washington, DC: ODNI, 2009), www.dni.gov/reports/IC_Consumers_Guide_2009.pdf.

38. U.S. Department of State, "State 2000: A New Model for Managing Foreign Affairs" (Washington, DC: U.S. Department of State, 1992), 212.

39. "Chairman of the Joint Chiefs of Staff Posture Statement before the 106th Congress Committee on Armed Services," United States Senate, February 8, 2000.

40. Thomas A. Schweich, "America's Broken Interagency," *Foreign Policy Research Institute*, March 2009, www.fpri.org/enotes/200903.schweich.americasbrokeninteragency.html.

41. "Civil-Military Cooperation in a Time of Turmoil," December 21, 2004, Woodrow Wilson International Center for Scholars,www.wilsoncenter.org/index.cfm?fuseaction=news.item&news_id=102532.

Index

Abizaid, John, 163

Account 150 assistance, *106t*, 106–8, *107t*

"active security," 47, 149

Afghanistan: alleviation of food insecurity in, 102; IMET assistance, 111; Taliban and illegal drug trafficking, 18–19; as weak state, 21

Afghanistan (U.S. military operations in): Central Command, 45, 88–89; coordination challenges, 181; counterinsurgency operations, 66–67, 68, 69, 88–89; and European militaries, 35; and fourth-generation theorists, 67; and future defense planning, 70–71; as "good war"/"bad war," 163; human security and development issues, 88–89; interservice rivalries, 84; intervention lessons, 102–3, 163, 173; irregular warfare school, 67, 68, 69; Marine Air-Ground Task Force, 63; and military modernization, 13–14; and modernist warfare, 66–67, 68; and mutual defense treaties of alliance, 34–35, 50n11; and NATO, 34;

traditionalist warfare school, 63, 70–71

Africa: FMF assistance, *112t*; and Global Fleet Station, 132–34; GPOI peace operations and training centers, 115, *115t*; IMET funding, *110t*, 111; IUU fishing and EEZ losses, 125–26; maritime security challenges, 125–28, 132–34, 135–39; piracy, 4, 18, 126–28, 136, 150; security destabilization and nontraditional threats, 19

Africa Command, *81f*, 162; and "active security," 47, 149; African countries' reluctance to support, 60, 133; and Bush administration, 1, 8n1, 47–48; DCMA position, 90; and Global Fleet Station, 133; institutional reluctance to support, 56, 60; interagency orientation, 43, 58, 88, 180; J-code system restructuring and directorate of outreach and communications, 92–93; jointness with civilians, 86–87; measuring effectiveness, 175–77; mission and responsibilities defined in UCP, 82; personnel/staff size, 4; and preventative

About the Author

DEREK S. REVERON is a professor of national security affairs and the EMC Informationist Chair at the U.S. Naval War College in Newport, Rhode Island. He specializes in security cooperation, democratization, political violence, and intelligence. His books include *Inside Defense: Understanding the 21st Century Military* (coeditor with Judith Hicks Steihm; Palgrave Macmillan, 2008); *Flashpoints in the War on Terrorism* (coeditor with Jeffrey Stevenson Murer; Routledge, 2006); *America's Viceroys: The Military and U.S. Foreign Policy* (editor; Palgrave Macmillan, 2004); and *Promoting Democracy in the Post-Soviet Region* (Mellen Press, 2002). He serves as a senior editorial board member for the *National Intelligence Journal* and editorial board member of the *Naval War College Review*. He is also a contributing editor to the *New Atlanticist*, the blog for the Atlantic Council of the United States. Before joining the Naval War College faculty, Dr. Reveron taught political science at the Joint Military Intelligence College, National Defense University, and the U.S. Naval Academy. He received a diploma from the Naval War College, and a master's degree in political science and a doctorate in public policy analysis from the University of Illinois at Chicago.

DATE DUE

Demco, Inc. 38-293